Men's Dreams, Men's Healing

Men's Dreams, Men's Healing

Robert H. Hopcke

Shambhala
Boston & London
1990

Shambhala Publications, Inc.
Horticultural Hall
300 Massachusetts Avenue
Boston, Massachusetts 02115

Printed in the United States of America

Distributed in the United States by Random House
and in Canada by Random House of Canada Ltd.

Library of Congress Cataloging-in-Publication Data

Hopcke, Robert H., 1958–
    Men's dreams, men's healing / Robert H. Hopcke.—1st ed.
    p. cm.
    ISBN 0-87773-561-1
    1. Men—Mental health.   2. Gay men—Mental health.   3. Men's
dreams—Psychological aspects.   4. Masculinity (Psychology).
5. Psychoanalysis.   6. Jung, C. G. (Carl Gustav), 1875–1961.
I. Title.
RC451.4.M45H67   1990   90-55067
616.89'0081—dc20   CIP

BOMC offers recordings and compact discs, cassettes
and records. For information and catalog write to
BOMR, Camp Hill, PA 17012.

Contents

Acknowledgments   vii

Introduction   1

1. A Dream of Ants and Spiders:
    Men and Feelings   9

2. The Dream of the Adolescent Cop:
    Men and Authority   41

3. From Iron Lung to *Ménage à Trois:* Heterosexual
    Men, Femininity, and the Anima   75

4. Dreams of the Dark Young Man: Gay Men,
    Masculinity, and the Male Anima   106

5. The Dream of the Italian Father: Fatherhood as
    Embodiment and Redemption   139

6. The Dream of a Daughter's Baptism: Fatherhood as
    Initiation and Relationship   170

Notes 199

Bibliography 207

Index 211

Credits 219

Acknowledgments

While in the process of writing this book, I went to lunch at a Chinese restaurant and got a fortune cookie which reminded me that "Behind every great man there are always other great men." Now I don't know about my own greatness, but the truth is, behind this book there have been men and women with greatness of intellect, creativity, and friendship that have made my writing possible. They deserve my thanks for their support.

First, the folks at Shambhala—particularly Jonathan Green, Emily Hilburn Sell, Dave O'Neal, and Kendra Crossen—and Rebecca Nowakowski, the freelance copyeditor, merit recognition. Their professional talents and personal interest make it a joy to work with them. Their hard work on my behalf, for this and my other books, continues to be greatly appreciated.

Next a group of people should be named for contributing to this book in a way that they themselves perhaps do not know, mostly by relieving me of that particular kind of intellectual loneliness that afflicts writers who work without the support and affiliation of an institution. Their conversations with me about my work and about their own were often short, but were in fact sometimes just what I needed to resolve a problem or muster the necessary enthusiasm to forge on. In this regard, I am grateful to Scott Wirth, Karin Lofthus Carrington, John Beebe, Dan Fee, Mitch Walker, Mark Thompson, Ken Pinhero, Tom Caldarola, Gareth Hill, Larry Jaffe, Howard Teich, Christine Downing, Kimn Neilson, and the Operation Concern Men's Team. Similarly, I would like to thank Ray Campton, Joanne Howell, Judi MacMurray, Helene Jia Hershel, and Martha Ruske Kassin for providing me—through my consultations with them—an opportunity to refine and reflect upon the particularities of men's individuation process; as their supervisor or consultant, I have learned at least as much from them as they have from me. Raymond Kilduff I would again like to thank for his dedication to my own individuation process, out of which so much of the present book has grown.

Then, last, I thank my friends who again may not realize how important they are in enabling me to write: their care for me and the relaxation we share is the foundation for my mental health in the course of a process which can be frustrating, isolating, and sometimes indescribable. Terry Huwe and Steve Risch, Cliff Adams and Steve Cattano, John Mendelson and Tanya Wilkinson, Jill Johnson and Rich Noronha, Rick Cotton, and Steve Elerding all mean a great deal to me and have assisted with their love in this book's creation.

Men's Dreams, Men's Healing

Introduction

That a book such as this one, in which the inner lives of men take center stage, should be inspired primarily by feminism is perhaps an ironic comment on psychology today. Yet in seeking to articulate what has impelled me to write this volume, I find that the impact of feminist thought on my life as a man and as a psychotherapist has been to show me just how sterile and outworn previous conceptions of men and conventional masculinity really are, and how the therapeutic process can give men a place to revise and expand what they think and feel about themselves as men in contemporary society. To say "feminist thought," though, is not to say very much, simply because by now this term encompasses so much and carries such an emotional charge. (A colleague of mine, when asked by prospective clients if she is a feminist, responds rhetorically, "What therapist in Berkeley would say they aren't?") Since some people would consider it a conundrum that a book on the inner lives of men was inspired by feminist thought, being more specific about how this book came to be is probably wise.

One might say actually that feminist thoughts, rather than some nebulous, general body of feminist thought, gave rise to both the purpose and the method of this examination of men's psychological healing. One such thought is the feminist critique of socially assigned sex roles—the cultural relativity of these roles, their one-sidedness, their inherent injustice, and the pain they cause women and men who attempt to fulfill their impossible demands. While

women are treated as "inferior" in the roles to which they are assigned, and while men ostensibly profit from the social benefits of
their "superiority," by now, twenty years into the contemporary
women's liberation movement, most observant people would agree
that really no one profits from gender-related roles when such roles
rigidly ignore the reality of the individual personality.

The freedom women have won and are continuing to win for
themselves from the constriction of their roles throws an unavoidable spotlight on the male half of this sex-role equation, personally,
socially, and psychologically. The suffering and the ultimate un-
workability of conventional, or as Jungians might say, collective
standards of masculinity often drive the men I see in my practice
into psychotherapy. Though the immediate symptoms are the ones
we shall see again and again in the various chapters that follow—
failed marriages, insecurities concerning fatherhood, compulsive
dedication to work and to achievement, fear of intimacy, lack of
even minimal feeling awareness, a virtual phobia of any sort of vulnerability, and inability to accept love from other men—the cause
of these symptoms I locate in traditional sex roles, which feminist
analysis and political action have helped to transform.

The second feminist thought informing this work on masculinity
is the validation, indeed the prizing of, that which is often denigrated and trivialized: the world of inner experience, of feeling, and
of intuition. To be masculine traditionally has been a quality mea-
sured by externals—physical attributes, success and achievement,
instrumental expertise and ability—a world with little room for the
inner reaches of the soul, with its tides and currents, its murky
depths, and its shimmering, elusive lights. While feminism has redeemed this inner world for women and has insisted on its importance in making women and those around them whole, it goes
without saying that men and men alone must find this other inner
half of their selves, not in the women they know and love, but
within themselves. Though they may not have any conscious sense
of this when seeking help for their suffering, men soon realize in
psychotherapy the importance of their inner lives in resolving the
conflicts they must resolve in order to go on with their lives. Psy-

chotherapy, they find, is a unique place in which to discover this *terra irridenta,* the unredeemed land, of their inner lives.

Thus, I have chosen in this book to frame the various issues I see contemporary men wrestling with in therapy nowadays by using that psychological marvel that exists only within—the dream. To use men's dreams as the conceptual and imaginal anchors for the discussions that follow is a move grounded more in the insights of Jung than in anything anyone could call feminist. Yet, in one sense, for all his overtly sexist attitudes and conceptions (for which contemporary feminists and others quite justifiably criticize him), Jung in his writings emphasizes aspects of human experience that are quite in tune with contemporary feminism. He consistently upholds the importance of the individual over the collective, showing himself to be a champion of feeling and intuition over rationality and instrumentality, a devotee of what he called Eros, the principle of relatedness, rather than of Logos, the principle of knowledge. (One telling example of this Jungian love affair with Eros can be found at the Jung Institute Library in San Francisco, where, in doing research, I discovered four times as many cards in the catalogue on Eros as on Logos.)

The dream stands at the center of Jung's thought, and his contribution to dream theory in contemporary psychology is perhaps the most elaborate and far-reaching ever developed. His insights into the purpose and workings of the dream, its sources, its connections, its transformative power, and the ways one can work therapeutically to unleash some of this healing force in the real lives of patients are insights unique in twentieth-century psychology. To ground my discussion of the issues men typically face in therapy these days by using the dream is to locate the following discussions in the rich tradition of Jung's psychology and to give the inner lives of men an all-too-rare place of prominence.

With regard to the dream, I am often asked to explain the differences between dream work, dream interpretation, and dream analysis to various interns when helping them work with their patients' dream material in therapy, and though they are subtle these distinctions are perhaps important to make. For me, dream analysis is a

process whereby the dream is broken down into its various constituent elements, in line with the original meaning of *analysis*, "to
dissolve or break loose." In Jung's method of dream analysis, the
dreamer is asked to associate to each of these elements, to bring into
the discussion whatever particularities or fleeting thoughts the dream
images bring up for him or her. Given the open-ended and highly
condensed quality of so many dream images, which are often really
images upon images upon images, this process of association in the
course of dream analysis may itself be quite an undertaking. In the
dream analyses that follow, we see just how intricate such material
can become.

One hopes that each of these elements of the dream (for example,
the images themselves, the succession of episodes, the qualities of
the dream images, the emotional tone of the dream, and its lasting
effect on the consciousness of the dreamer) when examined for its
meaning to the dreamer will lead to a point at which dream *interpretation* can occur, that is, a formulation or a series of formulations
reflecting the importance of the dream, its message, and its significance. The process of discussing a dream in therapy therefore does
not stop simply with analysis and the gathering of associations, as it
might in other therapeutic models, but proceeds toward a point of
conscious formulation, toward some kind of statement, or more frequently a series of statements, which may even at times be paradoxical, statements that somehow sum up the import of the dream
for the dreamer. This process of interpretation is vital to bringing
the power of the dream into the waking life of the dreamer, for
without conscious formulation, the individual ego may have experienced the dream quite deeply but has nothing to hold onto as his or
her inner process goes forward to other inner experiences, other
dreams. Interpretation is a way, however imperfect or tentative, of
pinning the dream down momentarily and learning from it in the
context of growth.

Of course, analysis and interpretation could both be understood
generically as "dream work," falling as they do under the category
of working with, that is, handling or examining, the dream material.
However, I see "dream work" as pertaining more to the way in

which analysis and interpretation of dreams occur in conjunction with a larger therapeutic enterprise, the "work" of therapy, as it is called in the psychodynamic tradition. For Jung and Jungians, the word "work" has a resonance, a double sense derived from Jung's alchemical researches, which heightens the dream's significance for psychotherapy.

The "work" of alchemy, the *opus* as the alchemists called it in Latin, was what most people probably associate with alchemy, the work of changing lead into gold. Jung's own familiarity with the medieval alchemical literature, though, revealed to him quite a different picture. While many practitioners of this obscure art undoubtedly went about the various processes and procedures unimaginatively seeking the material transformation of metals, Jung found a great number of alchemists who just as undoubtedly saw the work, the *opus,* in a less materialistic and more metaphysical way. This is clear both in the way they describe the alchemical process in often baroque and complicated imagery almost entirely unconnected with anything like a chemical process, and in the way that the goal of the work, the *opus,* is described, for example, as the "philosopher's stone," or with cryptic statements like "Our gold is not the common gold." Jung saw these alchemical descriptions for what they were: not chemical recipes for material transformation, but rather a body of writing in which the alchemists projected out onto the material reality of their substances the inner transformation, the coming to wholeness that they sought to produce within themselves spiritually. This *opus* Jung saw as a parallel to the work to be achieved in psychotherapy, and this movement toward wholeness, the recognition of conflicts and their resolution within the individual psyche, is what the dream work of psychotherapy is meant to enable. To do dream work, therefore, goes beyond the simple examination and formulation of the meaning of dream images and engages in the *opus* of one's inner life directly, which is the goal of psychotherapy in the largest sense.

For modern men, this work, this psychological *opus* as it occurs within the container of the therapy relationship, is of urgent importance. Modern men are broken in many ways, and traditional places of healing often seem cruelly only to exacerbate the pain. In turning to organized religion, many men find simply an ontological recapitulation of the one-sidedness and lack of creativity that landed them in their psychological predicament in the first place. The institutional church, therefore, may be simply one more instrument of alienation, rather than a place of deep self-knowing. Taking refuge in work is nowadays an equally chancy proposition. The character of the American workplace and the formerly undisputed economic dominance of the United States is in a state of profound world-wide transition, with challenges from all over. As a result modern men face either unprecedented professional insecurity—mass layoffs, high unemployment, the decline of industry, and almost unendurable entrepreneurial competition—or, on the other hand, equally unprecedented pressures to conform to a work world dominated by massive corporate structures that threaten to swallow their lives whole. Nor does the institution of the family seem to hold out much promise of stability these days for men who continue to seek wholeness outside themselves, since the family as an American institution is in a state of profound transformation as well. Perhaps it is on the road to something better than the previous state of nuclear-family isolation, but this road right now is characterized by disruption and anomie, not by rest and satisfaction. Thus finding nowhere to go for solace, many men I have seen think to flee their pain through alcohol, drugs, food, sex, gambling, or other compulsive behaviors, only to find, tragically, that their suffering has been multiplied rather than diminished, for in addition to the psychological, emotional, and spiritual conflicts they sought to avoid, these men also discover that they have now acquired an addiction to struggle with and through.

Such is the state of many men who walk through my doors for help, and while many of the explanations for the outward causes of their suffering come from feminist insights, it is their suffering as men, their search for a whole and workable sense of their masculinity, that grips me in the course of my work with them. As a man, I can validate their brokenness, having found those broken places in myself. As a man, I feel their suffering and lostness, for I share in it too. As a man, I see the various issues that have been pressed upon them by their dreams and their lives emerging in my life as well. The intention of this book is to bring forth some of these recurrent themes in the suffering and redemption of modern men's inner masculinity, and to do it by means of the dreams that we have been privileged to work on together. For those interested in Jungian dream theory, this book may present, in a way that few books have the time or space to, just how profound such dream work can be. For those interested in the inner lives of modern men and their struggles, this book may be quite a journey. The discussions at times become intricate, especially as the dream images that appear herein become amplified by symbol and myth, one way Jung found to lift up both the particularity and the universality of each individual's inner life. Happily for some, though, I do not assume familiarity with Jungian concepts, but instead take pains in the course of the various discussions to illustrate terms in analytical psychology that Jung and his followers have developed and that are relevant to the issues at hand. The point of even the most wide-ranging of the analyses that follow, however, is to arrive at the same place: to move toward a newer understanding of what it means to be a man in contemporary society and to do so in a way that is faithful to the individual soul. The reader may judge the success of my attempt.

We meet two men in this book, men who stand for a number of men with many of the same issues whom I have met over the years of my practice. Should the critical reader therefore claim that I am attempting to make sweeping generalizations regarding male psychology on the basis of two cases, my defense is that the range of issues I have chosen to focus on here is neither narrow nor meant to exclude others. My choice of these issues and the dream material that I use to illustrate these issues did not emerge *ex nihilo* or whimsically, but rather out of repeatedly encountering such issues in the course of thousands of hours of therapy and supervision work with a wide range of men. Within these particular cases, moreover, these issues were central to the healing process, so that if the reader were to read this book only as a pair of detailed case histories, the same purpose perhaps would be served.

The dream material is reported here with exactitude, as are the patients' associations, our interpretations of the dreams, and the outcomes of these interpretations, but the reader should know that many extraneous particulars of these men's lives have been camouflaged to help maintain their anonymity and limit their feelings of exposure. In addition to the fact that such disguising is ethically required, the sensitivity of some of the material that must be discussed for these dreams to be understood fully demands the alteration of nonessential information. Both patients have given their consent for the use of this therapy material with this understanding. To these men, and to all the men I have seen as a therapist, I dedicate this book.

1 *A Dream of Ants and Spiders: Men and Feelings*

I am asleep on my bed, which is beneath the window at the back of the house. Then I feel something on my chest—light, almost tickling. I open my eyes and see that ants and spiders are crawling across me. It's strange—I observe them calmly and make no move to brush them off or kill them. I simply watch them go their way as they walk across my chest, down onto the bed, then up the wall and out the back window. Watching them I notice that they are in orderly columns, in formation, like soldiers. The ants are large, like big fire ants, but these don't sting at all. The spiders are smaller and more delicate, and it strikes me that some of these are carrying others piggyback—don't ants do this? Still not moving but simply observing, I let my eyes follow their trail backward and notice that they are coming through the front door of the house, marching in a straight line through the living room, dining room, and then into my bedroom, up the bed, across me, then out the back window. The whole thing has a strange calmness to it—it is very early in the morning.

I asked Pete, after he had finished describing the dream, what he thought about the dream, which was the first he had reported in our sessions for at least six months. Unlike past responses in which he had dismissed dreams by simply saying, "I have no idea," this time he answered me quickly and directly, "I think the ants and spiders are my negative feelings."

Of course, negative feelings had been the latest topic of our meetings for at least the month prior to this dream, but not for the reasons the outside observer might suppose. For Pete, like many men, negative feelings had become the topic of his twice-a-week therapy sessions, not because of an abundance of such feelings, but rather, unfortunately and typically, because negative feelings were so rarely felt and Pete found himself quite unable to even identify such a feeling. Tellingly, feelings, negative feelings, had become merely the topic of our discussions, not yet a living presence in therapy. My intuition was that the dream, as dreams often do, was functioning to point out to the two of us precisely what Pete's relationship was to these much-discussed but as yet still abstract negative feelings he only very dimly perceived himself having.

But before we go on to examine Pete's dream in more detail, a little background is in order. I met Pete when he came to me for therapy at age twenty-five, a short, stocky gay man who found himself now three years past the time when he should have graduated from college. He seemed clear on the reasons for this delay: though an architecture major, he found himself often unable to draw. "Well, not really unable to draw," he told me in what I would find was a characteristic pattern of self-qualification. "I am able to draw; it's just that I'm not ever happy with what I do, so I find myself endlessly correcting it, trying to make it better, but what usually happens is that I end up somehow ruining the project, or having to start over. Well, I mean, sometimes I start over. Sometimes I am unable even to begin. When I start, I usually can't finish it, though. And when I do finish it, I usually hate the project and start over anyway."

For this reason, Pete decided to enter psychotherapy and, again in the words of many of my other male clients, "get the problem fixed" so he could at long last graduate. When we began our work together, he still had quite a few classes to take before he could graduate; he told me that academically he was considered a junior. Since his university no longer considered him eligible for student loans, he was forced to find part-time work as a word processor at a wage high enough to support himself. His need to work obviously cut down even further on his time for school, and, as he described his dilemma, I felt a sense of entrapment and desperation. Knowing men, I wondered if he was at all aware of these feelings.

"So it sounds as if you're coming here feeling kind of stuck and anxious, looking for a solution," I ventured.

"Exactly, a solution. It just can't go on like this."

After a short pause, I said, "You sound as if you're feeling kind of desperate."

"I just need to be able to draw and get my projects done." He looked at me with brown eyes wide.

"I'm wondering what you feel when you say that to me."

"I feel as if this has gone on too long and I need to get my act together. That's why I am coming to you."

Trapped in a situation with no clear out. Anxious about his ability to perform, to succeed, to produce. Desperate, as he grew older and as former classmates graduated and began their careers. As I listened to him and sensed the mood in the room, the urgency of his speech, and the directness of his stare, I conjectured further. Afraid perhaps, afraid of failure? Certainly needy: he was coming for help, having found no solution on his own for years. Panicky? This I dismissed. He seemed quite controlled, well-dressed, actually very professional-looking and sounding, a clean-shaven young man who paid meticulous attention to his hair and nails; his shoes were shined, his shirt cuffs ironed.

What other feelings did I pick up from him? Oddly I felt no uncertainty from him about my ability to help him. He seemed from the very first to trust my ability to "fix the problem" and "get him working" again, as he put it. I wondered if his faith in my abilities might not be due to the good recommendation I had received from the colleague who had referred him to me.

"You seem to be pretty sure that therapy with me is the answer."

"Marty said you have helped a lot of students with this kind of problem, so here I am."

"Do you have any feelings about coming here for help? Sometimes, people have feelings about going to someone for something they feel they can't do on their own." I felt myself push him a bit here, in order to evaluate whether he would be the exception or the rule.

Again, there was no pause or hesitation. His responses came back to me quickly and articulately. I was to find that silence would be a stranger in the room with us. "Feelings about coming here? Not at all. I just want to solve this ridiculous procrastination problem and get on with my life."

I nodded my head and merely said, "Oh." I had gotten the answer to my tacit question and felt a familiar sadness. Once again, like nearly every man I had ever seen as a therapist, like nearly every male patient any of my interns had seen, Pete found himself unable to identify much, if anything, of what he was feeling.

Of course, much has been written about men and feelings, but even those men I see in therapy who have read this now plentiful literature often begin their work with me in the same way Pete did: treating their difficulties as mechanical problems to be repaired, a process into which the inner life of their feelings enters not at all. Just as reading books on playing the piano is not quite the same as practicing scales, so, despite all the books on feelings, the situation of the vast majority of my male clients remains much like Pete's: no feelings about coming to therapy and talking to a stranger, no feelings about whatever the difficulty was that led them to pay for professional help, no feelings about any of the situations in the past that undergird their present relationships and are reexperienced in their present difficulties. And of course, no feelings about having no feelings. The anesthesia of male socialization, I have found, is still quite effective.

For this reason, unless given evidence to the contrary, I find myself often devoting the better part of the first year of therapy with a male patient simply to the development of workable emotional awareness. Interns I supervise, especially female interns, find themselves incredulous when I tell them that it might take that long for a man to acquire what I would consider the basic tools of therapy: emotional awareness, a sufficiently discriminating feeling vocabulary to express what they are feeling, and, sometimes hardest of all to develop, the necessary trust with me to actually feel the feeling in the therapy room. Many female interns, though, are not all that shocked. Their own myriad experiences with fathers, boyfriends, and husbands have taught them to expect little from men on this score. Many of the interns, male and female, do, however, share with me the sadness I felt with Pete in our first session, sadness at meeting yet another man whose inner world has been muted, discredited, and exiled. In my experience, such mistreatment of the psyche, especially the banishment of feeling from the inner realm of men's self-awareness, is both pervasive and insidious, and it is therefore nearly always the first and thus perhaps the most important issue men meet in psychotherapy with me again and again.

Pete and I indeed spent the first year of our work together focused on this task of feeling development, most of the time with him on one side of the room, intellectually analyzing the difficulties with the razor edge of his mind and reporting the results of this benumbed self-surgery with seeming ease and clarity, while I on the other side of the room often simply remained silent at the barrage of words that came at me. As time went on, though, I found myself more and more drawn into a certain kind of circular argument between us that would usually begin when I reflected feelings seeming to lie beneath his awareness. Pete's responses to such feeling statements would be a pressured torrent of counterassertions, rationalizations, and detailed but essentially irrelevant meditations on the how, why, where, and when of the situation. Though aware on some level of the danger he sensed in these feelings, I too often fell into the pattern of continuing to insist on these feelings, which naturally was nothing but an invitation to further counterassertions and rationalizations. The bottom line was that feelings were not safe, and my noticing them certainly did not make them any safer. On the contrary, my empathy seemed to draw out even more dangerous feelings—exposure, vulnerability, transparency, helplessness—and so around and around we went for some time.

More therapeutic, I feel, were those times when I simply noticed the feelings that seemed to be there and sat back, allowing Pete's intellectualized responses to fill the room with words, words, words—anything but those dreadful feelings. The atmosphere would then become dry and sterile between us without any of the juice of an emotional life lived in the present, and soon I began to feel the same sense of entrapment and desperation. Was I now caught, as Pete was, between his defenses against feelings and the anxiety that feelings—feeling anything—always provoked? Did I need to learn how to tolerate and work through this desert of intellectualization before Pete could find his way forward, too?

Often in the course of psychotherapy, certain people close to a patient seem to act in a way that furthers the psychotherapeutic agenda at various points. For example, Pete's only sister, who was two years older than he and had returned to school recently for a master's degree in fine arts, found herself taking an elective women's studies course in which the differences between male and female socialization took center stage. Synchronistically, in the midst of our work, she began likewise confronting Pete on his lack of feeling awareness, particularly the lack of feelings he had about shared family experiences that she had felt as painful or enraging. Similarly, a ex-lover of one of Pete's friends died rather quickly of AIDS-related pneumonia in the months after Pete had begun therapy, and his friend's grief and anxiety made my continual focus on feelings more and more comprehensible for Pete. As I began to notice how words seemed to be used to substitute for experience in the room between us, and to wonder also what might be kept at bay by so few silences and so much verbal communication, Pete began slowly to see exactly what I had been noticing.

"But I *don't* feel anything," he'd tell me poignantly. "Am I just supposed to make something up to please you?" Other times he would admit a feeling, a mild one, but then dismiss it as useless, unimportant. "Well, I did feel a little annoyed, but then I figured why dwell on it? What's the use?" Then there were those times when his family background was used as an explanation. "We weren't supposed to feel," he would say quite seriously. "Scandinavians don't have feelings."

His mother was described in almost stereotypical terms: of Danish descent, evangelical Lutheran from the Midwest. Unable to bear children, she and his father adopted his sister first and then Pete. His father, also Danish, described as large and taciturn, was largely absent, a self-employed accountant who spent long hours at the office and would return home tired and grumpy. Each of his parents, I learned, had no brothers or sisters. His mother's parents were from Denmark, spoke little English, and lived in an isolated rural enclave in Wisconsin. His father's parents had both died before Pete and his sister came along.

The picture was one of an isolated childhood, a certain kind of frozen loneliness, and I felt the Scandinavian winters in the barrenness of Pete's emotional life. When I would ask what it was like to not have many relatives, to know he was adopted, to feel very little relationship to his father, and to grow up gay in the Midwest, his responses were again typical of so many men. "I never thought about it much," he would say, or, "It wasn't really a problem," or, "I just decided I wouldn't care, and so I didn't," responses that revealed how thinking was used to control and dominate feeling, which was conceived of as problematic or dysfunctional, or, to use Pete's favorite term of derogation, "irrational." His being gay, contrary to the stereotypes, did not seem to afford him any special advantage in the feeling department either, for though he had been self-consciously gay since the age of thirteen and "out" to his friends and family for years at the time I saw him, his feeling awareness was every bit as stifled and difficult as any heterosexual male I had seen.

Sometimes he and I would clash. After a few months of working together, when it became clear his feelings were both valued and sought by me, I would specifically focus on whatever seemed to hold the most promise for feeling in any given session: "I keep wondering how it must have felt to come out to your parents." "When you describe being caught stealing candy, it seems there must have been quite a few feelings going on then." "It sounds like your grandmother's house was one of the few places you felt comfortable and warm." Ripe with some of these feelings and obviously longing to share them, he would nevertheless see my technique and fight back just as directly: "There you go again. Even if I did have feelings then, I don't have them now. That was all years ago."

At these points, I would then change direction, quickly and, I hoped, imperceptibly. Could I sneak up on his feelings? "It sounds as if you are kind of annoyed that I keep asking about your feelings."

"It gets tiresome, you know." His eyes fixed me steadily. "It's annoying."

I tried a bit more. "What's annoying when I wonder about your feelings?"

"Your insistence on it, like I need to produce something I don't know how to, something I've never been taught to produce."

"And when you're annoyed with me, what is that like in here?"

A precious, precarious moment of silence would ensue, a sure sign that the barrier of words had crumbled a bit and a real emotion was being felt, and he would then draw back, catch me at my game, and compose himself. "I really don't see the point of talking about my negative feelings in here with you. You are here to help me, I am here to be cured, and let's go on with it."

The brief skirmish over, I might then underline the point of what our latest go-round had meant therapeutically: "So it is hard for you to see what your feelings have to do with the problem you have come in here for."

"Especially negative feelings," he would say, looking away. "What good are they? They just get in the way."

Raised on a steady diet of messages that treat men as machines made to produce and achieve, an ideology of functionality perhaps endemic to a patriarchal, technological culture, Pete and many male clients miss the connection so obvious to psychotherapists: feelings influence behavior, unconscious feelings make for unconscious behavior, and unconscious behavior, without the guide and anchor of conscious awareness, all too often is unadapted to the outward demands of the individual situation. If we do not know what feelings engender our responses, we risk having our responses to situations and people fall into either familiar but inappropriate patterns or into exaggerated, bizarre forms of response that do not work.

Pete's "home remedies" for his drawing block are good examples of how feelings, when kept unconscious because "they get in the way," serve then to pervert and even destroy the very wish for functionality that their suppression is meant to preserve. A classic example of this dynamic would regularly occur when Pete would need to do a project for class. Rather than allow into his awareness his various feelings about having to forgo more pleasurable pursuits for work, he would simply fall into the familiar pattern of sitting down and forcing himself to draw, often with the thought, "I could just sit down and draw in high school, so why shouldn't I be able to now?" Although his conscious fear was that his negative feelings about working would get in the way of his drawing, the fact was that, in screening out and repressing these feelings, he could not come upon a creative resolution of the tension and was forced to adopt an inappropriate, outdated mode of behavior around work that did not fit who he was as an adult. Likewise we discovered that when his present abilities did not match his fantasized abilities he would further repress his negative feelings of disappointment, anger, and frustration, with the result that these feelings were then turned onto himself without his being aware of it. Having been taught to value himself for what he produced, not for who he was or what he felt, Pete had no choice but to attack himself for his failure to achieve. This internalized self-hatred, as well as various homophobic attitudes he had internalized through his development as a gay man, thus gave rise to various forms of unconscious self-punishment, for example depriving himself of fun until his work was done, wasting time in various irrelevant and often equally unpleasant tasks such as cleaning house and doing dishes, or being pestered by elaborate fantasies of humiliation at the hands of professors and classmates. We made some progress in bringing this self-hatred to awareness in one session when we were finally able to give voice to the running inner commentary, "the little voice," as he put it, that accompanied his work-avoidant behavior, a voice that continually chided and harped, "You can't do anything. You're just wasting your time at this. Why don't you just sit down and do this? You're incapable of managing your time and your life."

The connection between unconscious feelings and dysfunctional behavior may be obvious to psychotherapists, but most men I have met feel more like Pete. Feelings are the enemy, and they must be exterminated. Pete's sessions therefore grew more and more heated, as I maintained a steady lookout for any feeling whatsoever, good, bad, pleasurable, painful, mild, or extreme, and as Pete began to find himself sitting more and more on the fence between consciousness and unconsciousness, now all too aware of precisely how unaware he was of his inner emotional life.

Responding to my suggestion early on that remembering and discussing his dreams might be one important way to gain information on the source of his problems, Pete began to bring in dreams occasionally. I wondered briefly if his growing awareness of his unawareness might not have made dreams attractive, in that they seemed to hold the promise of getting to those feelings we were always talking about without necessarily forcing us to feel them. I had found dreams sometimes to be used by men as a way to avoid true feeling, especially with intellectual clients fond of analyzing the dreams symbolically rather than experiencing the dream affectively. One clue that this might be what Pete was up to unconsciously was that sometimes Pete presented the dreams explicitly as an offering to me. I wondered if this was intended as a sop for the feelings he was still unable to deliver. "You'll like this one," he might say, or, "I thought of telling you this dream as soon as I woke up." Comfortable or not in this role of psychic taskmaster, I had no choice. Unable to honor his feelings himself, Pete obviously needed someone to hold the banner of their importance waving until he himself was up to the task. So I listened and, not to his great surprise I am sure, continued to inquire about what feelings the dream and the dream situations brought up for him.

His initial dreams were quite dramatic, nightmarish really, clear compensations for his nearly complete lack of emotional awareness, as if the dreams were working to shock him out of his emotional numbness with gruesome and frightening images. They also seemed to catalyze those negative feelings he repressed in his thralldom to the patriarchal god of functionality, feelings that came to him in the dream images instead: sadistic killers, monsters, walls of water, and bottomless pits. Clearly such a situation would not do. Rather than move him away from his feelings, dreams, Pete found, landed him smack in the middle of them and in a way that could not be ignored or rationalized. The images were too vivid, their horror too real, and the sensations too well remembered on waking.

We thus entered another round of argumentation and intellectualization, but this time with a particular twist as befits a university student: feelings became a topic of conversation and an object of study, rather than a mode of interaction or a real experience in the room. He wanted to read literature on feelings, argue the various advantages or disadvantages of feelings, and wonder about their biological function. When he found me uncooperative and unchanged, continuing instead upon my steady course of noticing the feelings in the room and conjecturing about their existence outside of awareness, negative feelings began to emerge for Pete, first as a topic of conversation, and then in earnest, negative feelings about me in particular, about my ineffectiveness, about the irrelevance of my remarks, about my vacations, and about the fact he had been coming here for almost a year and still was not "cured."

Then, into this relationship at this moment for this man came the dream of ants and spiders.

Jung's idea of the dream is that it is an accurate representation of the current unconscious situation of the dreamer, a kind of photograph of the dreamer's psyche. Rather than using the idea of unconscious censorship to explain the weirdness and incomprehensibility of dreams or taking this incomprehensibility too seriously and thereby dismissing the dream, Jung found that the dream's strangeness lies in the fact that this photograph of the unconscious is composed of symbols, images pointing to something that can never be fully known. The oddness of most dreams, therefore, according to Jung, is due to the figurative language they use, the language of visual (and sometimes auditory and tactile) symbolism.

Like familiarity with a foreign language or, more analogously, with the artistic conventions of, say, Italian Renaissance painting, fluency with the language of dream symbolism allows one to discover meaning where there at first seemed to be nothing but a jumble of meaninglessness. Without knowing the various properties and qualities attributed to the pomegranate during the late

Middle Ages, one can hardly understand why certain fifteenth-century Italian painters show the enthroned Virgin Mary with a split pomegranate in her hand. Likewise with dreams: as natural phenomena, Jung assumed that they serve a purpose, that all their constituent elements serve a purpose, and that the purpose must be a psychic purpose since the dream is a psychic phenomenon. In assuming meaning, Jung found that dreams do indeed have meaning, but only after that meaning is created through the sometimes laborious task of familiarizing oneself with the language that the dreams speak.

In contrast to other psychologists, Jung upheld almost obsessively the importance of the individual for the study of psychology. To familiarize oneself with the language of dreams, therefore, is in actuality to familiarize oneself with the peculiar private symbolic language spoken by the inner lives of each individual patient. Despite the many parallels one might uncover to amplify and deepen our understanding of the dream of ants and spiders we are about to examine, the dream remains Pete's and only Pete's. Nevertheless the somewhat extensive introduction to this dreamer and the context of the dream ought to make clear how common Pete's situation is for contemporary men with regard to the life of their feelings, and how especially common the dilemma becomes for men in psychotherapy who find themselves faced with developing a long-atrophied side of their psyche.

The dream's first symbol is the delicious doubling back not uncommon in dreams. While sleeping in real life, Pete is presented in the dream as asleep as well, asleep beneath the open window at the back of his house. Is he dreaming in the dream? Many patients report dreams of dreams within dreams, being in movies in their dreams, which are actually movies about making movies, in plays about plays. Here there are no dreams, though, to trouble this sleeping sleeper. His unconsciousness is unruffled, his sleep undisturbed. Moreover, he is carefully tucked away in his bedroom at the back of his house, hidden from view of the street and the outside world, in a realm unperceived by the public at large. "At the back of his psychic house asleep" is in fact where Pete is located in relationship to his feelings, and the image stands as an excellent metaphor for the position of many men in the beginning stages of psychic healing. Not alert, not awake, and not at all in a place of communication or interaction, they wake up only to find that they have been asleep to their selves, blissfully unconscious of their psychic surroundings, of who they are, and of what they are feeling. In Pete's dream of sleeping, only the open window hints at what is to come: the way out and especially a back way out, a way not really yet usable, not a door but a window high up on the wall opening out. Onto what? Asleep, one cannot know. Aware and alert to the life of psyche, one might perhaps peek out and see.

Just as the window is open, suggesting that such peaceful sleep is not all there is to this bedroom at the back of the house, vague sensations begin to trouble Pete's sleep, sensations that tickle: an awareness that there is more to the self than has previously been encountered. The tickling seems once again an exquisitely appropriate symbol for the subject of this dream's commentary, since, like itching, tickling is a sensation that lies in an ill-defined place between pleasure and pain. Having not felt much of anything for so long, rendered senseless by unconscious necessity and by the norms of conventional masculinity, Pete experienced feelings as ticklish, prickling pins and needles while the psychic Novocaine of his defenses wore off, something not quite pleasurable—too intense, too distinct—but not quite painful either. Tickling is a sensation that draws forth a response, an interaction: one is tickled as the blood flows back into the immobilized limbs, as awareness again returns.

Pete's dream makes a further and more positive statement beyond the simple tickling, beyond the mere return of feeling to a life from which it has been too long exiled. The tickling awakens him. It cannot be ignored. The response that this tickling draws forth does not allow continued slumber. As the sensation crosses his chest, his heart, the very seat of feeling, Pete finds himself unable to maintain his unconsciousness. What is the source of this pleasure-pain that pierces his sleep, that forces him to open his eyes and look about him?

The collective situation of contemporary men, I think, is well represented here in this individual dream. Whatever all those wonderful childhood stories of awakenings have meant to women throughout the ages, like Sleeping Beauty, Snow White, Little Red Riding Hood, or Dorothy in the poppy field outside the Emerald City, this dream shows how this image of awakening applies equally to the inner lives of contemporary men as they find themselves unable to maintain blithe unconsciousness of their feelings and must open their eyes and shake off their sleep. Moreover, because the dream occurred within the context of ongoing psychotherapy, the imagery of awakening here, I feel, also makes a comment on what psychotherapy is for men today: to be healed as men, we must open our eyes to what is happening in our psychic surroundings, however uncomfortable, vague, or ambiguous the sensations may be. To ignore the tickling over our hearts would be to invite this tickling to grow into something more painful than pleasurable, just as an itch ignored quickly becomes a torment.

The collective situation of present-day men can be seen here in the dream of this individual man. Having ignored feelings until they have turned into nightmares of pain, Pete and many of the contemporary men I see in psychotherapy are now more attuned to their feeling lives; they are still asleep in some ways, but in the safety of the psychological relationship they become more apt to awaken and pay attention before the sensation turns to hurt and rage. Had my constant attention to feeling rendered Pete sensitive to the tickling on his heart? Had it been the greater sensitivity to men's alienation from emotion that he had found in the workshops he had begun to attend and in the literature he had begun to read? Has the old patriarchal masculinity of power, control, and reason finally worn itself down and become thin-skinned enough to awaken to truer awareness simply through the touch of an insect?

As the central symbols of the dream, the ants and spiders allow us to draw out the dream as a comment on men and feelings, especially Pete and his feelings. Following Jung's lead, I always assume that the dreamer knows the most about his own dream, if not consciously, then at least unconsciously in the form of the various themes that emerge as he and I work together on associating to the

various images presented by the dream. For Pete, the first association was really the only association: the ants and spiders were
clearly symbols of the various negative feelings he had been keeping at bay from our sessions.

When teaching dream interpretation to interns, I try to stress the
importance of the various qualities of dream images, rather than
focusing on simply what the image is. If the ants were associated for
Pete to his negative feelings, especially the negative feelings kept
out of the room and out of our relationship, then it is significant that
these ants were not the small common black ants of everyday experience, but the rather large fire ants of desert habitats. These were
feelings grown large in a hostile environment, feelings that normally bite and sting and that know quite well how to defend themselves against those who seek to invade their underground nests.
They were fire ants, fiery in their biting, fiery in their color, red and
passionate, angry and corrosive, aflame. To know that Pete dreamed
of ants is not enough; we must know and appreciate that fire ants
were the ants that crossed Pete's heart.

This very precise image made sense of the force behind Pete's
wish to exterminate these feelings from his life, a force behind the
wish of so many men who want to turn these fire ant feelings out of
their psychic homes. Who would want such vicious biting animals
living under one's roof and crawling over one in one's sleep? Ants
do get in the way, do they not? Stealing our food, invading our
spaces, they live in a counterculture poised to raid senselessly and
mercilessly. Like feelings, there is never just one but always a horde.
One can never feel just disappointment without more feelings coming along for the ride: anger, hurt, disillusionment, sadness, a whole
society of teeming feelings carried piggyback in a parade, one on
top of the other, a whole species of life just beneath the surface of
our calm, orderly homes, the conscious selves we think we know
ourselves to be.

Dreams of animals have a special potency, I have found, in giving image to what is essentially psychic. From the Latin *anima,*
soul, "anima-ls" are beings with souls, those who share a kinship
with all that is alive. If dreams compensate our consciousness, as

Jung believed, presenting us with what is missing from our everyday awareness, then dreams of animals seem to be telling us that we
too are alive and have souls, that we share in the life of all that
breathes and feels and propagates. As the overdevelopment of rational technology robs modern people of a sense of participating in
nature, animal dreams seem meant to restore this sense of the natural to us, to compensate the peculiar state of soullessness that afflicts
contemporary men in their search for that lifeless masculine ideal,
the perfectly functional, rational life. Such alienation from self is
certainly Pete's situation at the beginning of the dream and in the
beginning stages of his psychotherapy. Asleep to his soul, to his
own "anima-l" self, he is awakened by a more natural form of life,
which his feelings, his negative feelings, represent.

These considerations often give rise to what might be called a
standard Jungian intepretation, particularly among Jung's immediate followers, in which dream animals are seen to represent what
these Jungians call the more "instinctual" self—the animal self that
survives in human beings in the form of automatic, natural responses: the urge to live, to eat, to mate, and to carry out the most
basic functions of human life. In considering what the dream presents as the unconscious state of things to the dreamer and his
therapist, it is often fruitful to consider how close to human a dream
animal is in order to get a sense of how hard a patient might need to
work to relate to whatever instinctual processes the dream animal
symbolizes for him psychically. In Pete's dream, we see his negative
feelings represented by animals quite distant biologically from human beings. Unlike a dog, a cat, or a chimpanzee, animals with
whom most people could find a way to develop a relationship, very
few people would be able to relate in a meaningful way to an ant or
a spider. On the contrary, these are animals that if anything inspire
automatic horror and repugnance in most people. Considerably less
complex than human beings, ants and spiders are closer to the earth,
closer to the origins of life; they are animals whom Pete may have
quite a time trying to understand and care about.

Speaking psychologically, therefore, the appearance of ants and
spiders as symbols for Pete's negative feelings represents the rela-

tively undeveloped state of such feelings. They are not animals with whom one can easily have an individual relationship but are rather indiscriminate, basic, primitive, collective animals, acting on instinct more than on conscious reflection; they are automatic and unfeeling in their responses and behavior. In the 1986 remake of *The Fly*, Seth Brundel, the scientist who is turning into a fly due to a genetic accident, makes this point quite chillingly when, in attempting to protect his girlfriend from his more violent fly nature as it emerges, he asks her rhetorically: "Have you ever heard of insect politics? No? Neither have I. Insects don't have politics; they are very brutal, no compassion."

However, simply to notice the undeveloped, impersonal, collective state of Pete's feelings, as symbolized by ants, is really not to notice very much. This information I already had in abundance from our therapy sessions, and so an interpretation around the primitivity or collective nature of his feelings tells me nothing I do not already know. What the dream does reveal to me through its use of the particular animal images of the fire ant and the spider is the way that natural, instinctual processes such as feelings are characterized by Pete unconsciously. Distant from him in kind and size, they are potentially dangerous and invasive. They urge him out of a comfortable sleep to a world of greater awareness. Pete's dream is an example of how the dream symbol per se often does not give us as much information as the *qualities* that the dream symbol possesses, the often minute particularities of the symbol in the dreamer's dream.

Pete's situation is also the situation of many contemporary men in psychotherapy, whose feelings are imagined similarly and kept at bay. To let one in is to let in a horde, and so all feelings must be exterminated if the status quo is to be maintained, if life is not to be disrupted. Of course, the irony of this extermination ethic is that, by refusing to participate in the realm of the animal where soul and instinct meet in nature, men find themselves wrapped ever tighter into a hermetically sealed cocoon of control and isolation that disrupts their lives more completely than the more natural disruption posed by the presence of fellow creatures on earth. Certainly the boomerang effect of such patriarchal control and heartlessness is evident today as our atmosphere warms dangerously, as oil spills murder countless millions, and as pollution soils us from within and without.

Pete's dream strikes a positive note at this point, for the ants and spiders in their parade across his heart manage to disrupt his isolated sleep. They awaken him. Has psychotherapy and my own insistent focus upon that which represents Pete's truer, more instinctual and spontaneous self, his feelings, at last worked the disruption he has come to therapy to find?

Contrary to appearances, all patients come to psychotherapy seeking a disruption of their lives. While they may call this disruption various things, such as "change," "improvement," "cure," or "healing," the emotional reality is that change, improvement, cure, and healing are always experienced on some level as disruptions, both sought out and warded off, feared and desired. Pete's dream symbolizes this ambivalence in its use of ants and spiders as symbols for his feelings. In that these are animals normally not welcomed into the home, their disruptive presence and their closeness to his heart in the dream lead him to a greater awareness of his surroundings.

Having looked at ants as symbols of feeling and therefore symbols of both instinct and disruption, we find ourselves wondering if perhaps there may not be more to the ant symbol than what is contained on the level of personal unconscious, that is, in the dreamer's own associations and the characteristics of the particular ants and spiders in the dream. At such a point in dream work, a technique Jung developed is often useful for flushing out even deeper layers of meaning in the dream images; this is called the technique of amplification.

Amplification entails looking at the ways a particular dream image or situation has appeared over the ages in the myths and legends of the world. In putting the dream symbol in a wider context historically and imaginally, amplification serves to broaden the meaning of the dream for both dreamer and therapist and helps each to glimpse what enduring patterns of human behavior and imagination can be revealed by the dream. Jung called these patterns of behavior and imagination "archetypes," borrowing the term from the early church fathers, who themselves borrowed the concept from Plato. Dream amplification allows one to note what archetypal or collective situation is being enacted in the unconscious of the dreamer, and for the therapist such information enables a greater sensitivity to the broader human task in which the dreamer is participating. Amplification of Pete's dream is particularly appropriate, since Pete's dream was chosen by me for examination not just as a symbol for Pete individually, but as a symbol for the wider collective situation of contemporary men who find it necessary to develop another kind of relationship to their feelings.

To those who consider symbol amplification and world mythology irrelevant, a kind of gratuitous, academic distraction from the real work of psychotherapy, one can only respond that in one sense they are right. Amplification of dream symbols does serve to move one's focus away from the level of the personal content of a patient's dreams and directs one's gaze to the wider context in which the patient's growth is occurring. Jung's intention here was that, by putting a patient's personal process of change into a broader perspective, he might help a patient to see the way in which his or her personal conflicts and processes were connected to common human experiences and patterns. In this way, amplification enables patients to find facets of their essential humanity through their individual quests for resolution and wholeness. Certainly symbol amplification can be used in a distracting and unhelpful way in therapy, especially if it is carried out programmatically or made more important than the patient's own associations and experience. When used judiciously, however, amplification serves the function of enriching the therapist's understanding of the patient's inner life and at times deepens the patient's own appreciation of the forces in and around him.

Because we are concerned with Pete both as an individual and as a symbol of a particular set of masculine attitudes and patterns that I have met numerous times in my work, amplification of the ants and spiders seems especially in order, to shine some light on both personal and transpersonal meanings that the dream embodies for men today.

The Myth of Aeacus: Logos, Eros, and Our Native Soil

As one may imagine, there is hardly a huge body of myths concerning ants. Unlike some animals whose various attributes have rendered them legendary in ways that survive even today, for example the wolf, the eagle, the dog, or the lion, ants have fallen into the cracks of the ancient storytellers' repertoire. Besides Aesop's well-worn (and not very symbolic) tale concerning the thrifty ant and the flighty grasshopper, ants seem to have been put into the same category as Pete's negative feelings—too small to notice or bother with, and too much trouble to observe or spin a tale about.[1] However, one Greek myth does elevate ants to a position of importance. We will find that this tale, along with its historical background and its variants, is quite well suited to our discussion and explicates to some degree why ants, rather than eagles or lions, appear in Pete's dream as the best possible representation of his long-ignored negative feelings.

Psychotherapy, especially in its function of reconstructing the past, is testimony to the enduring human desire to discover and explain the origin of things. To see nothing but this in myth is, to be sure, a gross oversimplification of the myriad complex impulses that give rise to myth in a society, and yet with equal certainty one can say that one of these many impulses is indeed the common fascination all humans modern and ancient share in knowing where we came from. The myth of Aeacus is thus, first and foremost, a myth of origin, a tale meant to supply the history of a small but long-inhabited island off the coast of mainland Greece, the island of Aegina.

Surrounded by the waters of the great inland sea only later called "our sea" by the victorious Romans, this bit of land had not always borne the name of Aegina. Once called Oenone or Oenopia, a name that alludes to bountiful wine from its vineyards, the island was forever transformed when Zeus, king of the gods and insatiable womanizer, stole Aegina, the youngest daughter of the great river god Asopus, away from her father's home. After reducing her indignant father to a lump of burning coal with lightning from on high, Zeus brought the young girl to Oenopia for a love tryst. Made queen of the island by virtue of her relationship with the mighty Zeus, Aegina soon found that she was with child and in time bore the king of the gods a son whom she named Aeacus.

Zeus's wife Hera, however, whose immortality made her no less jealous and vengeful than any earthly wife would be in a similar situation, eventually found out not only about Zeus's extramarital adventure but also about the existence of his son Aeacus, and those familiar with Greek myth know that Hera's jealousy is a natural force to be reckoned with, against which few mortals prevail. Aeacus in the meantime had grown to manhood and succeeded his mother to the throne of the island, which he had named Aegina in her honor. Under the force of Hera's wrath, Aeacus and the inhabitants of Aegina, innocent as they were of wrongdoing themselves, nevertheless became victims of plagues visited upon them from the infuriated goddess: a poisonous snake hatching equally pestiferous eggs through the waters of Aegina's rivers; harsh winds and darkness laying waste to its harvests. Painfully and slowly, the island died, strangled by Hera's curse.

In his desolation and loneliness, Aeacus cried up to Zeus. His realm now ravaged and empty of life, Aeacus wandered the once-bountiful land, without companion, stricken, lost, looking for a sign that might indicate the end of the pestilence and give hope for the island's now decimated population. Putting his entire faith in the power and care of his father, Aeacus worshiped Zeus, observing the rituals sacred to the god and attending to the holy places his father had established on the island. In this state of dire necessity, powerlessness, and desperate longing, Aeacus lay down one night and dreamed of a shower of ants from the venerable oak tree on the island, a tree sacred to Zeus. These dream ants, though, were not the common black ant of ordinary experience, for when these dream ants touched the ground, they instantly arose as full-grown men, repopulating the island in such number that even the relentless plagues could not obliterate these new inhabitants. Upon waking, Aeacus thought the dream foolish, as many of us would, a product of an overactive mind in desperate straits. However, his young son Telamon came to him quickly, pointing out the bedroom window to a huge crowd that seemed to be approaching the palace. Were these men or ants? Still far away, they seemed so small and so numerous that Aeacus thought at first they could not be anything but yet another plague, this time a devouring horde of ants. Yet he discovered that his dream had not been mere fantasy but rather the sign of a miracle taking place, for what approached the royal palace were certainly not ants but full-grown men, men created from ants by Zeus to repopulate the island devastated by Hera. Aeacus named these men Myrmidons, from the ancient Greek word for ant, *myrmex,* and the name of this population lives on in history thanks to Aeacus's grandson Achilles, for whom the Myrmidons served as unswervingly loyal fighting companions in the subsequent Trojan war.

Such is Aeacus's story, retold of course for modern ears, a tale whose symbols, themes, and mythic purpose have a great deal of psychological relevance to contemporary men like Pete. To see this relevance, though, one needs to disabuse oneself of the naive notion that ancient Greek myths were told simply to pass the time or to entertain the hearers. As mythologists such as Robert Graves and Jung's long-time peer Karl Kerényi show in their own accounts of the tale, the myth of Aeacus had a political purpose for the Myrmidons and was meant to establish them as the indigenous inhabitants of the island instead of the rather greedy mainland Greeks who in their imperialistic expansion overtook the outlying islands and claimed them as their own.[2] The myth therefore portrays the Myrmidons emerging like ants from the land, autochthonous in the literal sense of the term, "of the earth itself," defiantly repopulating the devastated land with their own multitudinous kind. The Myrmidon-Aeacus myth both on its most obvious level and in its historical context tells the story of the reemergence of life from the native soil of one's home. For modern men and especially for Pete, who like Aeacus had been sent a dream of ants, the message seems to be that the ground of our being has the capability of generating new life if we, again like Aeacus, open our hearts to this renewal. The message of hope in Pete's dream is reinforced by this myth of renewal from the earth.

Another modern misconception concerning myths that one does

well to lose is the notion that a myth can be viewed outside its historical context as some sort of eternal, unchanging tale. The reality of myth is that there is nearly always another story hidden beneath the manifest story, a historical subtext that gave rise to the tale as we know it. One ought not to come at a myth too credulously. This tale appears to be a men's myth *par excellence,* the story of a rape by the father god of Olympus whose issue founds a race of heroic men, the story of an island kingdom destroyed by a goddess but saved by the fecundating power of Zeus. Yet the clue that all is not what it seems in this myth comes from the central symbol itself, for the ant, as Graves points out, is not an animal sacred to the father god of ancient Greece but is rather the animal-emblem of the mother goddess worshipped in the ancient Greek region of Thessaly.

Thus, like so many other myths, this myth represents in its struggle between Zeus and Hera nothing remotely as banal as the supposedly eternal "war of the sexes," but rather the much larger, more fundamental religious conflict in Greek civilization, namely the conflict between the older mother goddess religions of the pre-classical era and the newly emerging, rapacious, and patriarchal Olympian Zeus religion that had come to dominate Greek life in ever-expanding ways.[3] The subtext of Aeacus's myth is, therefore, not on a personal level, that is, concerned with representing the strife between husbands and wives, but is rather on a deeper, transpersonal or religious level; it represents the struggle between what Jungians would call the archetypal feminine, the Mother Goddess Hera and all she represents, and the archetypal masculine, the Father God Zeus and all he represents. The fact that the myth as it survives today portrays Hera in such a derogatory fashion, as a jealous shrew whose wicked vengeance upon innocents ultimately does not prevail, shows how complete the triumph of patriarchy has been. In contrast, the fact that Zeus disrupted nature's unfolding by stealing the daughter of the great river god Asopus; that he secreted her away from her origins, isolated her upon an island of his choosing, and bade her do his will; that he in this way betrayed his own relationship to his wife and queen and continued his deceit, though it meant devastation to the kingdom of his own son—these facts tend to be forgotten in the dazzle of the miracle Zeus produces at the end of the tale. Only our knowledge that the ant is sacred to the mother goddess, not to Zeus, and our awareness of the historical conflict that existed between matriarchy and patriarchy in Greek civilization allows us to see these figures, "heroic" Zeus and "vengeful" Hera, in a different light. Instead of such a masculine myth, the historical context has the myth tell a very different story, a story of what happens when the feminine is wronged and raped.

Jung developed and used two terms that give image to this masculine-feminine struggle. More evocative and poetic than clinical and precise, the terms Logos and Eros came to be used by Jung to delineate two principles of human life that Jung had discerned in operation among men and women. Logos, Greek for "word," Jung termed quite appropriately the "principle of knowledge" and described it as a principle traditionally identified with men and masculinity. Logos seeks out knowledge, analysis, clear-sightedness, light, hard edges, and well-defined spaces. Eros, on the other hand, derived from the name of the goddess Aphrodite's son, is what Jung called a "principle of connection," a principle traditionally identified with women and with femininity in general. Eros seeks relationship, connection, warmth, oneness, interaction of feeling, life, spontaneity, and merger.

In his own words, Jung says: "Eros is an interweaving; Logos is a differentiating knowledge, clarifying light. Eros is relatedness. Logos is discrimination and detachment." He also acknowledges elsewhere that he regards Eros and Logos "as intuitive ideas which cannot be defined accurately or exhaustively. From the scientific point of view this is regrettable, but from a practical one it has its value, since the two concepts mark out a field of experience which is equally difficult to define."[4]

For Jung, these two principles of human life are well represented by the various gods and goddesses of the Olympian pantheon, though the ascription of Eros or Logos to exclusively one gender or the other is both wrong-headed and overly literal, a point on which Jung was not often clear. Even among gods and goddesses, the facile equation of Eros with femininity and Logos with masculinity is inaccurate. Athene is every bit as representative of the Logos principle in her role as goddess of wisdom as the male god Eros himself is representative of the Eros principle with his power to instill (often fatal) attractions between people. Further support for such cross-gender identification of Eros and Logos lies in the parentage of this goddess and this god, since Athene sprung from Zeus's head and thus in some ways represents patriarchal masculinity, while Eros is his mother Aphrodite's helpmate, the eternal child bound to this personified feminine principle of love and relationship.

Using these two Jungian concepts to make deeper psychological sense of Aeacus and the Myrmidons, we see the myth portray what occurs when Logos masculinity proceeds forward untrammeled and unbalanced by Eros or by femininity. Seeking simply his rights and prerogatives as king of the world, Zeus ignores the relationship to and feelings of his wife Hera, just as his lust overrides the attachments of his young prey Aegina. In his figure we see the way the rising patriarchalism of Greek culture scorned and swept away with little respect the preexisting religion of the Greek provinces, in which the various mother goddesses and their son-consorts balanced masculinity and femininity, Logos and Eros. Aeacus's story, when seen through these lenses, tells of what happens when men become identified with Logos masculinity and lose touch with their native soil, their origins, and their relationship to the feminine. The land of their soul grows barren, plagued with many ills. Life dwindles, their hearths and homes grow still and dead, and a ghost town emerges from what once flowed with the wine of conviviality. King Aeacus wanders alone among the ruins of such a patriarchal overvaluation of the masculine, beset by isolation and at the end of his hope for renewal.

The parallels to the situation of modern men like Pete ought to be obvious. When Logos and Eros are torn apart and seen, not as formless psychological principles shared by both sexes but rather as discrete psychological patterns to be enacted and indeed enforced along gender lines, with men the Logos carriers of all humanity and women the bearers of Eros for generations upon generations, the

Aeacus myth with its historical context warns us to beware. When masculinity consists of lordly power, control, and analysis and when men find themselves enjoined to embody this one-sided masculinity so highly prized by patriarchal cultures such as our own, they wake up, like Pete, like Aeacus, and like countless contemporary men, to find their kingdoms devastated and their companions destroyed. The split-off and despised femininity that these men have sought to exterminate returns their efforts in kind, withdrawing its enlivening hand and allowing men's lives to wither and die. If qualities typically termed "feminine" are projected out onto women exclusively, if women are made to bear men's feeling, men's fertility, and men's creative, spontaneous, and free-spirited sides, and if men do not understand how as men they too possess what is called "feminine" by a patriarchally unbalanced culture, then a man's native land, his masculinity itself, dries up, the water of his inner life bears death instead, and harsh winds blow unmediated through the hollow halls of masculine glory.

The ants of Aeacus's myth, like the ants of Pete's dream, are positive signs, however, of a return of the Mother Goddess and her ability to populate from the very land itself. The ants are archetypal symbols of the essential humility and earthiness of the Great Goddess, the Queen Ant of Phthiotian religion.[5] Prepared by months of digging in the course of psychotherapy, Pete's native soil, his inner self, suddenly finds feeling and life returning; Eros reemerges after a fruitless, crippling search for a perfect Logos masculinity of control and correctness. There can be no creativity without feeling, true feeling, both positive and negative, and for modern men, there can be no feeling if conventional conceptions of masculinity and femininity continue to be applied unthinkingly to literal men and women. Men, in understanding Eros feeling and Eros connection as exclusively feminine, betray an essential part of their humanity and enjoin the women in their lives to bear a terrible burden that can only invite outrage and vengeance. Slowly, and usually only at the end of great suffering, we see the Goddess creep back into our lives in humble form through the cracks under our psychic doors.

Ancient myths do not exist in canonical form, set down in one fashion and only one fashion for all time. Orally transmitted, myths flow, change, and develop, with motifs and symbols popping up in numerous variants that amplify and complete each other in various ways. The man (or woman) identified with Logos psychologically may find such mythic inexactitude unbearable, but those with a taste for story and a tolerance for interconnections are presented with yet another "mytheme," that is, a theme or motif common to a number of myths, a mytheme that ties together the ants and spiders for Pete and for contemporary men in search of masculine healing.

Myrmex and Arachne: Hubris, Patriarchy, and the Return to Instinct

In his retelling of the Aeacus myth, Graves includes an interesting coda to the longer myth presented above.[6] According to Clement of Alexandria, the Myrmidons are reported to have been named as a people after the nymph Myrmex, who claimed that she invented the plough. When Athene, the real inventor of the plough, heard of the nymph's bragging, she turned Myrmex into an ant as punishment for her pride.

Conveniently enough for our purposes, this shorter myth on the origins of the Myrmidons allows us to turn our gaze toward the other insect symbol in Pete's dream, the spider, since this briefer Myrmex-Athene story bears a striking resemblance to the better-known story of Arachne, told by the Latin poet Ovid in his compendium on the many forms of the gods, *Metamorphoses*.

Arachne, a princess of Lydia, a region known for its dyes and textiles, came to the attention of Athene because of Arachne's accomplishment at weaving, one of the many arts practiced to perfection by the goddess herself. Affronted by Arachne's seemingly superhuman skill, the goddess challenged the mortal woman to a weaving contest, and, after finding no fault in the great tapestry that Arachne had finished with speed equal to Athene, the enraged goddess tore

Arachne's cloth to pieces. Humiliated in public, Arachne fled and hung herself, only to have Athene turn her into a spider, an animal that Athene held in great contempt.

A story familiar to many people, the Arachne myth is much more than a fabulous nursery tale meant to explain the origins of the spider. The ancient trade rivalry that existed between Athens and Lydia forms the historical subtext for the contest between the two protagonists and certainly informs the denouement of the tale, which ends with Athene's (that is, Athens') eventual victory and her humiliation of the defeated Lydia. Moreover, again using historical background to put this myth into its proper context, the transformation of Arachne into a spider as a symbol of contempt is also derived from the rather thorough-going devaluation of feminine symbols carried out by the patriarchal political system of Olympian religion, since the spider, like the ant of the Myrmidon myth, is a symbol of the archetypal feminine, especially the power of the archetypal feminine to give and withhold life.

Legendary for their "mate and kill" behavior, the black-widow spider, for example, represents the power the female possesses over the male of the species, a power that men often negatively characterize as bewitching, manipulative, or devious. This "black-widow" theme is a special favorite of moviemakers who, in such *films noirs* as *The Postman Always Rings Twice, Mildred Pierce, Double Indemnity,* and *Black Widow,* represent the same theme of the scheming wife and the hapless husband.

Thus, the spider's web adds another layer of symbolism to this image of feminine power, the feminine's power to bind and snare. The symbolism of the spider's spinning and weaving, traditionally female occupations, in turn bring to mind those other awe-inspiring female spinners of Greek myth, the Fates, who share much in common with the spider, creating or destroying the web of our lives with a turn of the spindle or a snip of their scissors. The spider in this connection stands for the primordial feminine, the Great Mother, who as Erich Neumann points out holds in her hands manifold forms of life and death.[7]

Of course, when seen through patriarchal lenses in which all that is supposedly masculine is revered while all that is supposedly feminine is feared, the spider and all her attributes—her web, her ability to spin and weave, her smallness, her darkness, her creativity—can only be characterized in a negative way. The term "spinster," for example, is hardly a complimentary term, nor do spiders figure high on the list of people's favorite insects. Woody Allen capitalized on this feeling toward spiders to comic effect in the scene in *Annie Hall* in which a spider in Annie's bathroom is reported to be "the size of a Buick" by Alvy, who in his terror uses an enormous broom to exterminate the tiny insect.

This male madness nevertheless has serious consequences when mortal men attack and suppress women's power, the power of the spider. Rather than speak positively, as feminist Carol Gilligan does in her book *In a Different Voice,* of women's ability to weave a "web of interconnectedness,"[8] patriarchally socialized men (and women) often feel women's power, their connection to the mysteries of life and death, as a threat, a way to strangle the autonomy and independence insisted upon by overvalued patriarchal ways of being in the world.

In this way, the two brief myths of Myrmex and Arachne touch upon another theme, endemic to Greek mythology and all too relevant for the souls of contemporary men: the theme of hubris and its effects. As the Greek term for that overweening pride that leads mortals in self-inflation to challenge the very gods and goddesses themselves, hubris is a theme that pervades Greek myth and drama. Again and again we find characters gripped by this destructive pride—Daedalus flying too close to the sun, Phaeton unable to control the sun's chariot that he steals, Oedipus thinking to outsmart the Delphic oracle's dire predictions—men swollen with arrogance in the literal sense of the term, arrogating to themselves a perfection that belongs only to immortals. Arachne and Myrmex supply female examples of hubris myths, women daring to arrogate to themselves technical perfection belonging to the realm of Athene. Myrmex's braggadocio is more evidently hubristic than Arachne's abilities, and yet Arachne is foolish enough to accept Athene's challenge to compete. In the end, both maidens find themselves humbled, transformed into the two insects of Pete's dream, the ant and the spider.

Through the lenses of patriarchy, such transformations are portrayed as punishment, humiliation, a lowering of status and species. However, our analysis of these myths and Pete's dream challenge us to see the animal symbolism more positively. As symbols of the feminine, transformation into ant or spider, as in the stories of Arachne and Myrmex, may not simply be a punishment but rather a return to the kind of natural humility that hubris-ridden competition destroys. To re-interpret the animal symbolism of these two short myths here is supported to some degree by the Aeacus myth in which the ant is a positive symbol of the chthonic feminine and its vital role in restoring life to a lifeless, feminine-denying island.

Certainly nowadays conventional conceptions of masculinity reek of what the Greeks would call hubris. Pete entered therapy because of the destructiveness and desolation caused by that stereotypical masculine virtue of functional productivity. In his studies and career, Pete's external achievements were all that mattered, and, like Myrmex and Arachne, his hubris invited the drawing block that drove him into finding another path forward, the path of ants and spiders, the way of greater humility.

Between Pete and me, Pete's inability to cede a point and thereby relinquish control in our sessions led, as we have seen, to our engaging in repeated fruitless argumentation, unenlivened in any way by those qualities one might consider "feminine," in this case, an ability to be interdependent, to take in another point of view, to hold and quietly reflect on something brought inward, to gestate a feeling within. As a man, I was as prey to such patriarchal hubris as Pete, and my insistence on points I ought to have simply noticed and then passed over contributed at least as much to our wrangling as Pete's difficulties around control.

Thus, to be an ant or a spider, to find oneself in a form closer to archetypal femininity, closer to the ground from which we all have sprung, closer to the realm of the natural—is this a punishment or is it salvation from masculine hubris? Remember: in Pete's dream, the ants do not sting, and the spiders help each other along the way. If these animals represent the feeling realm split off from Pete's masculine self that needs to come back into his psychic home, then these feelings have their own order and their own goal, for they are in formation as they pursue their own important journey forward.

Pete sits back finally and simply watches. He does not threaten, he does not control, he does not guide, he does not exterminate. He simply watches these "anima-ls" flow over his naked body, as the dawn appears in the window. The myths of Aeacus, Myrmex, and Arachne point out the larger conflict Pete and all men struggle with if their deeper, feelingful self is denigrated and suppressed in favor of a shallow, one-sided masculine ideal that excludes this spontaneous, grounded sense of oneself and others. The historical context of the myths seems also to indicate how this conflict between masculine hubris and a more relaxed sense of one's masculinity that admits "feminine" characteristics afflicted even ancient Greek men's ways of envisioning the world and was at the root of the ongoing conflict between the older matriarchal religion and the newer, male-dominated Olympian religion of Zeus. When men learn to sit back and let be, like Pete in his dream, like Aeacus in his dependence on forces greater than himself, then the realm of the spider and the ant come forth, dark, low, and small, but with purpose and intention, marching through the window of opportunity to a wider world and a new dawn. As the pose of conventional manliness is relinquished for a more fluid, emotional way of being, so often called "feminine" but clearly as necessary to men as to women, then the macho insanity of technological inflation cedes to a simpler, more basic self, the instinctual animal self, which is the ground of all enlightenment.

By rediscovering and revaluing this forgotten side of masculinity, psychotherapy, through dreamwork and the therapeutic relationship, can bring forth from the souls of men like Pete the spidery web of feeling and the ant-like deliberation so needed on that journey Jung called individuation. An individual, that is, a person whole and undivided, is the aim of psychotherapy, and Pete's dream of ants and spiders illustrates one important piece of the individuation process for men born and bred within a patriarchal culture. Recognizing and honoring one's feelings is one step toward men's healing. For another step along the way, we turn to another man and a pair of arresting dreams.

2 *The Dream of the Adolescent Cop: Men and Authority*

I'm in the car on my way to a special occasion in my hometown. My three sisters and other women are in the front seat, while my father and I are in the back seat. Dad is on my right and I am sitting right in the middle, though there is no one on my left, so I am sitting close to Dad, which is unusual. Dad is driving, but my sisters and the women distract him, pointing out various sights. I realize we're lost and that Dad doesn't know where he is going. Up ahead I see a conflict in the road between a group of adolescent boys and some policemen, who shoot the boys when they are threatened. I feel myself getting anxious, a kind of "Watch out!" feeling. That's when this adolescent cop walks in front of us and stops our car. He's pimply-faced, redneck-looking, swaggering, and brutal, mostly, I feel, because he is insecure. He looks at my father and me and says, "That's what happens when you mess with us."

It took some doing for me to clear away the raft of feelings and associations this dream evoked in me so that I could get about the business of helping Nick become conscious of what this dream might mean for him. In the first place, as sometimes happens, I felt the dream on a visceral level, felt the anxiety, the impending violence, the sense of being lost, felt them all in a way that I have come to recognize. I was having Nick's feelings for him, often the first step in therapy with men alienated from their emotional life. But of course, too, our relationship had been unconsciously structured in the last six months so this would happen, so that I would carry the "work" of our work, and I was aware of this unconscious dynamic between us as well. "At last," I said to myself. Perhaps through work with the dream I could somehow give back to Nick what he had been assiduously giving over to me to carry and make sense of, session after session: the emotional experience of his inner life.

If Nick felt any of these gut feelings, if he was swamped with associations, his outer appearance did not betray it. He reported the dream with the same dedicated diffidence that characterized these first few months of our relationship, with a manner that might have been mistaken for detachment except that it had more the air of a dutiful performance. He rarely looked at me, but kept blue eyes downcast, his longish brown hair framing his face in such a way as to make him seem twenty-five, rather than thirty-five. He brought himself here, week after week, more, I felt, out of a sense of having to than of wanting to.

"What do you think the dream is about?" I asked tentatively, after some moments of silence.

He too paused, thought, and then characteristically shrugged. "I don't know. I was hoping you could tell me."

His submissiveness was striking. After all, he was a fairly big guy, sturdily built and rather rough-looking. Because our sessions were at 6 P.M., right after his work as a tile setter's apprentice, he came dressed in his workman's clothes, redolent of sawdust and construction, flannel shirt pulled out, hands blotched with mortar or tar. From the outside, Nick looked like the ideal American male: hard-working, handsome, strong; the kind of guy who can wield a wrench, fix a car, support a family; not at all someone I would expect to come to me with lowered eyes and ill-concealed helplessness; not at all someone who would be caught at a loss before a problem. On the other hand, dreams, relationships, and feelings, I have found, often seem to stop many men dead in their tracks.

Was Nick really at that much of a loss before his inner life, or did he just seem to be? I wondered about this question a fair bit during the early part of our relationship. He had begun therapy with me in a rather unusual way, as half of a couple. His wife, Judy, had made the appointment with me, but when the hour arrived, I found only Nick in my waiting room. "It's just me today. Judy isn't coming."

Bringing him into my office, I was all set to handle the situation in my standard fashion and explain to him why I could not see him for marital work without Judy present. He beat me to the punch. "Judy and I have been talking and we have decided that the real problem between us is my dependence on her, so that's why I think I should be in therapy alone. The problems with our relationship are more about me than about the two of us together."

"Dependence on her, you said. What does that mean for you?"

"Well," he shifted a little nervously, looking away from me, unused to putting these things into words. "I'm dependent on her emotionally."

"Which means . . . ," I prompted him.

"Which means . . ." He sat in thought for a while, searching for the words with a baffled expression on his face. "Well, I don't know. The way Judy puts it is that she feels like she's my mother. She's always doing things for me."

"Doing things? You mean around the house or . . . ?"

Again, nervous shifting. I realized he was dressed up but not comfortable with what he was wearing, as if in his Sunday best. Had his wife dressed him to come here? He cleared his throat. "Yeah, but not really. More like in the relationship. She doesn't have a whole lot of time to do stuff around the house, but it's like if we do anything together it's because she initiates it. If there are problems between us, she's the one who starts the discussion."

"So I guess I'm wondering how it feels to be here since Judy's the one who made the appointment. Do *you* think individual therapy would be helpful?"

He looked at me as if I had called an already-settled matter back into question and so did not really know what to think. "I guess so," he finally said. "What do you think?"

This time I took a moment, mostly to take stock of my reservations: the issue was "dependence" and he had not even made his own appointment; he was more here, I felt, to please his wife than out of a burning sense of his own suffering or unhappiness. And yet, how else would—could—such a man initiate psychotherapy if he needed it? After all, having not even known me for five minutes, he waited for *me* to tell him if *he* could use therapy! Rarely had the presenting problem been so perfectly demonstrated so quickly. But how could I answer him without furthering the dependence?

"What I think, Nick," I told him with as much empathic tact as I could muster, "is that I am willing to explore what's going on for you for a while until we see whether or not *you* think seeing me is helpful. How does that sound?"

"Okay by me." He sat still, and an awkward silence lapsed in which he took in my office, attempting to appear nonchalant. Then he met my eyes again. "So where should we start?"

Clearly, I told myself, dependence is the issue.

I was soon to find out that a great deal came under the heading of "dependence" for Nick and that the roots of it ran deep. In his present relationship with Judy, there was certainly the emotional dependence he had mentioned, dependence that ironically he had depended on her to point out to him. I got a full dose of this emotional brand of dependence in our sessions, since his lack of feeling awareness made it necessary for me to take the lead often in inviting him to explore himself—no doubt, I imagined, the way his wife often felt with him.

She, I learned to my surprise, was a junior partner in one of the big law firms in San Francisco, a "capable and decisive" woman, as Nick described her, four years younger than he. In exchange for his supporting her through law school, she was now the primary provider for the two of them as he attempted to make a go of learning tile setting as a trade at minimal pay, the third such attempt at a career he had made. His appearance in my office, I found out, had been preceded by now almost twelve years of directionlessness, a long period following college in which he had wandered around the country taking odd jobs here and there. After a brief stab at beginning a restaurant in the Southwest, where he met and married Judy, the two of them moved to San Francisco for her law-school education where, through the intervention of his father, he was hired as an office manager for a financial-investment firm run by a family friend. This last job he left two years earlier, and when I asked what prompted him to leave, he had no real answer. "It was time to go, and besides, Judy was earning enough by then for me to start to take it easier." In explaining his present choice of career as tile setter, his thoughts were equally vague: "I've always liked working with my hands and besides, my friend Brian, who is now my boss, thought I would be good at it."

As therapists are prone to wonder, I was interested to discover what kind of family might have produced such aimlessness, and, as is often the case, I found a life lived in clear reaction to childhood. Nick's father was a Lutheran minister—"American first, Missouri Synod second, and Christian third" was his father's self-description, Nick told me—who had grown up in St. Louis, a third-generation German-American of Prussian descent. Nick's mother, also born and bred in a long-established Missouri family, had married his father with the knowledge and intention of pursuing a full-time career of sorts as a minister's wife. Of the two, I heard far more about his mother than his father in the first few months of our meetings, and she was always described with many of the same adjectives with which Nick described his wife: resolute, capable, in charge, strong, achievement-oriented. Nick was the self-described "baby" of the family, with three older sisters very much raised in the mold of Mother—academically successful, fully involved in the church, mothers themselves of large, church-going families. One session, when talk of Mother and sisters had dominated our conversation, I wondered aloud, "And where was your father in all this?"

Nick smiled. "Maybe I should tell you what my mother used to say when I would ask her. She used to say, 'He's out doing the Lord's work.'"

I noted the somewhat bitter undertone and simply lifted my eyebrow. "What did you say to that?"

His smile remained but grew a little tighter around the edges. "What can you say, I mean, to the Lord?"

The answer to that unanswerable question, I soon found out, came not in Nick's words but in his deeds, past and present. As with Pete, my concentrated reflection of the various feelings I heard beneath Nick's statements gradually began to sink in over the course of the work, and again, as with Pete and so many other men, Nick too took on feeling awareness as an inner task, a project to be accomplished, a challenge to be met. The feelings, however, that he succeeded in dredging up were of a particular hue, and a dark one at that—guilt and shame.

This slow disinterment of his guilt and his shame began modestly. First came the admission that he smoked cigarettes. Then the fact that Judy didn't know he smoked. Then the admission that, not only did he smoke cigarettes, but he also smoked marijuana, not just occasionally but almost every night, and had since college. In another session I heard about feelings of guilt around a grade-school incident in which he had cheated off the paper of a fellow student during a test and had gotten the best grade in the class. "You," he told me earnestly, charged with embarrassment, "are the first person I have ever told about that." In a subsequent session he recounted a rather elaborate story about being taken to a "titty bar" in the South by some high-school friends, trying to resist and maintain his family's standards of Christian morality, but eventually succumbing to his curiosity and, as he put it, "my animal lust." Many more of his moral lapses, past and present, soon came to be displayed to me, most minor, some major, none grossly illegal but always sufficiently troubling for him to feel as if I "ought to know."

The confessional tone of all this was not lost on me, but the question remained: how to proceed with this therapeutically? The unconscious rebelliousness of this minister's son was certainly clear enough, but far more striking was the way in which I felt in session with him: as if I was being invited, even pushed, into the role of judge and jury. The way he would present these incidents suggested to me that he thought I would be shocked or dismayed to find these

things out about him—that he had stolen library books, mastur-
bated to *Playboy* magazines on the sly, found a method for beating
parking meters—and I felt frustrated that my nonjudgmental presence and straightforward reflection of his feelings was not being internalized. Indeed, my neutrality seemed only to lead him to continue the stream of confession.

Finally, though, one day, at a propitious moment, after yet another confession of sin, rather than simply explore or reflect his feelings, I decided to work on this transference. "What do you imagine
I think about these things you've done?"

"What do you mean?"

"I mean that I've noticed that you seem to use our sessions as a
kind of ritual of confession. I wonder if you think I'll be shocked or
judgmental, or whether I don't really care one way or the other. . . ."

He sat for a moment thinking—he was extremely thoughtful
throughout our relationship—and then said, "Well, actually, you
just seem to sit there and accept it all, you know, as if you aren't
really all that interested in passing judgment on me."

"And how does that feel?"

Another few moments of silence. "Actually, it feels kind of good."

The following week, Nick did not show up for his appointment
and did not call to cancel.

Thus, the carefully presented "rebellious bad boy," secretly sinful
beneath his facade of Christian all-Americanism, became a living,
breathing reality for us. No longer content to talk of rebellions
major or minor, Nick began to act recalcitrant. Appointments suddenly became difficult to make after months of perfect attendance
and promptness: six o'clock no longer worked; it was too tiring
to come after work; he needed time to unwind. Money also suddenly became a problem: my fee was too high; monthly payment
was too frequent. He would forget his checkbook. Couldn't I bill
him twice yearly, like tuition? The structure of our meetings came
under discussion as well: They were too artificial, too intense. They
didn't occur when he had feelings. Couldn't I see him every other
week? Couldn't we just go out to lunch together every month?

While Nick's repeated attempts at questioning the structure of our relationship certainly were neither enjoyable to endure nor particularly gratifying to oppose, in a strange way this "acting out" felt like progress. Instead of testing my judgmentalism in words only, he now clearly felt that we had enough of a relationship to put it to the test, to see whether or not I really was the punitive authority figure of his negative transference fantasy, the stern judge whose image hid beneath his impulse to confess. To test me and our relationship so actively meant, therefore, that we did have a relationship, and to my mind this is always progress.

Moreover, by "acting out" and testing my limits, he was not acting arbitrarily or without unconscious intention, for his rebellious behavior served to put both of us in the paradoxical conflict he had surely felt himself with his upbringing and his unsuccessful life choices. To accept my authority and be submissive would preserve our relationship, but would also make him more dependent, only this time on me. Had he not come to therapy in order to be less dependent? However, to rebel against the structure I had set for us meant to jeopardize a relationship with someone he had repeatedly experienced as nonjudgmental. Was independence and autonomy worth the isolation that such rebelliousness brought with it?

It took a number of sessions to demonstrate the function of this "acting out" for the two of us: how his difficulties with our structure brought to the fore his painful conflict between dependence and independence, between dominance and submission, between relationship and isolation. Having thus raised this unconscious conflict to our conscious awareness in this way, we took an important therapeutic step forward, only to find that there was as yet one last form of resistance left untapped in those early days. We soon came to know it well.

Gradually, Nick understood how the structure of our relationship provided constancy, safety, and regularity, a container for the various difficult feelings that were to emerge. His objections began to wane and his attendance and promptness improved. Interestingly enough though, now when he came, there was suddenly very little to talk about. Life was normal; Judy was fine; their relationship went okay; work went well. Never a very talkative person to begin with, Nick allowed long silences to ensue. He would look out the window, sigh, examine the floor, glance at me, and then look out the window again. "Not much going on, I guess."

My attempts to intuit the feeling level in the room met with little success, for there was not much feeling in the room, except, that is, the feeling of distance and vagueness. My questions, when I roused myself to ask them, were met with monosyllabic answers. After a number of such sessions, sometimes interspersed with minor incidents of day-to-day interest but mostly filled with emptiness and boredom, I commented on the big picture of our process, how we had moved from a point of conflict to, for lack of a better way to say it, a repeated experience of "nothingness." Nick (ever the tile setter) named this experience the Wall, and the name was especially apt. While I in my extraversion experienced his behavior as withdrawal and distance, he repeatedly told me that his experience, in line with his more introverted attitude, was much more of being cut off from himself, as if a wall suddenly descended between him and his inner life. He felt alienated, empty, bored, and directionless. I wondered silently if the unconscious function of this defense was to establish a kind of independence from me, to find a kind of autonomy in refuge from a relationship to that fearsome judge he expected me to be. Yet I felt that such interpretations, however on target intellectually, were not as important as learning to tolerate this experience of self-alienation with him, to be present to him even if he could not be present to me or to himself. These sessions continued and the Wall became more and more a palpable separation, pained, draining, until finally, after seeing me for six months, Nick brought in the dream of the car stopped by the conflict in the road, the dream of the adolescent cop.

Patriarchy, Perpetual Adolescence, and Authority: Where Personal Meets Collective

There is a Jungian dictum (some might say superstition) that the initial dream in therapy is a herald of the entire course of the analysis. Of course, one might cavil on the definition of the initial dream:

the first dream after therapy has begun? the first dream the patient brings in? the first dream before the first appointment? the first dream ever? The point remains, however, that, even if not profoundly prophetic, at the very least the first dream a patient brings in for analysis usually serves to give form to some of the most basic issues that led the client to initiate treatment.[1]

This first dream of Nick's dramatically illustrates through symbol and image what on some level had already become clear concerning his inner life. The automobile, that symbol *par excellence* of the modern individual who is expected to be, after all, "auto-mobile," that is, self-moving and independent, here in this dream is lost, blocked, hindered. In fact, Nick has psychically not yet even left his hometown or his family, who are the occupants of the car. As for the "special occasion" that is the destination of this dream journey, when I asked what it might be, Nick imagined it might be a wedding or a church service of some sort, possibly with his father as officiant. If this car is, as cars so often are in dreams, a symbol of Nick's ego, the dream provides a poignant symbolic depiction of the inner lostness that undergirds the external aimlessness of Nick's life, the very problem he brought into therapy under the rubric of "dependence," that is, how to leave home and live as an adult.

This sense of being lost is a common, one could even say archetypal, midlife phenomenon, immortalized by Dante in the first lines of the "Inferno" in the *Divine Comedy:*

> In the middle of life's pathway
> I found myself in a darkened wood
> Having lost the right way forward.
>
> What words are there to tell how hard the sight
> Of this rough wilderness was to me—
> The mere thought of it renews my fear.
>
> Only death could be more bitter. . . .[2]

What distinguishes Nick from many of the men afflicted by middle-aged anomie is that Nick did not really lose his way in life but rather had never developed one that fit him. His is not a case of disaffection with prior commitments, values, or life choices, but a case of never having even chosen yet. Consequently, we see in the dream that Nick's father, not Nick, drives the car, and that what stops the car is not an adult conflict but an adolescent clash. Even Nick's position in the car is telling; rather than sitting on his own in the back seat, he is still "unusually close" to his father.

On the personal level of the dream, therefore, on the level of Nick and his relationship to his family of origin, the dream indicates where Nick finds himself developmentally, namely, in adolescence with all its related psychological tasks: the formation and consolidation of an adult identity, risk-taking, social integration, and greater independence and responsibility. In a sense this initial dream serves as a bit of encouragement, a positive sign, in that we are not forced to go back to infancy or childhood, and yet the immaturity of Nick's inner world cannot be ignored. He is still at home, still driven by Dad, beset with violent adolescent conflicts that completely impede his growth.

Would that this psychological adolescence, this state of arrested development, were an anomaly, confined to this individual man and to his particular nuclear family. Unfortunately, my experience has been quite the opposite (hence my choice of this dream and this patient): such delayed developmental progress for modern men is both common and perhaps unavoidable. Men in their twenties and thirties are all too often still working out the conflicts of late adolescence which Nick presented: dependence, lack of roots, absence of a satisfying career or vocation, and unclear identity or self-image. One explanation for such collective male adolescence, put forth by Jung initially and developed by a number of his followers, rests on the observation that modern life and the growth of our technological civilization results in a progressively greater alienation from a natural, more instinctual way of life. By losing touch with the normal rhythms of our physical world and our bodily processes, therefore, modern men and women have little sense of what psychological development actually consists of, and so often have little sense of how to proceed constructively. For this reason, the Jungian literature is rife with research and reflection on initiation, especially the psychic effects of the peculiarly modern absence of initiatory ritual for contemporary people. The psychological necessity of such rites of passage, a term coined by the anthropologist Arnold van Gennep to describe collective rituals that aid social and psychological movement forward from one stage of life to another, becomes more and more clear as the prolonged adolescence, anomie, and aimlessness of modern men becomes a malaise of epidemic proportions. Many Jungians thus conceive of analysis as one such form of initiation, perhaps the one most perfectly suited to modern Western culture with its emphasis on individual achievement and insight, which would account for the social success enjoyed by the psychotherapeutic model during the last century.[3]

However interesting and debatable, these Jungian observations on the result of modern alienation from instinct, I feel, elucidate only one part of what keeps modern men in the state of perpetual adolescence as portrayed by Nick and his dream. His dream suggests, in an intriguing and convoluted way, how patriarchy itself, in its rigid distinction between male and female, in its overvaluation of the masculine and denigration of the feminine, is detrimental to men's development. Nick's dream shows how patriarchy is oppressive to men, particularly in the way its one-sidedness robs men of true psychic maturity and growth.

In Nick's dream, this point is made in the way his dream functions as compensation for patriarchal attitudes. Jung's concept of compensation, that is, the way dreams as products of the unconscious often function to furnish "the other side of the story" to a consciousness that is overly rigid in one particular attitude or feeling, grew out of his own personal and clinical experiences. To give just one example, Jung reported dreaming of a patient whose treatment had become more and more frustrating, eventually reaching an impasse. The topic of Jung's dream, that he was walking through a valley at sunset and espied a woman atop the highest balustrade of a castle, so high in fact that he had to hurt his neck in bending back to see her, led him to understand the dream as compensatory.

> From this I concluded that if I had to look up so much in the dream,
> I must obviously have looked down on my patient in reality. When
> I told her the dream together with the interpretation, a complete
> change came over the situation at once and the treatment shot ahead

beyond all expectation. Experiences of this kind, although paid for
dearly, lead to an unshakable confidence in the reliability of dream
compensations.[4]

As with Pete's dream in which his position in the back of his
house held psychological significance, so with the physical posi-
tioning of the dramatis personae in Nick's dream, for here we see
reversals of all that might be expected within his psychic automobile. The driver's seat is not on the left and in the front, but
rather in the back and on the right. Consequently, Nick's sisters and
the women friends sit not in the back of the car, where they would
normally, but rather in the front where they function as distractions.
Nick, rather than sitting in the front and on the passenger side of the
car, sits in the back and in the middle of the car. The oddness of this
physical layout and the consistency of its reversals indicates that the
dream is attempting to compensate for the patriarchalism of Nick's
family. The Prussian father-pastor is demoted to the status of back-
seat driver, where his performance and control is obscured by, again,
the unusual position of the women in the front seat of the car. This
clear compensation for Nick's conscious experience of his father, a
father largely absent in the service of sacred duty to God as Lord,
occurs in tandem with a compensatory elevation of the feminine
element of the family, Nick's sisters, who in real life simply served
as adjuncts to Father's ministry. Though we will be examining men
and fatherhood more specifically in a later chapter, it is important to
note how Nick's dream and its compensatory intention arise directly
out of the role most fathers, including Nick's, seem to play in patriarchally structured families. This role, termed "Sky Father" by
Arthur and Libby Colman in their book *The Father: Mythology and
Changing Roles,*[5] is the powerful father whose providence occurs from
a distance and whose occasional presence in the family is striking
because of his more usual absence. Because Nick's family was organized around his father's profession, which was itself organized
around the father principle of an especially patriarchal form of
Christianity, Missouri Synod Lutheranism, we find Nick's unconscious attempting to counteract, mollify, and devalue this patriarchalism—father and son are put in the back and the women are

placed up front, while Nick's actual distance from his father is compensated by his closeness in the dream, a closeness Nick found "unusual."

Thus, what is obvious in the dream and its dramatic compensatory imagery is that Nick's difficulties with an adult male identity arise from patriarchal attitudes and ways of being that do not—cannot—aid Nick's process of individuation, his coming to psychological wholeness. On the contrary, because of the one-sided exaltation of men and concomitant devaluation of women, such attitudes set off a chain of unconscious compensatory reactions that impede and eventually halt all psychological movement forward. Adult masculinity is feared and devalued, resisted and fought—Nick's negative transference image of me and his struggle in therapy is an illustration of this form of compensation. At the same time, the long-denied femininity is exalted and honored—all women become the competent, all-encompassing Mother. In this way, patriarchy ensures a kind of eternal psychological adolescence for men.

On the level of external socialization, men's prolonged adolescence is even more powerfully reinforced. Encouraged through a network of one-sided cultural attitudes to conceive of themselves as lords and masters, endowed with outer power and authority not because of qualities developed through individual work and hard-won inner insight but rather simply because of anatomical particularities, patriarchy inculcates an especially pernicious misconception into men, namely that the privileges and power they enjoy socially and politically exempt them from having to work at psychological wholeness. In the field of psychology, this patriarchal misconception takes the form of defining psychological health according to those qualities identified with "masculinity" in Western culture, qualities trained into boys and discouraged in women—independence, drive, ambition, productivity. At the same time, the qualities associated with psychological abnormality or pathology bear a suspicious resemblance to the female sex role in Western societies—emotionality, passivity, physicality. Thus, patriarchal attitudes delude men into thinking, altogether erroneously, that to be a man is to be psychologically whole by definition, or at the very least that the patriarchal sex role assigned to men, the John Wayne ideal or the Playboy Paragon, represents a self-fulfilling promise of happiness.

The reality behind this delusion is shown quite graphically by Nick and his dream. Far from being a recipe for growth and wholeness, this patriarchal equation of "man = health" functions instead to condemn men to a kind of perpetual adolescence, depriving them of the real tools needed to move forward psychologically, tools like humility, an appreciation of interrelatedness, an awareness of the importance of inner reality, and a true experience of feeling. Thus, Nick and his father are placed with a kind of artistic deliberateness in the back seat, and their movement forward via patriarchal conceptions of maleness, the "automobile," is thwarted by the appearance of the feminine and eventually stopped altogether by the very immaturity of their own masculine counterparts in the dream. One cannot move forward if one thinks one has already arrived. Such cocksureness is a hallmark of immature masculinity.

Unfortunately for many men, the psychological bankruptcy of such patriarchal arrogance does not become clear until the inner immaturity has created catastrophe, for themselves, for those around them, or most frighteningly for society at large. For Nick, this situation took a form somewhat different from that of many male clients. Driven to therapy not by the irresponsibility of his personal habits or by a painful inability to enjoy intimacy, which in my experience are the most common manifestations of this patriarchally induced male immaturity, Nick's catastrophe was of a more benign sort: he woke up one day at age thirty-five still without direction, without fulfillment, without, in a certain way, a life of his own, dependent on his wife financially and emotionally, and still living in his psychic hometown, driven by his father. Adulthood had eluded him, indeed, had been consistently refused unconsciously, even though he had lived half his life, and instead dream adolescents ruled his soul and ruled it badly, stopping the forward movement of his self with rebellion, violence, and conflict.

The appearance of conflict in Nick's dream is a positive sign: all is not dead, immovable, blocked. On the contrary, the dream conflict is dramatic and violent, vital and frightening, and the aspect that opposes the adolescents provides both the dramatic tension of the dream and our passageway into understanding the more collective level of Nick's dream, namely the policemen, most especially that curious, swaggering, pimply adolescent cop.

In situations, as with Nick, in which a kind of therapeutic stalemate has occurred, it sometimes feels to me that a client's dream is a kind of flag raised by his unconscious, a signal, often completely outside of his awareness, that is designed to communicate to me as if by secret semaphore in what direction I should go, as if the client's unconscious, via dream symbols, is waving to me, saying, "Not over there—over here, over here." With Nick's dream, the policeman put me on the scent of the true conflict, a conflict that lay both on the level of Nick's personal unconscious, that is, with his parental complexes and the particular transferential form they had already begun to take with me, as well as on the level of the collective unconscious. The real issue was not "dependence" really, but rather what the policeman in his dream stood for: in a word, authority.

Besides cars, which rank high in frequency of appearance in dreams, policemen, in my experience, are among the most common of dream figures. Rarely does a week pass for me when a patient does *not* bring in a dream with a policeman in it. Of course, other authority figures tend to be numerous and intriguing in people's dreams—ushers, ticket takers, tollbooth workers, border guards, Nazi soldiers, military commandos—but policemen are ubiquitous and significant, important collective symbols. But symbols of what?

In my work on gay male individuation, I found policemen often carried for gay men the potent, powerful masculinity that is often denied to gay men in modern society through an identification of homosexuality with effeminacy or passivity. Thus, for gay men individually and for gay male culture in general, policemen tend to be cast as sex symbols, objects of intense longing and desire.[6]

For women, policemen in dreams have probably as many meanings as there are individual women. Yet two of the more common dream cops I have encountered in women's dreams are the brutal policeman, a symbol of phallic, oppressive, patriarchal masculinity, and the more neutral, though distant, figure of policeman as regulator, the one who assures order, regularity, and productivity. In Jungian terms, these two types of policemen would be understood as negative and positive animus figures, respectively, inner masculine figures for a woman representing parts of her psyche to be brought into her wholeness as a woman.

Behind all these different sorts of symbolic policemen, however, including the policemen in Nick's dream, there lies a common theme, the theme of authority, and in particular the authority of the social order, which in patriarchal societies is cast as an attribute and function of men. Interestingly, while the two words, "police" and "authority" do not share a common etymology, they do share a common conceptual base. "Police" is derived, as one might be able to guess, from the Greek *polis,* the word for "city" or "state," a word that carried connotations not only of a particular geographical place but of a whole way of being, a whole form of society. *Polis* was city, state, government, society, civilization, and political order all rolled up into one. Thus, "police" is what protects and preserves *polis;* police are the civilizing, regulating force that assures the continuation of society and the safety of civilization.

"Authority" on the other hand finds its root in the Latin *auctoritas,* an abstract noun derived from the simpler *auctor,* that is, "author," "originator," or "promoter," which is in turn derived from an even more basic verb form, *augere,* meaning "to increase" or "to generate." Authority, thus, is that principle by which something is generated, its "author-ity," and obviously, when used in the abstract sense to refer to a social or political principle, it shares with the word "police" the sense of "that which assures the generation and increase of society."

In amplifying the appearance of the police in Nick's dream in this manner, I found myself reconceptualizing his problem and our therapeutic process in a way that not only was more fruitful for Nick personally but that also forged connections beyond Nick to the more collective level of how patriarchal masculinity is wounded, how, in a perverse kind of way, such masculinity continues to wound itself. Rather than seeing Nick's primary difficulty, therefore, as dependence or psychological immaturity, his dream and its policeman disclosed how his most basic conflict centered upon authority, or more precisely, on his difficulty in developing an internal authority, that is, a principle of generativity, increase, and power that would be self-centered (in the positive sense) and psychologically effective. Without such authority, without a genuine principle of power and strength based on his own individuality, Nick's masculinity could only be dependent, immature, adolescent—the masculinity of rebellion, not the masculinity of adulthood.

Of course, as we have seen, many personal factors went into this authority problem. Certainly among the most obvious and prominent was the ambivalent authority of Nick's Sky Father, whose presence had a kind of divine, undisputed dominance over the family but whose absence and distance spoke with far more emotional authority to the developing psyche of his only son. The result is a pattern of father-son relationship so common nowadays that it is almost a psychological cliché, a pattern which Québecois analyst Guy Corneau has named to perfection in French, *père manquant, fils manqué,* "absent father, failed son." The second and related personal factor is without a doubt the unacknowledged but perhaps all the more powerful authority of the feminine within Nick's family; he was the sole boy in a sea of capable, successful women who nevertheless, as the dream makes amply clear in its compensation, took the back seat in a traditional, religious, Prussian-German family. In this regard, the absence of Nick's mother in the dream stands in striking contrast to her constant presence in our therapy discussions, indicating that her authority, too, was for Nick highly ambivalent, double-bound by patriarchy: exalted and devalued, honored but denigrated. Thus, we see a man whose search for personal and collective authority was stuck in a tangle of cross-purposes and false values. The ostensible head of the family, Father, was actually absent, affectively distant, with a divinely endowed but largely ceremonial authority, and the effective (and affective) authority of the family was Mother, whose real emotional presence was relegated to the role of "pastor's wife" and whose gifts and contributions met with contingent acknowledgment.

From this morass of ambivalence and devaluation, Nick (and so many modern men with similar family experiences) had to fashion a sense of effective personal authority. As one can see, he did the best job he could. In line with his maternal complex, he located a woman who was sufficiently ambitious and sufficiently maternal to serve as a life partner, upon whom he might have depended his whole life, had Judy not been astute enough to see what was happening or strong enough to confront him honestly. Likewise, with me, one of the few men, I was to learn, with whom he experienced anything like emotional intimacy, Nick tripped into the mare's-nest around authority that characterized his paternal complex: setting me up as the divine authority in the role of father-confessor, rebelling against me in the role of unempathic father–rule giver, and walling me out of existence in the role of the distant, absent father.

Thus, the adolescent policeman of his dream, he who stops the car with his threats and swaggering, is a representation of the whole strained, conflicted amalgam of authority and insecurity that faced Nick and that, on a wider level, men in a patriarchal society have to make sense of, day after day. For the authority men are told they have in a patriarchal society is not a true, inner authority, authority in its radical sense of "author," the principle and power that grows out of an individual's own creativity, generativity, and achievement. Authority for most men is more like a brutal, insecure adolescent of Nick's dream, an authority based on the uniform, a nightstick, and a gun, an authority located in a costume.

To use a Jungian term, this sort of authority is based on the persona. Drawing from the Greek word for "mask," Jung coined the term persona to describe that section of the personality formed by collective expectations and meant to mediate between the individual and social norms and standards. The persona is the social face we use in everyday relationships and situations, a mask that both permits us to function in society and that hides our unique inner self from the eyes of those around.[7] For these reasons, a persona-based authority, relying on outward equipment and brute force rather than on any authentic generative power is, like the adolescent in the dream (and like most adolescents), inherently insecure and frightened, attempting to cover his shallowness with overcompensation— a swaggering, bullying bravado of gun and badge.

His persona, however, is obviously flawed: his social face is pocked with pimples, eruptions from within, and patriarchy's pus, its inner decay, cannot be hidden forever, no matter how crisp the uniform or well polished the gun. Rage shows through, as does fear and emptiness, and this figure of adolescent manhood would be a poignant symbol, were he not so profoundly dangerous and disruptive. In this quality of the adolescent cop, we see that other archetypal figure that stands in reciprocal relationship to the persona, that which Jung called the shadow, an inner figure that incarnates all that we find unacceptable, painful, dangerous, or immoral about ourselves and often seek to hide from others beneath a flawless and burnished persona.

Another Jungian dictum states that the brighter the persona, the darker the shadow, and this insight seems especially applicable to the psychic situation represented by Nick's dream and its central figure. For Nick, this adolescent cop is a symbol of his self, a representation of the kind of masculinity and authority that he is bringing into therapy to contend with. The dream, thus, shows how the much-feared negative image of me that held sway early on in our relationship was actually a shadow-projection of the violence, rage, and judgmentalism that he himself felt within and that his determined dependence on others and aimlessness in life served to ward off. In this way, Nick demonstrated the positive function that Jung often attributed to projection. By projecting judge and jury onto me, Nick met those shadow aspects of himself that he had sought to avoid. His rebelliousness, his so-called "acting out," served the function of raising to our mutual consciousness the very psychic conflict he intended to side-step. For these reasons, Jung understood the psyche as a self-corrective system, for even those maneuvers intended unconsciously as defensive often ironically work to present in external form that which we must eventually encounter within ourselves.

Though the violence, rage, and arrogance of this adolescent policeman can easily be laid at the doorstep of Nick's father or mother, both of whose connections to a positive, nurturing masculinity left much to be desired on many levels, Nick's personal unconscious, however influential, is not the whole story. In the figure of this insecure teenage cop, we see a process and a polarity inherent in what Jung and Jungians call the archetypal masculine, a collective cycle of authority and rebellion in which Nick, his family, and all of us within a patriarchal culture are caught and with which we all must contend. For modern men, however, because the cycle is an integral part of the masculine and because patriarchal authority is becoming ever more sterile and unworkable, consciousness and resolution of this archetypal masculine cycle of authority and rebellion is more difficult than ever to discern, while at the same time being a matter of psychic life and death. To see the archetypal roots of this cycle and its ramifications, we look to a myth of life and death, to the masculine creation myth of Ouranos and Kronos.

Authority, Rebellion, and Polarities of the Masculine: The Myth of Ouranos and Kronos

This story begins not "once upon a time," but rather at the very beginning of all time, before humans and all their joys and complications, before plants and animals. *In illo tempore,* in that time, Ouranos the Sky Father came nightly to mate with his wife Gaia, the Earth Mother, covering her each evening with the whole of his body and uniting with her, out of which repeated unions came a line of children. However, whether due to the perceived threat to his authority or simple unreadiness to acknowledge fatherhood and responsibility, Ouranos took each of these children, whom he hated from the beginning, and hid them within the body of Gaia the Earth Mother, condemning them to darkness. Full thus with the weight of her progeny because of Ouranos's hateful behavior, Gaia turned to her six sons and six daughters and pleaded with them to cooperate with her in devising their escape and in punishing their father for his oppressiveness.

Of Gaia's children, only one, Kronos, stepped forward to volunteer his help. Outraged with the shamefulness of his father's behavior, along with his mother he set out a plan: he was to hide in a place near his mother's bed and, using an iron sickle provided to him by Gaia, Kronos would attack his father when he came for his nightly conjugal visit. This Kronos did, waiting for Ouranos to come to his wife "inflamed with love," as Kerényi puts it,[8] a sunset sky nightly covering the earth with his blood-red passion. Before the union could occur this time, Kronos grabbed his father with his left hand and, using the sickle, cut off his father's genitals, throwing them behind his back.

Blood-red passion thus turns in our myth to children of blood, as the blood from Ouranos's wound seeped into the womb of Gaia the Earth Mother, and from this Gaia gave birth to the Erinyes, the goddesses of vengeance and remorse, and to a race of Giants and the Nymphs of the Ash Tree. Falling into the ocean behind Kronos, the castrated genitals of Ouranos gave rise to yet another goddess, the most beautiful in the pantheon, the great Aphrodite, the goddess of love. Through this deed of rebellion against patriarchal tyranny, therefore, Kronos ended his father's reign over the earth and took his place as ruler now of the universe.

And yet, how often is it that the younger generation learns from the old, sons from their fathers? Kronos, though now ruler of creation, found himself afflicted nevertheless with the same problem as Ouranos. Jealous of his power and authority, he acted against each of the children born to him by Rhea, his sister and his wife, not by hiding his offspring but rather this time by swallowing them whole one by one immediately upon their birth. Like Kronos's own mother, Rhea found her husband's practice just as abhorrent and intolerable as his father's before him, and so she prayed to her own parents, Gaia and Ouranos, for help. The answer to her supplication involved yet another subterfuge intended as deliverance.

Rhea went away for the parturition of her youngest son Zeus, hiding him in a cave and emerging from her confinement with a decoy, a stone wrapped as a baby. Hungry to ensure his domination and reckless in his authority, Kronos seized this false child and swallowed it down, not knowing it was but an inanimate rock, not knowing his real son lived. Away from his father, Zeus grew strong and, in learning of his father's oppression, he, like his father before him, acted with cleverness and strength to overthrow Kronos's rule. By feeding his father an emetic, Zeus forced Kronos to throw up the children he had swallowed. By this act, and with the help of his brothers and sisters, Zeus thus founded the race of the Olympian gods we all have come to know, continuing the cycle of authority and rebellion through yet another generation.

Dare we say that this cycle continues even until our own time? Without being overly literal concerning this creation myth, even readers unsophisticated in myths or their psychological meaning can discern how relevant this myth is to the patterns that Nick found himself living and reliving in his life and with me in therapy, patterns given form and shape by his dream of the policeman. Nick's position at the beginning of his analysis was not too dissimilar from Kronos or Zeus after him. Swallowed whole by his father complex, that web of images, feelings, fears, and experiences of his father's authority, Nick languished in the nether world, without connection to brother or sister, without power or direction. His real-life rebelliousness, not nearly as victorious or violent as that of Kronos against Ouranos or Zeus against Kronos, nevertheless carries the same themes: the son, in order to live, strikes at his very origins, castrating the father's phallic authority, in Nick's case through indulgence in minor vices and sins of the flesh prohibited by the father principle of his patriarchal religious upbringing.

Graves reports the more ancient Hittite variant of this myth, in which Kronos does not use a sickle to castrate his father but rather bites off his father's genitals with his teeth.[9] This interesting variation shows the unconscious intention behind the son's rebelliousness, which is not simply to castrate and depotentiate the father but to go further, to attempt to incorporate some of the father's adult manhood into himself and thereby make himself powerful. The homoerotic image here, amply supported by the homosexual character of so many male initiation rites in native societies, does not point as much to literal homosexuality as to the fact that the authority conflict addressed by all these myths is a conflict endemic to the archetypal masculine, in which two poles of the masculine seek union and resolution, obviously an equally important issue for gay male relationships.[10]

The oppression of the feminine element here—remember, Nick's mother is wholly absent from the dream and his sisters are in the front seat in order to compensate for their actual status in the family—is given image in Gaia's affliction and Rhea's grief. If this is a universe ruled by the masculine, then motherhood is torment, fecundity a burden, and instinct a source of pain and loss. The result for Nick and for all under the sway of such authority is what the myth depicts. Life, growth, health, happiness, and all good things are blocked and can go no further. If Sky Father rules and Earth Mother serves, then masculine and feminine become deadlocked, eternal antagonists. By emphasizing one authority at the expense of the other, creation grinds to a halt.

In this way, revolt seems built by nature into patriarchal conceptions of the world, for only revolt can break the standoff, allow life to flow, and let the children live. Significantly, the revolt in the myth is led by those most oppressed by patriarchal attitudes, mother and son, Gaia and Kronos, Rhea and Zeus. We are reminded again by this myth that one-sidedness fosters revolt and invites the violent and powerful return of what has been split off, devalued, and repressed.

The idea that revolt is inherent in patriarchy due to its one-sidedness is supported by the most noteworthy aspect of this mythic conflict: its repetitiousness. While one could arrive at the same conclusion through a simple review of the history of Western culture with its continually recurring wars and conflicts, the repetitiousness of this cycle, on a psychological level, points to the way in which myths depict processes and cycles inherent in the human condition, eternal features of existence. Rather than providing the literal, historical truth as myths sometimes claim to do, for example how the world began or how the gods came into being, myths, as Jung saw, instead put into symbol and image psychic experiences shared by all cultures and experienced in some way or other by all men and women. This common psychic heritage was what he called the "archetypes of the collective unconscious." The repetitiousness of our myth forces us to acknowledge that an archetypal reality lies behind this cycle of authority and rebellion: what Nick is going through as he attempts to throw off the weight of his past and locate the authority of his own life is a struggle common to all men, not just a personal problem of overstrict upbringing coupled with an absent father. An awareness of the archetypal themes of Nick's struggle places what is happening within the context of a wider human community.

However, the repetitiousness of this cycle points at the same time to a lack of development, to an unconsciousness that seems to condemn the gods and humanity to cyclical oppression and cyclical upheaval. Ouranos's lack of awareness, his unthinking reliance on his Sky God's rights and privileges, teaches his son, of course, nothing but the same, for Ouranos's unconsciousness is matched by Kronos's, who ascends to the throne of the universe seemingly with a case of amnesia around what he himself suffered at the hands of his father. Nick's dream holds out a promise to him and me—that in our work toward consciousness we might be able to break this cycle of oppression and revolt, personally, and on a deep archetypal level, one hopes, for Nick.

The Ouranos-Kronos story is a creation myth obviously patriarchal in both its origin and intent, and so it stands as a vivid, unadulterated portrayal of the archetypal masculine and its elements. Because, as Jung noted, all archetypal constellations are composed of two opposite aspects, polarities in conflict and yet part of a unity in themselves, perhaps by discerning the poles of the masculine presented for us here we can get a better sense of how patriarchy entraps itself. In this myth, the polarities of the masculine emerge in the conflict between father and son, with father carrying the authority principle, that is, the generative aspect of the masculine, and son carrying the necessity of rebellion, that is, the dependent, contingent end of the masculine that seeks its own establishment and permanence. In this way, the myth does not stray too far away from the everyday lived reality of real fathers and real sons, upon which the voluminous father-son literature of Western culture finds both its personal and archetypal basis. In understanding this myth and Nick's dream conflict, however, as an archetypal process, it behooves us to remember what we may often forget in the heat of the conflict—that "father" and "son" are two sides of the same masculine unity, images given to an archetypal reality that goes beyond our own fathers or our own sons. Myths, and especially the psychological application of myths, in this way help us to move beyond too literal an attitude toward life and to bring to bear our capacity for imagination and transcendence by reminding us of the unity of the masculine that we may miss on the personal level of our everyday lives.

For this reason, it is helpful to discern what exactly "father" as symbol carries in this myth. Progenitor and source, he is essentially conservative, wishing to hold onto his preeminence and not wanting to be challenged, attacked, or competed with. Fitting, therefore, it is to identify this aspect of the masculine with sky—that which vaults above it all and encircles everyone and everything. His counterpart in Nick's dream, the policeman, shows his affinity with this half of the masculine—that which preserves and encompasses, that which is ultimate and above all others, that which holds the power of generativity and generation of power. Clearly, "father" is an apt image, but the image is not the principle, and to identify this too closely with "father" is to risk an unhealthy literalism.

I find it more helpful to adopt a term James Hillman uses to describe this half of the masculine: *senex,* the Old Man.[11] Of course, this term includes father and husband—"old man" carries that connotation in colloquial English. To frame this aspect of the masculine as *senex,* however, is one way of extricating oneself from what Nick and so many men, including myself, have gotten caught in—literal rebellions against literal fathers—rather than seeing how our *own* masculinity contains an admixture of *senex,* and with it all the aspects Hillman describes, using the image of Kronos's Roman counterpart, the god Saturn: heaviness, age, decay, depression, and inertia.

Against this set of masculine qualities, archetypal reality pits "son," the rebellious adolescent in dream and myth. What does "son" carry imaginally in our myth? What is his pole of the archetypal masculine? Kronos and Zeus both are, fittingly, their father's youngest sons, and so bring with them a particular form of masculine youthfulness: vitality, a sense of forward movement, a closeness to instinct and feeling, and a ferocious appetite for experience, independence, and adventure. The same danger lurks for us, however, if we saddle our sons alone with this aspect of life: the danger of continuing what our myth depicts as cyclical, the splitting and mutual attack of father and son.

An awareness of the more abstract, imaginal quality of this characterization is helpful, and for this again Hillman is instructive. Against *senex* he positions *puer,* the Eternal Youth, that archetypal pole of the masculine that is authority's issue and that carries those qualities Jung sketched out in his article on the Divine Child: the sun hero, a sense of futurity, freshness and fire and effervescence, creation and life.

Thus, beyond the father-son conflict is an archetypal pair of opposites, that of youth and age, *puer* and *senex,* and this more fundamental opposition I posit as the essence of the authority-rebellion conflict. Though quite naturally this conflict is often incarnated in the father-son relationship, with fathers as *senex* to their sons' eternal *puer,* the discernment of the archetypal level of this conflict is necessary in order for men to rise above what the repetitiousness of the myth and Nick's dream so devastatingly illustrates: namely, that to cast the problem as a father-son conflict exclusively is to miss the fullness of the masculine and to become entrapped in a cycle that is never ending and eternally self-wounding. It is to identify with only one pole of the archetype and project the other onto someone else, father or son, church or secular society, ingroup or outgroup, so that one's authority is never really located within but always elsewhere, in someone or something else.

Of course in one sense the very polarity of the archetypal masculine and any archetypal constellation makes for a cyclical kind of self-wounding if the opposites are not discerned and made conscious within ourselves. This myth seems to say that, in particular, within the realm of the masculine, within the realm of authority and generativity, such wounding is inevitable: to grow up and be free, we must both strike at and incorporate our origins, be both father and son, if not literally, then figuratively and emotionally.

What makes Nick's dream so poignant and instructive, therefore, is its central and most dramatic figure, the adolescent cop. He stands as a symbol of how the two poles of the masculine, *puer* and *senex,* have not yet been differentiated from one another in Nick's awareness but instead are fused together, confused, confusing. It is as if, for Nick, Ouranos and Kronos are still one person, attempting like Siamese twins to pull apart and strike at each other to win their freedom. The result, of course, is that this conflict halts all movement, but examining the more archetypal level of the dream discloses more precisely why: Nick, and perhaps all rebels, fight not only the oppressor but, on a deeper level, their own nature as well. Continued unconsciousness of this archetypal level of the conflict can only lead to the repetition seen in so many revolutions, in which the new regime simply repeats (and in often much more gruesome form) the very mistakes of the old regime, bringing progress, as in Nick's dream, to a painful, violent standstill.

However, to my mind, this myth also demonstrates one fatal flaw in patriarchal attitudes and in the male-based structuring of societies and consciousness: to base a system—or a personality—on only one set of archetypal polarities is to create a situation in which war, violence, and conflict are inherent, a system of escalating self-reference out of which there is no issue. Patriarchy condemns men to live out the eternal Ouranos-Kronos or Kronos-Zeus struggle, in which cycles of dominance and submission continue ad infinitum, and in which authority equals paternity, rather than something more creative, more growthful, and more imaginative.

To some degree, this overstates the case, since after all the myth does portray the emergence of something new for the world attendant upon Ouranos's castration, but here too we simply see another archetypal polarity emerge. From the blood that seeps into Gaia's womb emerge the Erinyes, the goddesses of revenge and remorse, the "strong ones," bringers of a new moral order and consciousness, guardians of justice, while alongside this fearful face of the feminine, we see arising from the sea one of the most powerful and beautiful goddesses of all, Aphrodite, the "one born of foam," in whom love, beauty, and creativity reside.

In a lecture on this myth, Swiss analyst Mario Jacoby frames the birth of these goddesses as a symbol of what occurs on an archetypal level when an individual moves, as does Kronos, as does Nick, toward individual self-realization, or in Jungian terms, individuation. By stealing the power of father's authority, by loosing his stranglehold on our life, by striking at the root of his generativeness, his "author-ity," we free ourselves not only into a greater creativity and awareness of the value of others, symbolized by the goddess of love, Aphrodite, but also into civilization itself, emerging from the womb of the family into a wider world of adults, into a new moral order ruled over by the Erinyes, goddesses who also were called the "Eumenides," the "kindly ones." This alternate name could be understood, of course, as a euphemism, an attempt to placate their fierce judgment, but I wonder if the name is not well chosen, since these goddesses of revenge and remorse ensure the order of civilization and therefore of life itself. As Jacoby puts it:

> Revolt has its archetypal foundation in the fact that no collective social order and no conscious value-orientation can satisfy the complexity of human existence forever. It necessarily tends to one-sidedness and throws a shadow, becomes with time stale and hostile to life's flow. . . . We can—and we have to—castrate the authority of collective social norms in order to liberate our nature and creativity: Aphrodite. Yet the Erinyes are born. We set new limits to a complete freedom of an autonomous ego because they represent the guardians of the natural world-order, of the Self. . . .[12]

Because this is a masculine creation myth and depicts the ground of masculine individuation, it is vital to appreciate the fact that from Ouranos's castration something new and different is given birth, two powerful aspects of the feminine—Aphrodite and the Erinyes. However, the cycle continues despite their birth, for Kronos learns very little from these two sisters of his. By ignoring love and remorse, proceeding in his stereotypically masculine way to once again enact the loveless, remorseless search for power and control, he continues the very situation he himself suffered, devouring his children, oppressing his wife, and forcing revolt.

The parallel with Nick, and with many men caught in this self-wounding patriarchal staleness, is represented I think most forcefully by the way Nick's sisters in the dream are seen as distractions and obstacles, not as the locus for contact with something new and different and potentially more helpful. In a patriarchal cycle of self-referential authority, the feminine has no place here, and her authority is ignored and trivialized. For Nick, the authority of the feminine is rather projected out, most notably onto his wife, for whom his maternal projection has become, like Gaia and Rhea, a burden too heavy to bear any longer, while the feminine authorities in the front seat of his psyche, their observations on the realities of the world around him, are not seen or taken in as a true part of himself.

In this patriarchal system of self-referential masculinity, the "collective social order" and "conscious value-orientation" of patriarchy, to use Jacoby's words, cast a shadow that falls on the feminine, which from within this "one-sided," "stale," and "hostile" system (how perfectly Nick's dream situation is described by just those adjectives!) is and can only be perceived as "Other." The feminine is something absent, something distracting, something exalted; she is given the front seat, precisely because she is devalued and because her "author-ity," her generativeness, and her strength are denied, encumbered, forbidden fruition or release.

This myth shows us two ways patriarchy entraps men on the level of the collective unconscious. In its one-sidedness it excludes that which is beyond itself, that which is Other, rendering the feminine a problem and burden, and it thereby consigns itself to a closed system ultimately doomed, as are all closed systems, to slow death by suffocation. Secondly, the ethic of masculine superiority ensures a kind of eternal self-attack; by confining power to *senex* masculinity, patriarchy invites everlasting *puer* revolt as the archetypal polarities of the masculine cycle again and again through the same twin opposites, unrelieved by any third value, any higher conscious standpoint.

This more extensive analysis of Nick's dream and the amplification of its conflict through archetypal parallels led me to see which way to go, which way we *could* go. The mythic cycle repeats with Kronos and Zeus because the authority-rebellion conflict is not supplemented by the sisters to whom it gives birth—love and the impulse toward relationship, passion, and creativity; remorse and the protection of justice through regret, guilt, mourning, and honesty. For Nick, without love or remorse, the only form of masculinity he had available was immature and violent, the adolescent cop. His authority resided outside himself, in father figures or mother figures. It thus struck me that Nick's distance, the Wall, could be conceived of as a kind of failure of love. Jung used the name of Aphrodite's son to name this psychological principle: Eros, the principle of relationship and feeling. Rather than let me into relationship with him in an intimate way and live Eros between us, I was kept out by distance, by silence, by withdrawal—silence defending against remorse, remorse substituting for love.

In turn, I began to see that the stalemate with his wife (they did after all intend to come for marital therapy) was in a certain way actually a failure of remorse. Rather than confessing his sins to her—his cigarette smoking, his drug use, his *Playboy* fantasies, his transgressions of the law—and thus beginning an honest relationship with an Other out of guilt and responsibility, he kept her out through what was termed as "love" but which Judy accurately named as "dependence," a sort of clinginess defended as love, love substituting for remorse.

The dream and its mythic background brought to my attention not only the splitting inherent in Nick's situation, but also the way in which patriarchy had failed Nick in an unfortunately characteristic way: if authority is conceived as only a masculine attribute, an eternal father-son affair, then this patriarchal attitude toward authority grows hostile to life, for it cannot really address, as Jacoby puts it, the "complexity of human existence." In its one-sidedness, it condemns men to a perpetual adolescence, because such a patri-archal attitude is endlessly self-referential, and provides a cop-out (pun half-intended) to a true confrontation with that which is the other coequal in creation, the feminine and all her forms: Mother, Sister, Love and her son Eros, Remorse, and Revenge.

I had Nick look at the dream carefully. Did he feel the rage de-picted? Did he feel the stuckness of his car? His honestly did not fail him this time, and he admitted that it had occurred to him that the Wall, his withdrawal, was a way to protect himself—and me—from his anger.

"And you are angry at . . . ?" I wondered aloud.

"Angry at your power over me. Angry that I am needy. Angry that I am still insecure like that kid in the dream. Angry that I am angry."

The room began to heat up and for once Nick looked me in the eyes, his annoyance building. The boredom and silence between us seemed to break.

"And how does it feel to be angry at me?"

He paused a few moments. "Frightening, like that feeling in the dream: 'Watch out!' I am afraid I'll hurt you."

"And if you hurt me . . . ?"

"Well, I can't afford to hurt you. I depend on you. I am coming for help. What if you reject me? What if you're threatened and throw me out?"

"So you can't imagine our relationship would survive your anger at me. You can't imagine my care would survive your fury. The car would stop."

He sat for a moment, struggling with a puzzle, caught in a rela-tionship, enticed out from behind the Wall.

"Actually, I am afraid I'd just be another one of those guys who yells and hollers and stamps and punches—."

"Isn't there any other way to exercise the authority of who you are? Does the policeman have to be a bully?"

"How else is there?"

"I don't know. You tell me. How would your father have handled the situation in the dream?"

"Oh, he would have simply ignored the whole thing and driven on."

"Is that what happened to you when you were angry or insecure? After all, the adolescent cop here is a part of you. Did your father just ignore your anger, your fear?"

I heard the echoes of Ouranos as Nick grew quiet and then said, "He was so above it all, as if much higher things than my feelings were the real issue in his life. But I wonder if he may not have felt threatened by me. If I learned the Wall from anyone, it was certainly from him. He was never around, and when he was, we never really talked or spent time together." He sat quietly for a few more moments and then said, "You know, it feels great to be angry. I feel, like, strong, in charge."

"Are you angry at your father?"

He responded in that familiar way men have of admitting to feelings without feeling them: "I guess so. I ought to be."

"The dream and what you are saying now seem to suggest a lot of anger at not having a father."

"I wonder if that's why I am so dependent . . ." His voice trailed off, resuming even more softly, "and keep so much from so many people." Again a look straight into my eyes. "It's strange being so weak and so strong at the same time in here, like it's empowering to know what I am feeling and yet what I am feeling is weak and needy."

I sat silent, allowing him to be with the paradox of strong-weak for a bit. "It reminds me of that adolescent cop—feeling weak and insecure and covering it over, rather than dropping the uniform and the nightstick."

A smile grew slowly on his face, but it had a kind of nervous sadness mixed in. "Too vulnerable, too naked. You might get to know me."

"And then we might actually have a relationship, rather than a game of 'who's up and who's down.'"

The sadness grew.

"You're right. We just might."

Two months later, Nick reported this dream:

> In a reform school under the control of ruthless guards, I am herded
> with others into a courtyard. So that my sister can escape from this
> place, I create a diversion: I break free from the crowd and run into
> a dorm and up to a balcony where I have a view of the whole court-
> yard. Down below I see a retarded boy playing ball with a very
> patient, loving social worker. The social worker wants to get to
> know the boy and give him money, but guards come by and hold
> him back from doing this. They threaten the social worker with
> death, but the social worker knows it's a bluff and continues to play.

Nick laughed a little when he told me the dream. "I guess you're
the social worker, huh?"

"And you're the retarded boy?" I arched an eyebrow.

"Not in this dream. I am not anyone. I've got a bird's-eye view—
I can see it all."

I played along. "And what do you see?"

"I see that there's a way out of the place and that the guards
really aren't all that threatening. I guess I also see that it's possible
to play ball even if you're not all that perfect."

"It strikes me that the guards aren't all that effective in stopping
the social worker and the retarded boy from relating to each other,
not like the dream of the cops and the car being stopped."

"So this is progress?" he asked me.

I merely looked at him, smiled a little and allowed the feeling
of connection to grow. At last the silence between us had begun
to warm.

From Iron Lung to
Ménage à Trois: *Heterosexual Men, Femininity, and the Anima*

I am working for an old pharmacist, a crusty character who criticizes everything I do and doesn't ever give me any praise. Finally, I get tired of hearing nothing but criticism and tell him so, tell him that I need affirmation and that I am not working for him any more.

I then leave the drugstore and go into the parking lot, which is very dark, to smoke, calm down. I am accosted repeatedly by a number of street people who bum cigarettes from me. I act friendly toward them, though they're really annoying, and end up giving away all my cigarettes, just so I can be alone.

After this I go home (it is a strange house, not my own or my family's) and avoid both my mother and Judy, because I am afraid they'll smell that I've been smoking. I walk into a room to find a deformed woman who is being held in an iron lung. The scene is grotesque, because the woman is having her breathing manipulated by technicians in an attempt to have her remember something which the doctor told her which will save her. The procedure is absolutely excruciating and yet the woman is cooperating. I can't bear to watch it and turn away, which is precisely the point when I hear the woman laugh. She has remembered! When I turn back, the iron lung has been turned off and the woman is free, cured.

I could see on Nick's face how affecting the dream had been. "There's a lot of feeling here, isn't there?"

"Absolutely. Especially that last episode. The whole scene is so awful and so liberating at the same time. . . ." He stared into my eyes in an uncharacteristically direct way, raising tears in both our eyes simultaneously. "Her suffering is so hard to watch. I can't bear to think of it even." I succeeded in holding my tears back, but saw a large drop slowly make its way down Nick's tanned cheek.

I hoped that my psychoanalytic supervisors were correct, that my emotional restraint would permit the patient to feel his feelings all the more deeply and not be distracted by my upset. Even without my tears, however, I was sure Nick sensed my involvement. His dream work had become the key to our movement forward, unlocking his intuitive and symbolic gifts in a way that probably nothing else would have been able to therapeutically. Now, one year into our relationship, when he brought in such profoundly affecting dreams, it felt very much like we both tumbled together into another, more enchanted, world.

Aware of my desire to do an analysis of the dream, to dissect the dream symbol by symbol in narrative sequence, I decided that perhaps my hunger for order was defensive, a way to use my thinking function to distance us from the dream's evident pain. I opted instead to simply be present.

Sometimes words seem such heavy instruments for something as delicate as men's feelings, and so I used a look and a gesture: I asked gently about Nick's tears with a look, turning my hand up to my face and knitting my eyebrows.

Nick understood my unspoken question. "Well, I woke up after the dream and realized that she is the part of me that I bring in here to you."

"So the tears are for the part of you that's here."

"It's deformed and so dependent. I mean, it can't even breathe on its own. It has to be kept alive through artificial supports. Which is bad enough, of course, but then, she—," he paused at the change of pronoun and shot me a knowing look, "she, it, whatever, she has to be manipulated to remember what it'll take to get well."

"If she's the part of you which you bring in here to me, I wonder if you feel manipulated at all by me." In recent sessions, manipulation had been a theme, ever since, at the end of one especially difficult session, Nick went to hug me and I refrained, mentioning that perhaps we should talk next session about his wish to hug, rather than acting on it right away. Our subsequent work had thus been focused on how our relationship was one in which my person and my technique both had a place, unlike a friendship or some other kind of social relationship. Nick began to see how I acted in deliberate ways to evoke and explore feelings, rather than cover them over or act them out, and responded with understandably mixed feelings: grateful at my ability to help him so powerfully, anxious and annoyed with my strength, suspicious of my motives, and concerned over being manipulated.

Nick's response to my current question, then, was a little surprising to me and in my mind signaled progress. "Well, actually, it feels more as if you're the doctor in the dream, not the technicians. You would be the person that had told the woman what it would take for her to get better, the thing she had forgotten."

"Which the technicians are trying to help her to remember."

"Yes." He lapsed into one of his long thoughtful silences. "It's so painful."

"It hurts to be here, to remember what you've gone through, to feel it again."

"If this is the iron lung, then our work is keeping me alive."

I wondered briefly if I should be more frankly interpretive, choosing in this instance to risk it and check the effect. "To be precise, we're keeping alive the part of you symbolized by the woman."

Although this dream was not the first in which a female figure had appeared, it was certainly the first of such intensity. "You mean she isn't a part of me."

I smiled. "She is—and she isn't."

His initial puzzlement smoothed into understanding; his capacity for paradox had grown considerably after so much dream work. "I guess so. But then, who—what is she?"

If I were teaching a course in dream work or supervising an intern, I might have presumed to answer the question with a simple, "She's your anima." But of course, men's healing these days seems less likely to come from snappy definitions or intellectualized understanding than from true inner experience, from learning to tolerate the mystery, paradox, symbol, and confusion of inner unconscious life without control, power, or security. And so I left the question unanswered, leaving it to Nick to find out who or what she might be and how he and I might build a relationship to this poor, deformed, dependent creature who ultimately, the dream seemed to promise, would remember the source of her cure and find herself freed.

The concept of the anima is certainly one of Jung's major contributions to the psychology of the unconscious and remains a cornerstone of his theory. Yet the psychological freight that this archetypal figure has been made to bear in analytical psychology has often made it difficult to come to terms with all of the anima's faces.

One such face, so to speak, can be discerned in the name: "anima" is the Latin word for "soul," and so Jung's coinage of the concept was meant to rectify the problem that Jung considered the source of the modern world's psychological malaise, namely the soullessness of contemporary life, the loss of that intense inner experience that in previous centuries used to be a living, breathing reality, the soul. This modern unconsciousness of the soul remained an abiding theme of Jung's psychology throughout his career. In fact, the title of one of his more popular works, *Modern Man in Search of a Soul,* could well stand as a summary statement of Jung's view of modern life.

For Jung, "anima" and "soul" were deeply intertwined conceptually. For instance, we can see in the "Definitions" section of *Psychological Types,* one of Jung's earlier works, how he conceived of this relationship between anima and soul.

> SOUL-IMAGE [Anima/Animus]. The soul-image is a specific *image* (q.v.) among those produced by the unconscious. Just as the *persona* (v. *Soul*), or outer attitude, is represented in dreams by images of definite persons who possess the outstanding qualities of the persona in especially marked form, so in a man the soul, i.e., anima, or inner attitude, is represented in the unconscious by definite persons with the corresponding qualities. Such an image is called a "soul-image." Sometimes these images are of quite unknown or mythological figures.[1]

In short, the anima is the inner figure that serves as the personified image of a man's soul. If we take the more common religious meaning of "soul" first and leave a more technical understanding for later discussion, we see Nick's individuation process, as illustrated by the first two episodes of the dream, result in the situation depicted by the third and most striking part of the dream.

We have already traced the way in which the acquisition of a true inner authority for Nick was hampered and blocked by a number of personal and collective factors. For Nick, his Sky Father's simultaneous absence and dominance resulted in a religious attitude focused upon sinfulness, judgment, and guilt, and in a pervasive dependence on other's attitudes and feeling for self-esteem and motivation. The first episode of the dream, in which Nick finds himself working in a pharmacy for a druggist long on criticism and short on praise, shows how our work on bringing his authority conflicts to awareness through their reenactment between us in the transference enabled Nick to stand up for himself and refuse to remain dependent on outer authorities. This greater inner autonomy, symbolized in the dream by his quitting his job under the tyrannical druggist and walking out, represents a rebellion against authority that is decidedly more mature. His previous rebelliousness, expressed through indulgence in behaviors and actions considered naughty, most notably smoking cigarettes and using marijuana, is seen here as on the wane. He leaves the drugs and the druggist behind, prepared to go it alone. Though in the second episode of the dream he still smokes and actively avoids his mother's and his wife's negative judgments, we see his dream ego giving all his cigarettes away, quite aptly, to those impoverished parts of himself that seek solace through drugs and stimulation.

The first two episodes of Nick's dream therefore show a transitional stage of individuation, in which the projection of authority—religious, moral, psychological, and emotional—has begun to be withdrawn from those around him. The result is a greater independence, an ability to go it alone, and a lessening of dependence on other people or on psychoactive substances. The third episode of the dream, therefore, is the one in which Nick finally and quite dramatically meets his own soul, his anima, in personified form, rather than living his life through the souls of others.

Though the face-to-face quality of the confrontation is hearten-

ing, the state of Nick's soul described by the dream is deeply disturbing. Coming to terms with the state of one's soul in analysis
through dream work is not often an easy confrontation, and hence
frequently requires a great deal of time and preparation. This horrifying scene of a deformed woman kept alive through artificial
means, dependent on technicians for life and breath, struggling
through her suffering to remember the prescription for healing, is
not, as one can plainly see, a confrontation that Nick could have
tolerated any earlier in his inner journey. Without an alliance with
me based on trust and empathy, rather than rebellion and suspicion,
without the greater autonomy, self-esteem, and inner strength represented by his walking out of the abusive pharmacy, and without
his own relationship to the religious tradition of his father and his
childhood, Nick could have easily remained a stranger to his soul,
unable to stand the pain of seeing his inner life face-to-face in its
weakness and vulnerability. For these reasons, modern men in
search of a soul often find themselves involved perforce in a process
completely unlike fixing a broken computer or repairing a dysfunctional engine. To know one's soul is a process that requires considerable time and patience, the result of which is not simple cure but
rather a more profound awareness of its brokenness.

To see the woman in Nick's dream as anima in the religious sense
of soul is to note the effect of his father's patriarchal strictures and
his own father's lack of relatedness to a true inner authority. In a
church in which instinct is suppressed in favor of obedience and in
which women hold an inferior place, Nick's soul, his religious life,
could really only take the form presented here in such unsettling,
graphic detail. She is deformed, stunted, alive but only through artificial means, unable to breath or move on her own. We find Nick
struggling with such religious issues as guilt, responsibility, sin, and
forgiveness, at first by the way of his hidden pleasures but then, as
our work progresses, by meeting his soul more explicitly in the figure of the anima—a religious life hampered, constricted, only half-
alive. Whereas the adolescent cop of the previous dream personified
the *character* of Nick's personal and collective conflicts, the anima
figure of this next dream might be said to present the *result* of this
conflict on his soul.

One must note that Jung adopted the term "soul" into his psychology precisely because of its manifold meaning. For Nick, the religious level of his inner conflicts and accordingly the shape of his anima are appropriate to examine, given his own personal history and the way in which a patriarchal religion of external authority contributes collectively to the deformation of the souls of modern men. However, the much more common use of the word "soul" and therefore of "soul-image" or "anima" in Jung's thought is the one in which the religious connotations of the word are exchanged for a more modern meaning, namely, as a synonym for "psyche," and here we move a bit more deeply into a technical level of discussion.

"Psyche," the Greek term for "soul" (and, interestingly, for "butterfly," too) was a word initially used by Jung not as a synonym for "soul" but rather in contradistinction to it. Again from his early thought in *Psychological Types:*

> I have been compelled, in my investigations into the structure of the unconscious, to make a conceptual distinction between *soul* and *psyche.* By psyche I understand the totality of all psychic processes, conscious as well as unconscious. By soul, on the other hand, I understand a clearly demarcated functional complex that can best be described as a "personality."[2]

This early distinction, neat as it may seem, gradually erodes as Jung develops a more complex view of human life, making such neat distinctions between soul and psyche impossible. In part, the eventual overlap between these terms is due to Jung's choice of the German word *Seele* (soul, mind, spirit), a word that requires consistently different translations in order to render Jung's ever-changing meaning of the word correctly into English.[3] Yet in reading Jung one comes to feel that this imprecision was meant unconsciously to make clear his belief that the object of the modern discipline of psychology, psyche, is very closely related, if not at times identical, to that which once bore the name "soul" in Western culture. For this reason, the anima as the personification of psyche for men is referred to by Jung interchangeably as the "soul-image" or even just simply "soul."

If we apply this idea of the anima as psyche personified to Nick's dream, we come to discern Nick's impulse to engage in psychotherapy, the healing of psyche as soul. If the woman in Nick's dream is "the totality of all psychic processes, conscious as well as unconscious," then Nick and I are faced with a grave situation. In an illustration of how the most brilliant interpreter of a dream is nearly always the dreamer himself, Nick's own insight that the woman represents the psyche he brings to therapy seems entirely accurate: the totality of his inner life is in serious condition, a condition whose gravity goes far beyond the aridness of his religious conflict or his struggles around inner authority. His nonphysical existence, his psyche, remains severely undeveloped and survives only through the skillful manipulation of others. His psyche thus resides in a vacuum, the prisoner of a machine that both compensates for and mirrors the withering within.

Of course, again, the dream does not present in any miraculous way what a trained observer could not have already deduced. A talented, creative, and intelligent thirty-five-year-old who had spent most of his adult life wandering without vocation, ending up dependent on his wife's financial and emotional resources, obviously could not be in a psychological situation any different than that depicted by the dream. As natural phenomena, dreams do not exist merely to supply information to interested psychotherapists. Rather, what dreams do best is what this one does for Nick, namely, present him with a personification of psyche in the figure of the anima, and so permit him to enter into relationship with his psyche. In this way, dream work serves both the purpose and source of psychotherapy: soul healing.

Rather than expressing these realities through concepts and notions, through intellectual definitions and distinctions, the dream uses symbols and figures to bring Nick into a relationship with something virtually inexpressible in word or thought. The measure of the dream's effectiveness can be seen most vividly in the tremendous feeling it evoked for Nick. Psyche is no longer "mind," "soul," "inner life," or any of the other verbal descriptors men typically use to handle and constrain that element of their existence over which they often have so little control. Psyche instead takes on the form and face of the anima, an inner figure who in Nick's case suffers so poignantly and is struggling so desperately to remember the formula of her cure and liberation.

As the personification of psyche for men, the anima's appearances in dreams and fantasies are occasions for much attention in psychotherapy, a process focused in essence on the healing of the soul. The decidedly clinical setting of Nick's dream depicts how many men experience such inner work: as if it were a medical problem analogous to polio or tuberculosis, in which vaccines, technological manipulation, and faith in the wonders of modern science are applied passively to their minds and hearts, resulting in complete remission from all symptomatology. Nick's own interpretation of the dream points in that direction, identifying me as the doctor on whom psyche depends for her informational cure, even though I do not appear in the dream. Earlier dreams of his pointed in a similar direction: Nick would be wandering in hospital hallways, meeting sick children, going to a clinic periodically for an injection.

By giving psyche form and substance, by imparting a face, a body, and an independent life to the soul, the anima of men's dreams and fantasies, as with Nick's lady of the iron lung, shows men that psychotherapy's healing has little to do with the medical model so often applied to the physical body, a model based on knowledge, control, power, and overarching wisdom. These qualities, representative of what Jung called the Logos principle, were identified explicitly by Jung as part of what he considered to be masculinity. What many men find, especially in these changing times, is that the insight and intellectual efficacy of the Logos principle can only take them so far, and, thus, often must cede its place to Eros, to the healing born of relationship and all that relationship entails: responsibility, vulnerability, interdependence, feeling, love, creativity, work, acceptance of imperfection, and abiding care and nurture. In this way, the anima as psyche personified brings men into relationship and leads them once again to discover the essence of who they are, their soul.

This confrontation with psyche in psychotherapy is, understandably, difficult for most men for a number of reasons. We see, in Nick's case, that he did not even glimpse the anima until nearly a year into his treatment, and then what he saw led him, in pain and fear, to turn his face away. Part of this difficulty, I think, lies in the fact that modern life does not support processes and relationships that take a long time or a great deal of effort, or that result in something less than beauty or perfection. In an age of jet travel, microwave cooking, and instant global communication, there is an ever-growing emphasis on speed and gratification. The social and economic conditions of modern life enable, indeed at times require, a previously unheard of mobility that often runs counter to what Jung would call Eros, the needs of relationship. A deep connection to another person may not really grow or blossom in the few months or years that one may have in one geographical spot before transfer or relocation, and so men are encouraged socially and economically to forsake the exigencies of human relationship for things that will ensure what is defined as "success" in our society—high earning power, ability to provide, social recognition, competence, and control. When faced, therefore, with the anima in psychotherapy, with the task of having to build a true relationship with psyche, the most frequent tendency is what we see in Nick's dream: medicalize the problem, that is, give it over to the hands of an expert, and turn your face away from the suffering. The shallowness of male "success" turns men's psyche into the sickly wraith we see in Nick's dream, haunting in her pain and desperate for cure.

As one can see, modern men's alienation from psyche is linked to the development of a civilization centered upon technology. As we grow ever more dependent on machines of ever greater sophistication and complexity, we depend less and less on other people. In contrast to the time of the industrial revolution, when technology was fairly closely linked to simple economic production—the production of material goods for consumption—nowadays we are caught in a technological way of life that goes far beyond the production of goods, in which machines are capable of carrying out processes once understood as essential to the definition of "human." Two striking examples of such a trend away from the human can be found in the realm of "artificial intelligence," in which computers have begun to supplant human thought with vastly superior intellectual capabilities, and in the realm of reproduction, in which biotechnology allows for conception, gestation, and birth without parents. However often we may hear the dire predictions concerning the psychological effect of such technological growth, such words often fail to make an impression on us, and yet a dream like Nick's can be seen as having a collective meaning, illustrating what Jung would call the *anima mundi,* the state of the world's psyche, as we grow further away from our basic ground in instinct and interdependence.

Technology is not all that stands in the way of men's psychological development. As we explore what is a familiar theme by now, we see how patriarchy, with its definitions, attitudes, and results, also alienates men from an ability to relate to their psyche, leaving them, like Nick, overwhelmed by the anima, turning their face away from relationship and life.

The Anima and the "Feminine": Jung's Conceptions and a Modern Critique

We have in the previous section looked at anima as both soul and psyche in both the religious and psychological senses of the terms. However, these are (unfortunately, in my opinion) by far two of the least common ways in which Jung and subsequent Jungians tend to regard or define the anima. The most common definition of the anima, I think, is drawn from the great body of Jung's own writing on the anima and is perhaps the most easily understood and most popularly accepted: the anima as the personification of a man's unconscious feminine side.

To be sure, the anima as a man's unconscious femininity is an idea fundamental to Jung's thought. For example, if we simply continue the previous quote from *Psychological Types,* published first in 1922, we see that Jung's idea of the anima from its very inception was linked to his ideas on the feminine: "With men, the anima is usually personified by the unconscious as a woman. . . . For a man, a woman is best fitted to be the real bearer of his soul image, because of the feminine quality of his soul. . . ."[4]

The following quotation from *The Relations between the Ego and the*

Unconscious in 1934 expounds on the sources of this femininity of the anima in greater detail.

> Among all possible spirits the spirits of the parents are in practice the most important; hence the universal incidence of the ancestor cult. . . . For the child the parents are his closest and most influential relations. But as he grows older this influence is split off; consequently, the parental imagos become increasingly shut away from consciousness. . . . In place of the parents, woman now takes up her position as the most immediate environmental influence in the life of the adult man. She becomes his companion, she belongs to him in so far as she shares his life and is more or less of the same age. She is not of a superior order, either by virtue of age, authority or physical strength. She is, however, a very influential factor and, like the parents, she produces an imago of a relatively autonomous nature— not an imago to be split off like that of the parents, but one that has to be kept associated with consciousness. . . .
>
> Here without a doubt is one of the main sources for the feminine quality of the soul. But it does not seem to be the only source. No man is so entirely masculine that he has nothing feminine in him. The fact is, rather, that very masculine men have—carefully guarded and hidden—a very soft emotional life, often incorrectly described as "feminine." . . . The repression of feminine traits and inclinations naturally causes these contrasexual demands to accumulate in the unconscious. . . .
>
> It seems to me, therefore, that apart from the influence of woman there is also the man's own femininity to explain the feminine nature of the soul-complex [anima]. . . .
>
> An inherited collective image of woman exists in a man's unconscious, with the help of which he apprehends the nature of woman. This inherited image is the third important source for the femininity of the soul.[5]

Thus, according to Jung, the femininity of the anima (here called "soul" or "soul-complex" according to Jung's early usage) is determined, first, by a man's experiences of actual women, starting with his mother; second, by a kind of inborn femininity within men;[6] and third, by an archetypal factor within the psyche that carries, as Jung says above, "an inherited collective image of woman."

One final quotation from Jung's later work *Aion,* published in 1950, should be sufficient to demonstrate that Jung's view of the anima as feminine remained throughout his life an essential part of the concept.

> The projection-making factor is the anima, or rather the unconscious as represented by the anima. Whenever she appears, in dreams, visions, and fantasies, she takes on personified form, thus demonstrating that the factor she embodies possesses all the outstanding characteristics of a feminine being. She is not an invention of the conscious, but a spontaneous product of the unconscious. Nor is she a substitute figure for the mother. On the contrary, there is every likelihood that the numinous qualities which make the mother-imago so dangerously powerful derive from the collective archetype of the anima, which is incarnated anew in every male child.[7]

As all this shows, Jung defined the anima as a man's unconscious femininity, the archetypal image of woman for men. Accordingly, the great variety of female figures in men's dreams and fantasies, the profusion of women who populate mythology and literature throughout the ages, and every place a man gives form or substance to an image of woman are all seen as a manifestation of the anima. Now, as the perspicacious modern reader will quickly discern, especially readers familiar with the feminist critique of sex-role stereotypes, Jung's image of the anima as feminine rests on a definition of "feminine" inherent in patriarchal sex roles and so, when Jung says above that the anima possesses "all the outstanding characteristics of a feminine being," these characteristics, as a review of his writings will disclose, are the ones traditionally assigned to women within Western patriarchal societies.

For example, we see Jung describing some of the anima's "feminine" qualities, and not the most flattering ones, when he writes:

> The anima is a factor of the utmost importance in the psychology of a man wherever emotions and affects are at work. She intensifies, exaggerates, falsifies and mythologizes all emotional relations with his work and with other people of both sexes. The resultant fantasies and entanglements are all her doing. When the anima is strongly

constellated, she softens the man's character and makes him touchy,
irritable, moody, jealous, vain and unadjusted.[8]

Anima femininity is, for Jung, closely tied to the traditional realm
of woman in patriarchal societies, the realm of Eros, the world of
feeling and relationship. For this reason, he writes of anima:

> The animus corresponds to the paternal Logos just as the anima
> corresponds to the maternal Eros. . . . I use Eros and Logos as
> merely conceptual aids to describe the fact that woman's conscious-
> ness is characterized more by the connective quality of Eros than by
> the discrimination and cognition associated with Logos. In men,
> Eros, the function of relationship, is usually less developed than
> Logos.[9]

One has to work to find in Jung characterizations of anima femininity that do not have a depreciating, pejorative edge, a fact that in
itself points out how Jung's ideas of the feminine are very closely
linked to the unconsciously devaluing stereotypes of women in patriarchal societies. The following is yet another example of how
even some of Jung's positive descriptions of the anima seem to
go sour.

> Every mother and every beloved is forced to become the carrier and
> embodiment of this omnipresent and ageless image [the "projection-
> making factor" mentioned earlier, that is, the anima], which cor-
> responds to the deepest reality in a man. It belongs to him, this
> perilous image of Woman; she stands for the loyalty which in the
> interests of life he must sometimes forgo; she is the much needed
> compensation for the risks, struggles, sacrifices that all end in dis-
> appointment; she is the solace for the bitterness of life. And, at the
> same time, she is the great illusionist, the seductress, who draws
> him into life with her Maya—and not only into life's reasonable and
> useful aspects, but into its frightful paradoxes and ambivalences
> where good and evil, success and ruin, hope and despair, counter-
> balance one another. Because she is his greatest danger she demands
> from a man his greatest, and if he has it in him she will receive it.
>   This image is "My Lady Soul," as Spitteler called her. I have
> suggested instead the term "anima." . . .[10]

The above quote shows how in addition to the realm of feeling and relationship, summed up by Jung in his use of the term Eros as a psychological principle, anima femininity carries another side of the traditional, partiarchal sex role assigned to woman, that of the "ideal," the "embodiment of perfection" that is the reward for a man's heroism and courage. The anima is especially suited to carry this traditional role of women in patriarchal societies by virtue of her archetypal nature. Unlike flesh-and-blood women whose imperfections and weaknesses, of course, eventually show, the anima as a collective representation of woman remains above the frazzle and fray of human life, always the Untouched Virgin, the Supreme Embodiment of Goddessness.

Because this equation of the anima with a man's feminine side is the most current and most heavily used within analytical psychology, it is important to see that this understanding and use of the anima has a number of problems, some of which actually seem to defeat Jung's more positive intentions in coining the concept. The first and most obvious problem is the one inherent in Jung's phenomenological methodology, in which he formulates the character of an archetype, in this instance, the anima, by a historical-cultural survey of images, symbols, and fantasies. Thus, in defining the anima as a man's femininity, his concept comes to reflect not some unsullied, pure conception of what the feminine might be, but rather a compendium of what has historically been called feminine in Western culture—which is something altogether different from what is implied by the phrase "archetypal feminine," with its ontological ring.[11] The problem here is the extreme patriarchalism that characterizes this culture, which denies, represses, devalues, and attacks what is understood as "feminine." Thus, the anima ends up becoming an archetypal vehicle for patriarchal sexism, carrying often the worst characterizations of patriarchal stereotypes of woman—unreliability, emotionality, seductiveness, eroticism, irrationality, and dangerousness. Even the best of her characteristics still remain tainted and problematic insofar as the anima is defined, again through an essentially patriarchal view of woman, as the Other, that which comes to men unbidden, unknown, unconscious, as something outside of his inherent masculine nature, something requiring integration and understanding.

Which brings us to the second problem inherent in such a conception of the anima. If the femininity of the anima is seen as the depreciated Other in the soul of the man, this characterization of the anima seems derived from the way that femininity is seen in patriarchal societies as a set of psychological qualities or characteristics that belong exclusively to women, while masculinity is that which is characteristic exclusively of men. Jung, again quite characteristically, casts the problem as an issue of opposites. Masculinity and femininity are seen as the dual poles of a wholeness represented archetypally by the image of the Androgyne, a symbol for the supraordinate Self or archetype of wholeness. But to cast the problem in this way is to continue in archetypal form the seemingly endless enmity between male and female seen in patriarchal societies.

Rather than going beyond culture with an archetypal theory, Jung finds himself trapped within his culture, and particularly within a cultural view of the feminine that simultaneously values it as the completion of a man's wholeness while casting it in the mold of "depreciated Other," inferior, unconscious, the source of illusion and irrationality. For this reason, within Jung's more traditional view of the anima, even the anima's most positive qualities, summed up perhaps most succinctly in her role as Eros carrier for men, still present men with an insuperable difficulty: these qualities are not seen as available to men as men, but rather as available to men only through women, only through the integration of anima femininity, not as inherent in their masculinity.

This rather extended discussion and critique of Jung's concept of the anima thus gives the reader, I think, a deeper sense of the collective nature of Nick's dream. For the anima, as a symbol of collective femininity in a patriarchal society, freighted with the most devalued half of the psyche, is very much like the woman in the iron lung in Nick's dream: deformed, manipulated, she lives a contingent existence, struggling to "re-member" herself, to put herself back into her body and free herself from the awful suffering into which she has been consigned. And Nick's task is the collective task of so many men in contemporary Western society: first, to face the suffering of the feminine and acknowledge their own complicity, and second, equally important, to begin to see the feminine not simply as an attribute of the women around themselves but rather as an archetypal reality essential to their wholeness *as men.*

In this sense, Nick's dream and his deep inner connection to the anima is again a positive sign. That he feels her suffering as his own, indeed feels it so deeply that he must turn away, not out of callousness but on the contrary out of intolerable empathy, shows how his outer dependence on women is simply the literal enactment of something that actually is better understood as an inner reality, namely, an essential and emotional tie to his psychic femininity. In this way, Nick is part of a collective shift in attitude toward the feminine, in which the suffering wrought on this constellation of psychological reality through stereotyping, projection, and devaluation is at last being seen and felt, not just by women but by men too, who like Nick find patriarchal definitions of femininity leading them down a path to a developmental impasse.

The whole context for Nick's tie to the anima is one of suffering and illness: however empathic his connection and compassionate his attitude, this is an anima lacking an ability to breathe, a soul image without spirit or life. Is this not the natural result of seeking the feminine outside, in women—wife, mother, sisters—in the Other rather than in the self? Doesn't Nick's injured anima reflect the result of patriarchy upon the soul of the feminine in both men and women, robbing her of her ability to breathe and live? Is it not important that Nick see this anima as a part of him and of all men, not simply an image of the Other upon whom relationship, feeling, and life depend?

What are some solutions for these problems? The first is to move beyond some of the false dichotomies inherent in patriarchal (and Jungian) thought and to refrain from continuing to define or assign femininity or masculinity according to biological gender. Certainly the highest intention of Jung's vision of the contrasexual archetypes of anima and animus was precisely to transform patriarchal masculinity into something more androgynous, something transformed inside out into a union of opposites. That his theory and his own attitudes did not always live up to this impulse toward wholeness should not deter modern individuals from keeping in mind that it is this androgynous union, not further division between masculine and feminine, that is the ultimate source and result of healing for Jung.

Another solution, the result of a greater consciousness of the causes and effects of sexism in patriarchal societies, is to acknowledge the subjective nature of our observations and to refrain from participating in the "other-ization" of the feminine or of women in general. We do well to hold Jung again to the highest and best of his intentions, namely, his attempt to bring back to Western patriarchal consciousness the archetypal reality of the feminine as a coequal half of human wholeness, which women, unjustly, must carry in a one-sided patriarchy that denies its value or significance.

A third solution to the problem presented by the sexism of the anima concept is to become aware of the continual transformation and development of the collective consciousness. The entire thrust of individuation is a movement on both a personal and collective level to greater and greater unity, not to ever greater antipathy and separation: the polarities of masculine and feminine are not static, unchanging, divine conceptions, but rather twin poles of a reality that changes with greater consciousness and discrimination. Perhaps the rigid contrasexuality of these archetypal polarities is in the process of softening and blurring, leading to a salutary confusion between male and female, masculine and feminine. The result of such softening, of course, need not be the abandonment of the anima as a psychological notion, but rather an acknowledgement of its transformation in its role as carrier of men's femininity.

Such considerations (at least for a Jungian) lead to myth, a very patriarchal myth that illustrates what Nick's anima dream implies. Here, through the darker face of patriarchal masculinity, perhaps another relationship to the feminine for modern men can be located and celebrated.

Hades and Persephone: The Queen of the Underworld
and Her Role in Men's Individuation

We have already heard of the establishment of Zeus's dominion over the sky, but we have not yet heard much about Zeus's brother, Hades. Granted rule over the much darker realm, the realm of the underworld, where the spirits of the dead dwelled and from which no soul ever returned, Hades reigned alone in his kingdom until out of his solitude he emerged and approached his brother Zeus for permission to take to himself a wife. The woman Hades had set his sights on, however, put Zeus in a bind, for Hades' intention was to have for his queen none other than his own niece Persephone, the only daughter of their sister the goddess Demeter. Knowing that sister Demeter would never permit her only daughter to become Hades' bride and queen of the underworld, Zeus neither gave Hades permission nor refused it, and allowed Hades to take his own course of action.

Finding Persephone alone one day as she picked flowers in the fields, Hades broke open the earth and rode up in his huge chariot, abducting the unwary girl, whose frightened cry rang so loud it covered the earth, rising even up to the heavens where her mother Demeter heard the shout before the earth closed up and cut it off. Disconsolate as any mother would be, Demeter madly rushed over the earth in a fruitless attempt to locate Persephone, receiving little help from either gods or from humans who, out of fear of offending Zeus or Hades, told Demeter nothing of what they had seen. The great goddess continued her mournful search, aggrieved at her terrible loss, neglecting her appearance, eating and drinking nothing, until she grew unrecognizable, and the bounty of the earth, over which she presided as goddess of the harvest, itself too withered and died. Out of pity, finally, and in response to Demeter's implorations, Helios, who as god of the sun saw all on earth, told Demeter what had happened, that Zeus had permitted Hades to abduct Persephone and make her his queen.

Furious at both the rape and the betrayal behind it, Demeter turned from Olympus and began her sojourn on earth, dazedly

wandering, still half-searching for Persephone. In her travels, Demeter eventually stopped by a well in the city of Eleusis and was
welcomed into the household of King Keleos by the king's four
daughters, who were moved to compassion and hospitality by this
poor lady's grief-stricken countenance, little knowing she was a
goddess. Metaneira, wife of Keleos, had just given birth to her son,
Demophoon, and gave Demeter charge of the baby, whose care
became a source of comfort to the now childless goddess. As a favor
to the house of Keleos, therefore, Demeter worked by night to
make Demophoon immortal, placing the child in the fire in order
to strengthen him, a plan which would have succeeded had not
Metaneira come upon the two of them one night, shrieking in
horrified misunderstanding as she spotted her baby son consumed
by the fire without realizing Demeter's intention. Only then did
Demeter reveal herself to the house of Keleos as goddess, rebuking
Metaneira for her ignorance but allowing Eleusis to receive great
renown and blessing for her if they would erect a temple in her
honor and faithfully keep her cult. Thus began the Eleusinian mysteries, the best kept and most important secret ritual of the ancient
world, honoring Demeter and her lost daughter Persephone, her
grief and her glorification.

Meanwhile, in the underworld, Persephone was devastated by the
loss of her mother and her life in the upper world. As the inconso-
late Demeter cast famine and barrenness upon the world above,
Persephone pined away in the shadow world of her husband below,
growing thin and sickly, having eaten nothing but a single pomegranate seed. Finally, Zeus sent his messenger Hermes below to his
brother Hades, asking for Persephone's release so that both the
earth and Olympus might once again enjoy the bountiful favor of
Demeter rather than the drought and dryness from which they all
were suffering. Given the consequences of his rape, which had se-
cured for him nothing but a reluctant slave rather than a willing
queen, Hades consented to allow Persephone to spend eight months
of the year with her mother above, drawing sustenance from the
living and from the love and care of her mother, but claimed Persephone yet as his bride. Since she had eaten in the underworld, he

would require her to fulfill her duties as queen of the underworld annually, descending to him for four months of the year, which is how Persephone, also known as "Kore," the Maiden, became a central figure in the ranks of the divine, spanning both earth and the underworld as both Hades' queen and daughter of the harvest.

In Persephone's story, we perceive again what we saw earlier in the myth of Aeacus, a shift from a goddess-based religion and world view to one characterized by male dominance and female submission. The structure and symbols of this myth, therefore, are nearly identical to those of the Aeacus myth. The action begins and revolves around the forcible abduction and rape of a female by a father god, the result of which constellates a reaction on the part of a goddess-mother, who then withholds her life-giving force until she is properly recognized and honored. This historical stratum of myth, referring, as Graves puts it so succinctly, to the "male usurpation of the female agricultural mysteries in ancient times,"[12] comes out of that transitional time when men began gradually taking to themselves what had been exclusively the province of women: the power of life, growth, and birth; the authority over production and increase.

However, I feel the myth is infinitely more evocative on a psychological and symbolic level than as a historical artifact. One piece of insight afforded by this tale, relevant to modern men struggling with patriarchal categories, is its illustration of the archetypal underpinnings of rape. By categorizing Eros—feeling, relationship, sensitivity, and passion—as "feminine" and thereby assigning such qualities literally to women or figuratively to the feminine in some archetypal sense, men find themselves alienated like Pete and Nick from the true fullness of psychic life and identified instead with a conception of masculinity in which force, control, and performance are substituted. The stage is thus set for rape as a brutal and ultimately unworkable "solution" to this painful split in men, in which men seek to penetrate and obtain for themselves literally or emotionally those qualities that have been given away to women.

I think the Hades-Persephone myth provides a view of the psychic or archetypal factors at work when rape occurs literally, but also reveals how the traditional Jungian understanding of the anima as the carrier of a man's femininity prepares the way for such oppression. To see anima principally as feminine simply reinforces the patriarchal split between male and female and redeems neither women nor men. In the myth, Hades does not elevate Persephone or fulfill her deity by making her his queen, but instead abducts her into the underworld, into his still unconscious masculinity. The reverse possibility, that Persephone through her marriage to Hades might lead him upward and out of his unconscious kingdom of power, does not and cannot occur within such a patriarchal context. Though the central figure of the story is of course Persephone, who is taken and then freed, we must admit that Hades does not undergo any transformation at all through the interaction; he is neither redeemed nor changed in any fundamental way. On the contrary, some versions of the myth even emphasize the shallowness of his consent to Persephone's liberation by having him secretly slip the pomegranate seed into her mouth to guarantee her continual subjugation. His figure here is demonstration that patriarchal masculinity is never made whole if femininity is located somewhere outside of a man's basic masculine identity, in the Others of men's external lives, their wives, mothers, and sisters, or in the Others of men's dreams and fantasies, the female figures or psychological constructs of femininity such as the anima. To saddle the anima with the full freight of a man's femininity makes rape not only an acceptable course of action for a man desperate for wholeness but also perhaps one of the only ways for a man to feel as if those denied and projected qualities of human life can be possessed and made his own.

The myth's interlude concerning Demeter's wanderings is of vital importance. The fertility of life comes to a standstill when the power of life is given wholly over to the feminine and then must be stolen back. Such an archetypal process robs the goddess not only of her future—her daughter—but of her very life, her essential authority and independence. The paradox is acute. The insecure masculine overvaluation of what is assigned to women as feminine does not free women nor make available to men *as men* those qualities called feminine, but rather serves to continue the subjugation of women to men. Whether this idealization of the feminine is perpetrated by men emerging from early matriarchal agricultural societies or by modern men standing on the shaky ground of one-sided patriarchal masculinity in transformation, the self-defeating quality of it remains the same. This myth depicting the origin of the Eleusinian mysteries establishes their importance as a surviving remnant of what Hades attempted to abduct, what the shift to patriarchy had attempted to suppress and own, namely an initiation into the fullness of women's participation in the feminine on her own terms and not through masculine ways of being, thinking, or creating. This view explains the significance of these rites in the ancient world and the absoluteness of their mystery in a world slowly possessed by patriarchal modes of thought and action.

Demeter's abortive attempt to redeem masculinity, her attempt to make Demophoon immortal through exposing him to her own divine nature, is eventually abandoned. The goddess cannot save masculinity from itself within a patriarchal context, with no help forthcoming either from the old-boy network of Olympus, who abandon her to wander upon the earth, nor from ignorant humans who can only experience her power as a trial-by-fire rather than purification and refinement, the burning away of imperfection to create a new, more durable nature. Demeter, therefore, demands her own worship and her own temple, and begins to seek her own healing and a recognition of her own power and authority.

The parallels with Nick's dream up to this point seem fairly clear and help us to sort out what may be going on archetypally for Nick as he pushes his way out of stereotypical, authoritarian masculinity and comes upon the figure of Woman within. Like the abducted Persephone, his figure of woman wastes away, entrapped in the machinery of masculine technology. One almost wants to say "enthroned," since Nick's anima figure finds herself elevated as the victim of patriarchal ministrations, not unlike Persephone, whose elevation as queen and object of Hades' attention comes at the price of her freedom and independence and is the source of her oppression. The male technicians are quite explicit about their tender mercies. Their manipulation of the controls is meant to heal and cure the woman. After all, they have her best interests in mind, do they not?

However, it remains to the dream figure to remember her own cure, to move past this dependence on technology for life and breath and reproduce for herself her own inner wisdom of "what the doctor ordered," what our therapeutic work together and its attention to his inner life had already suggested to Nick. From the Demeter portion of the myth we may therefore conclude that the autonomy of the feminine must be recognized by detaching woman from the burden of carrying for men this principle and all it represents. By removing this femininity from the "life supports" that foster both dependence and restriction, we prepare the way for a deeper level of masculine acknowledgement that sees this femininity as a part of himself that must be "re-membered."

For these reasons, I think we must move away from a definition of the anima that stresses femininity so heavily and in such obviously patriarchal ways, so we can recognize the anima (and her counterpart, the animus in women) in the more basic sense we examined earlier, as a figure for "soul" or "psyche." Only in this way can men like Nick begin to allow the healing of the dream to occur on an ongoing basis. To "re-vision" anima in this way urges us to interpret Nick's dream in a completely different light, not as the making whole of some contrasexual Other, but rather as a healing of something that is essentially his own—his own soul and his own masculinity.

As definitions of masculinity and femininity change and broaden, it is imperative to de-emphasize the gender of the anima. Such a movement can be supported by the distinction Jung began to make late in his career between the archetype in itself, which is essentially unknowable, and the symbolic representations of the archetype, which in the case of the anima can take many forms, not all of them necessarily female. (We will be exploring this point in greater depth in the next chapter as we look at the form the anima seemed to take for Pete, a gay man.) This does not mean abandoning the anima as a concept but perhaps reinterpreting the notion within a newer awareness of issues around gender and sexism.

One important clue to such a reinterpretation is suggested by the myth and by Jung himself, specifically, to define this archetypal figure through its most important function, that is, that of intermediary, that figure which, by personifying the soul, connects conscious and unconscious life. Jung speaks often of the anima as that which brings to our awareness the fullness of our unconscious experience. Again, from the definition of soul in *Psychological Types,* he writes:

> We can, therefore, speak of an inner personality with as much justification as, on the grounds of daily experience, we speak of an outer personality. The inner personality is the way one behaves in relation to one's inner psychic processes; it is the inner attitude, the characteristic face, that is turned toward the unconscious. I call the outer attitude, the outward face, the *persona;* the inner attitude, the inward face, I call the *anima.*[13]

Thus, we find Jung in his various writings referring to the anima as a "bridge" to the unconscious, the "mediatrix" or "psychopomp" in the soul of a man, a figure who leads men into the darker realm beneath his conscious, persona-based outer life,[14] and for Jung, as we see in the following quotation from his autobiography, this characterization of the anima was a reality in his life, not simply interesting psychological speculation.

> But the anima has a positive aspect as well. It is she who communicates the images of the unconscious to the conscious mind, and that is what I chiefly value her for. For decades I always turned to the anima when I felt that my emotional behavior was disturbed, and that something had been constellated in the unconscious. I would then ask the anima: "Now what are you up to? What do you see? I should like to know." After some resistance, she regularly produced an image. As soon as the image was there, the unrest or the sense of oppression vanished.[15]

A bit later in the same chapter, Jung comments:

> The soul, the anima, establishes the relationship to the unconscious. In a certain sense this is also a relationship to the collectivity of the

dead; for the unconscious corresponds to the mythic land of the dead, the land of the ancestors. If, therefore, one has a fantasy of the soul vanishing, this means that it has withdrawn into the unconscious or into the land of the dead. There it produces a mysterious animation and gives visible form to the ancestral traces, the collective contents. Like a medium, it gives the dead a chance to manifest themselves.[16]

In this way, the Persephone of our myth is the anima, not because of her femininity, but rather because of the way in which she exists on two planes, as both Goddess of Death and Daughter of the Harvest, Queen of the Underworld and Princess of Olympian Light. Her movement between these realms assures the continuation of the world and represents the cycle of life in which renewal prefigures death, in which death is necessary for rebirth. That Hermes is the god who secures Persephone's release makes sense, therefore, since Hermes serves for Olympus the same function as messenger and intermediary; his caduceus, the staff of intertwined snakes, is the symbol of healing through unity.

I submit that this function of intermediary between conscious and unconscious, and not the gender, of the figure earns for it the appellation "anima" or "soul figure." Furthermore, the fact that the figure that serves this function for heterosexual men is personified as a woman so often does not seem to me to be a result of something inherent to the archetype—which after all exists simply as a psychic potential without form or figure—but rather as a result of patriarchal sex-role assignations in Western society. Women are coerced into performing for men those social and emotional functions that the anima as archetype performs in the psyche; they serve as the carrier of relationship and the embodiment of soul as passion, sexuality, and life. The release of women's bondage to femininity provides freedom and cure for *men* as well as for women.

To go even further, we have seen how these sex role assignments rest upon an even more basic condition within a patriarchal society, namely, men's alienation from their own inner wholeness as men. The appearance of the anima as "soul figure" in the form of woman, therefore, may denote for men what feminist critics of the animus concept have already called attention to in the psyches of women: an estrangement from self that forces one's own psyche to appear to one as Other rather than as a figure of like nature. For heterosexual men who accept and enact such patriarchal definitions of "man" and "woman," this self-alienation is supported, not only by the splitting of sex roles, but also by one of the correlates of patriarchal masculinity, homophobia, the fear and hatred of homosexuality. To be in relationship to oneself as a man means fundamentally to both acknowledge and celebrate a kind of homosexuality, an enjoyment of one's own manhood as a man; this enjoyment is anathema in a patriarchal society whose dominant values and social structures are organized along heterosexual lines.

Hence, the heterosexual man's anima appears in female form, not necessarily because of the archetype's essential femininity, nor because a man's soul or psyche is somehow essentially feminine—both these views derive from the patriarchal literalization of "masculine" and "feminine" into "man" and "woman"—but rather because heterosexual men have been conditioned to see relationship as primarily a female concern, both as a part of the female sex role and because of the value placed on heterosexual relationships in modern Western societies. The result of this conditioning is therefore what appears to Nick in his dream and what is so horrifyingly illustrated in the rape of Persephone: patriarchal masculinity distorts men's view of the feminine, turning it into an Other that must be conquered or cured and into something dependent on masculinity for life and breath (though Demeter successfully resists this and establishes her own cult). In addition, this patriarchal conditioning robs from men an ability to relate to their own soul, locating their wholeness in women or in relationships with women. The contrasexuality of Jung's view of the anima can thus actually stand in the way of men's development and psychological liberation from patriarchal self-estrangement. However, by casting a man's relationship to anima less in male-female terms and more in terms of a man's relationship to whoever—whatever—constitutes his soul, his connection to the collective Self, perhaps collectively we may find a situation similar to the one in Nick's dream, in which the soul remembers its cure, leaping up from its bed of suffering and pain to move and breathe and live on its own, unfettered by patriarchal distortion or devaluation.

The reverberations of Nick's dream lasted long and initiated a whole new level of understanding. Feeling the woman's pain as his own and therefore deeply appreciating her cure and her freedom, he was thus tempted by the dream to begin to value the relationship to his own inner life, the poverty and sickness of which was among the prime motivations for his seeking sustenance from women in the form of his dependence. This movement inward further consolidated our therapeutic relationship as a place of healing through relationship.

And yet the heterosexuality of this inner imagery led us continually to knock up against those obstacles that patriarchal conceptions of men and women place in the way of the heterosexual man's individuation. How could I, as a man, help him in relationship? He had never really had very many significant relationships to men and truly did not know what intimacy with a man would be like. If his inner life was feminine, did this mean he was a "latent homosexual"? Wouldn't it make much more sense for him to be seeing a woman therapist? Or would that simply be a continuation of the dependency he had come in to resolve?

Socialized to think of inwardness and emotionality as feminine, Nick found his soul, the inner life of his feelings and his most fundamental self, personified unconsciously as a woman (actually as a series of women), with the result that continued relationship to these inner images felt to Nick as if a process of progressive "feminization" were occurring, something he found profoundly disturbing and something that I had to work against significant resistances to normalize. Rather than feeling as if our work were helping him reclaim a fuller sense of his manhood, his lack of a symbolic ground in masculinity simply made his relationship to his inner life a carbon copy of what did not work on the outside in relationships with actual women. This lack of a symbolic ground in masculinity was enforced by consistently female personifications of the anima in his dreams and by the continual specter of latent homosexuality should masculine figures of similar power and attraction appear.

Then, a dream:

> I am helping a man and woman make love standing up. The woman has a penis and I hold both of them together as the man brings himself and the woman to simultaneous orgasm. The man leaves and, excited by the scene, I leap into making love to her, thrusting hastily but finding that neither I nor she is able to come.

Nick found this dream incomprehensible and was extremely puzzled. His repeated attempts to come up with an interpretation in the session led to exactly the kind of rushed lack of attention and tenderness he evinced in the dream, and I said so. "It feels as if once again we see you working on your inner life in the same way you might approach this woman—very excited on your own terms, but having a difficult time slowing down enough to let a relationship develop."

Having had so many anima dreams, Nick understood my point. "There she is, again, the woman of my inner life." He sat quietly, pondering, looking troubled. "Which of course means that you are the man in the dream, the one who is able to bring the woman to orgasm."

I was quite taken aback and felt immediately guilty, as if I had somehow in the course of our relationship robbed Nick of his own ability to join with and enjoy his soul. "It seems as if you're saying that you feel I have a better relationship to your inner life than you do yourself."

"Don't you? I always feel as if you are much more involved and concerned with my feelings, images, dreams, fantasies, while there is always a part of me that is kind of standing, like in the dream, on the outside, holding the two of you up together. You accept everything, take your time, enter in deeply and fully, while I just stand outside and watch on some level."

"Why do you think that is?"

"I don't know."

I had a couple of hunches, mostly having to do with how little men are taught to value inwardness or femininity or relationship. But instead, I wondered aloud, "I wonder if it might not have something to do with the way this woman in the dream is not just a woman but a man, too. I mean, she does have a penis after all, which is kind of strange."

"It is strange, isn't it?"

"I wonder if the dream might not be saying to us that your inner life really isn't just like a woman, full of feelings and relationship and all the other things women are supposed to be, but that your inner life has a penis, too—that it is masculine in certain ways." I paused for this to sink in. "I wonder if this might not give you some problems."

"Well, I can tell you in the dream I was quite concerned how I would make love to her, I mean, what to do with this penis." He looked at me and smiled a little. "Here I am making love to this woman in the dream but actually worried that the dream might mean that I am gay."

"And I wonder if that might not be some of the problem between us, why it feels as if I have a better relationship to your inner life than you do."

"You mean because I am gay?" The question was rhetorical and meant as humorous but betrayed the anxieties underneath.

"No, I mean maybe you are afraid to permit yourself to value and love your inner life, really enter in and make love to yourself, because of how little experience you have had with intimacy with other men. To love yourself after all means learning how to love a man, not a woman."

He sat there rather absorbed, and I felt as if a piece of the truth had been reached and understood. "I never thought of it that way, but it feels right. Could that be why I am always looking to women to help me out?"

"And why," I continued for him, "you might be afraid to depend on me and my ability to relate to you fully?" I let a bit of silence pass. "Maybe what the dream is saying is that in order to relate to a woman you need somehow to relate just as fully to yourself as a man, that you need to learn how to make love to both women and men, not necessarily literally or sexually, but more figuratively and emotionally."

He had gotten it. "I *am* aware that in here with you, as a man, I am often thinking either that it doesn't count, it isn't important, it isn't real intimacy, or that if I really let myself get involved, that I am going to lose myself, you know, find out that I'm gay, or find myself crushed, defeated, judged by you."

"So it is hard for you to imagine that, figuratively speaking, you might be able to make love with both parts of your inner life the way you feel I do, loving the parts that are feminine *and* the parts that are masculine?"

"They're both me, aren't they?" he repeated distractedly. And then more firmly. "They're both me."

4 *Dreams of the Dark Young Man: Gay Men, Masculinity, and the Male Anima*

I meet two younger men, Eric and Mark, who I am supposed to interview for acceptance into my program. Both are very handsome but I am more attracted to Mark, who tells me he's Cuban and has the last name of Caballero. I have the sense that they are a gay couple but don't know it. Eric is chatty but Mark is reserved. They are not clear on why they are coming here and my attempts to clear it up fall on deaf ears. They leave, and I schedule another interview with them, but when the time comes for the second interview, only Mark shows up, dressed in tight-fitting clothes. He is tall, slim, dark hair and moustache, about twenty-three. I get the sense he is gay and think how I might have missed this interview if I had gone away on my trip as planned. When I ask him where Eric is, he tells me some excuse. The atmosphere is seductive, and Mark is just my type.

Pete reported the dream with relish. Our first year's work together, particularly with his dreams, had begun to unlock the natural world of his feelings so that images like those of the ants and spiders had begun to mature, take on more developed shape and form, and become imbued with a whole spectrum of feeling. He had begun to have dreams with impressive imagery that often stayed with him for days and days, so impressive, in fact, that dream work had become a sort of a hobby for him, and I marveled a bit that the rather constricted, perfectionistic gay man I had begun to see only a year ago had come to take such an avid interest in his inner life.

This dream, however, was one of the first that broached a topic about which he and I had talked very little, Pete's sexuality, and the emotional temperature of the room rose a few degrees as I asked him what he meant by Mark in the dream being his "type."

"My type, huh? Well, this character in the dream is pretty much the kind of guy I am usually attracted to—Latin, dark, younger than myself, fairly masculine. I don't know what it is about those guys, but there is something about them that I just find irresistible."

I listened to the description, thinking to myself that it was not really all that different from Pete himself, who was fairly youthful, dark, and not overly effeminate. My thinking mind wondered if perhaps this figure might be Pete's shadow in some way, a dream figure representing those parts of Pete's personality that he found unacceptable and difficult to acknowledge or integrate into his conscious self-image. If this were the case, then the twinship theme in the dream, in which Mark appeared with a partner, Eric, who resembled him quite strongly, might make some sense: figures appearing in twos can represent a hitherto unconscious complex coming to consciousness. On the other hand, shadow figures were usually repulsive, frightening, or threatening in some way. Furthermore, Pete and I had already had a number of dreams in which the shadowy elements of his personality, especially his judgmentalism and low self-esteem, had been personified into Nazi commandants and street people. We had already met the shadow, and the atmosphere of erotic attraction that this dream had brought forth signaled another kind of complex entirely.

"Have you had relationships with these kind of guys?"

Pete shifted a little nervously. We were moving into as yet undisclosed territory, having spent most of our first year together on, I imagined, the much safer ground of academic performance and work inhibition. "Actually," he cleared his throat, "the only relationships I have ever had have been with these dark young man types, beginning with my first boyfriend in high school, Tony. I feel almost like Tony in a certain way imprinted me on this type of guy. He was gorgeous and Italian and athletic, and we spent all of our time together during my senior year. He seems to be pretty heterosexual at this point—we still talk to one another about two or three times a year, you know, at the holidays and such—but during high school there was a lot of physical contact, mutual massages, sleeping together over at his house, and so on. Nothing overtly genital or orgasmic, but very physical, very sensual." Pete's eyes glittered. "I was completely head over heels in love with him. Still am to some extent. That's why dreams like this make me wonder if I am somehow still trying to recapture Tony when I find myself attracted to guys like the two here in the dream."

"You have had other relationships with men like this, I mean, besides Tony?"

"Just two I'd actually call relationships, one with a guy in college for a few months, Frank—another Italian—and then my last relationship, four years ago, with Joseph. But all the guys in between, you know, the ones I have been attracted to, or had crushes on, or have tricked with over the years, and what not, all of them have been this type of guy—dark, Latin, masculine, and usually younger than me, though not always." Pete smiled impishly. "I can get into older men as well."

One thing was for sure: whatever this figure in the dream represented, it was certainly endowed with a wealth of erotic energy. Pete's comment about older men was perhaps the first, and not all that veiled, attempt at seductiveness toward me, unusual given the way that many gay men use their sexuality as one of the primary vehicles for relationship to other men. I might have expected an erotic transference to emerge somewhat earlier on in our work, but perhaps it was only now that Pete's inner life felt safe enough with me to show itself, in the manner of many dreams, in personified form.

From this first discussion, there then ensued in the following three months a fairly consistent series of dreams containing this figure, whose aspects became more and more clear with each dream, and whose character became more and more developed.

Tony, my high school boyfriend, and I are in our apartment, a
messy place which I share with my mother and sister, about the size
of the vacation house we used to rent. He and I go into a darkened
room, sit on the floor, and talk about our friendship. I am very con-
fident and self-assured in a good way as I talk about my coming to
terms with my sexuality, and he starts to talk about how he has
come to terms with his homosexuality. This is a pleasant surprise to
me, and we do what I have been waiting many many years to do—
kiss him on the lips. It is wonderful and I am suffused with this
feeling of tenderness, making up for lost time, healing the past, and
sheer erotic pleasure. Mom pokes her head in the room, and Tony
and I cool it enough to appear to be talking, although he has his
head on my lap. When she leaves, we make love with him laying on
top of me, kissing me for a long, long time.

This dream, in which Pete begins to make his peace with his relationship with Tony from high school, led me to wonder if Pete's
attraction to this certain type of man was not the result of a kind of
projection, in which Pete unconsciously sought out men of a type
that corresponded to an inner fantasy that was actually a piece of
himself. The dream here presents Pete entering into a more mature
relationship with Tony, one in which the homosexuality previously
denied and sublimated in their relationship now is addressed directly by both participants and is acted upon with a great feeling of
satisfaction, tenderness, and excitement. And yet, this was all a
dream, not happening nor likely to happen in Pete's outer life; it
was a symbol of what was occurring within. Could this Dark Young
Man figure thus be a symbol of Pete's sexuality, or more specifically,
his homosexuality? And if so, with what was Pete striving to come
into contact through his sexuality?

For this reason, I asked a question that many male clients find
baffling, especially when the dream in question contains figures that
the client actually knows or has known: "If Tony in this dream were
a symbol of a part of you, what do you think he would represent?"

Pete, in this case, did not hesitate too long in answering. "The
first thing that comes to my mind is masculinity. Tony was very

masculine, a jock almost, but not a jerk about it. His family was very masculine also; his father, Signor Pacelli, was pretty dominant, and Tony had three brothers. There was something about him that was just so masculine, especially for me, not having come out as gay yet, that made me want to spend all my time with him."

"So your attraction to Tony and to this type of man might have something to do with finding your masculinity."

Pete thought a bit. "In a way, I guess. I don't feel particularly deficient in my masculinity. I suppose I should—gay men get plenty of messages about being effeminate, or wanting to be a woman, and so on, you know. For me it's more like being gay means having to have contact with masculinity, loving men, and maybe in that way Tony is a symbol of my own manhood. I remember, for instance, envying the fact that he had brothers, and in fact, the family used to call me Quinto, as a kind of joke. Quinto means fifth in Italian, and I spent so much time at his house that they just called me the fifth brother. Tony and I used to call ourselves brothers, and sometimes people even thought we were when we would go out."

"So part of the attraction to him was his masculinity, being part of a brotherhood of sorts?"

"Especially as a young gay man."

I continue my thinking out loud. "Which is why your mother might not have much of a place here. It is a strictly masculine affair."

Pete laughed. "In more ways than one!"

Another dream, a few weeks later, continued the development.

> A figure who is a combination of Frank, my lover in college, and Dan, a man who I have a crush on now, has gone running with me. He is wearing nothing but black shorts, and as we stretch in the wet grass, he is horny, has taken his pants down, and rubs his erection against the ground. Gently, I offer to help him. I spit on my hands and begin to stroke his hard cock. He comes quickly. He is very grateful and happy, and I say that I am open to helping him any time. I fantasize in the dream about how I would like him to penetrate me.

Pete reported this dream with a smile. "Here we go again, another dream of the Dark Young Man."

"It's begun to be quite a theme, hasn't it?" I said to him. "Which indicates that this figure is pretty important is some ways. I take it that Frank and Dan are both Dark Young Man types."

Pete nodded. "As I said, most of my sexual and relationship fantasies are about this type of guy. I guess I find it interesting that so many of these men are Italian or Latin, you know, dark curly hair, dark skin, fairly extraverted, close to their families."

"Not too much like your own family. . . ."

Pete paused and thought about that comment for a while, obviously a new piece of the puzzle. "I guess you're right, my family is pretty Scandinavian."

"Except you."

"Absolutely. You know, lots of people mistake me for Italian or Greek or Jewish."

I remembered at this point that Pete told me early on that he was adopted. Could the Dark Young Man represent more than simply a sexual or relational fantasy? Might it not be the case that in his attraction to these men, he was groping toward that part of himself that predated his adoptive family, part of himself that was genetically—dare we say—archetypally his most basic self?

"Do you know anything about your biological family?"

Pete shook his head. "Nothing at all, really. My parents claim to know nothing, though I guess I have always found that hard to believe. And as for me, people always ask me if I am curious, but in all honesty, I really am not. My life with my parents has been good enough, and I just don't feel like opening up another whole can of worms."

I did not respond but simply took in the information and continued to wonder about the Dark Young Man that had now become a regular feature of Pete's inner life.

"What do you make of Frank and Dan being put together into one person in the dream?" I asked after a time.

"I don't know. I guess that's pretty common. It makes me feel a little bit like all the outer men I get crushes on are almost inter-changeable. Almost as if it doesn't matter if it is Frank or Dan or Tony or any of the others. Who they are seems less important than the fact that they fulfill my fantasy of this type of man." Pete's intelligence sometimes outstripped his emotional awareness, and so occasionally he would stumble onto a truth about himself in our discussions that made sense intellectually but might actually be somewhat painful or embarrassing to admit emotionally. At times, like this one, he would stop and smile ruefully at me. "Maybe that's why I am not all that successful at relationships, huh?"

If he were right, if his relationships failed because they were based more on projection than on reality, then this was probably the case for reasons beyond Pete's own creation. Thus, I felt a bit more compassion for the dilemma and was moved to modify his insight to make it less stinging an indictment of his psychological maturity. "Maybe that's all you've been taught. Or maybe you're looking for something outside that might be best found inside instead."

He remained quiet. I wondered to myself if his silence equaled consent.

The next dream of the Dark Young Man followed two weeks later and seemed to show a bit of progress: the Dark Young Man was no longer someone Pete knew but now a stranger.

> A friend and I are in a deli, bending over a glass case, when a handsome young Italian man bends over me, pressed against my whole body, his crotch up against my ass. He embraces me from behind. I am pleasantly surprised and we flirt, making a date to go out. Later I find out that my friend knows him and that he is only fifteen years old, though he looks about twenty-one. I have some reservations about someone that young but am more surprised at how attracted I am to him, despite his age.

Pete looked a little concerned as he reported the dream. "My first thought upon waking was that our work together here was going backwards. I mean, the point isn't to begin making me into a child molestor, is it?"

"I sense your concern and anxiety, but I wonder if the dream is speaking symbolically rather than literally, inwardly rather than outwardly." Deciding that this was a bit too oracular even for me, I made it simpler. "In other words, what if this Dark Young Man is a part of you?"

"What part would he be?" Pete finished the question for me, and as opposed to the last time we addressed this question, the answer seemed harder to come by. Pete puzzled away but came up with nothing.

I noted how this dream was a bit more difficult to interpret, indicating the presence of stronger defenses. Pete's disturbance over it reinforced this observation.

I continued to prompt. "We could think about it in another way. What was this Dark Young Man's most prominent characteristic?"

"Either his youth," Pete answered slowly, "or his seductiveness. I mean, it reminds me of the kind of thing I wish I were able to do, or rather, wished I could have done when I was fifteen, you know, just go up to a guy I am attracted to in a public place and flirt. Gay people don't get to do all that stuff when they are teenagers."

"And your feelings right now?"

Pete looked away, out my window. "Sadness, like I missed out, and yet a certain kind of guilt, almost as if I don't deserve somehow to go out with the guy in the dream, even though he's hot and hunky and made the first move. I feel kind of stupid, young, like I don't know much about relationships at all."

Two weeks later, Pete reported another dream. "Only I'm not sure if it's a dream or a fantasy—it happened early in the morning when I was half-awake."

> I'm on a journey at the end of the street where I lived back in Wisconsin, walking along the stream there. I see three rocks and ask them the way forward. They cannot tell me. They say, "We know not the way. We are but symbols, markers of the way you must go." When I ask what they mark, they fall silent and do not speak.
>
> I see a tunnel downstream and know this is where I must go, so I go in. It's very dark inside and as I go into the darkness, with the

light fading behind me, I begin to hum. The sound reverberates and the tunnel lights up from within—brighter when the sound is loud, dimmer when it is soft. I see in the half-light that another figure is with me, a Dark Young Man with a beautiful voice who sings in patches of brilliance. I imagine following him to the end of the tunnel, where I see a huge field over which hovers a huge white lighted disk, a flying saucer ready to take me off to the heavens.

At times, especially with a series of dreams, dream work may consist less of interpretation or puzzling out a meaning from the symbols and become more simply a process of underlining much of what has been made amply obvious by the dream itself. In Pete's case, with our work together having stimulated him to begin to read a fair bit about dream and dream work, he was rather well prepared to tell me what he thought the dream was about.

"It seems pretty clear I am on a journey of some sort, which has something to do with back home. The symbols in my dream are markers of how I must proceed, which is to follow the flow of my life, or my childhood, back to its source. Right now that's been pretty dark, like a tunnel, but if I enter into it and keep myself company, bits and pieces of where I am get illuminated."

Not able to top this cogent summary of his therapeutic task, I contained myself and simply wondered, "And the Dark Young Man here?"

Pete laughed. "I think that's the best part! We have been paying so much attention to him, it's about time he does something useful."

"Meaning. . . ?" What Pete meant was a little lost on me.

"Meaning that in this dream or fantasy or whatever, he finally begins to act like my guide and companion on the road. In a strange way, I guess it's kind of what I have always yearned for in a lover or a friend. I almost feel like maybe having finally begun to pay attention to him is going to allow him to start bringing forth his real purpose in my inner life."

"Start" was the right word. In the subsequent four years of my work with Pete, he and I met this inner figure in nearly one hundred dreams, fantasies, and active-imagination exercises. In fact, he became so familiar that I followed Pete's lead and began to abbreviate his title to "DYM" in my notes, as Pete did in his dream journal. What we came to discover again and again was that this constant figure carried the various aspects of his psyche that these first few dreams present so simply and so well.

The Dark Young Man first and foremost on the emotional level always had a distinct and undeniable erotic charge. Many of the dreams in which he appeared, either as a dark handsome Latin stranger or in the projected guise of one of Pete's previous lovers or sex partners, were among the most sexual of the dreams Pete discussed with me in the course of his analysis. For instance:

> I am dancing in a disco with a large, dark man. My eyes come to the level of his chest, which is wet with sweat and clad in a torn purple T-shirt. I'm trying to move closer to him, and he remains noncommittal and distant. Then we begin to take off our clothes—will he be attracted to me? He reminds me of a classmate I know.

> I go into the rest room of a small disco in Wisconsin with a mirror like a dressing room, where I put on a white T-shirt and unattractive jeans. When I leave, I go out to the dance floor and make out with a dark, handsome bearded man whom I have seen here before. I have some compunction about cheating on Frank but continue to make out with DYM. The song "Shame" is playing in the background: "Why should I be ashamed? Sometimes I think I'm going insane."

> I watch Tony play soccer and whenever he makes a goal, he hugs me. The hugs get progressively more intense and erotic, with him caressing me, grabbing my ass, kissing my neck. It is wonderful but I fear being seen in the open. The last hug has him grab me so hard that he begins to make love to me. I fall backwards into a church pew at my father's church. I am so hot for him I wonder if we can find an empty room to go fuck.

> I am in my hometown with old friends Dave and Laura. We go into their apartment and he wants to try sex with a man. I oblige him while Laura looks on, approvingly.

As Pete told me, much of his sexual life, both outwardly and on the level of fantasy, had revolved around this type of man, and so in the course of many of these dreams I heard about the second aspect of Pete's psyche that the Dark Young Man seemed to carry for him, namely, his homosexuality, his specific erotic attraction to men and to their masculinity. For this reason, many of the Dark Young Man dreams had as the major character some of the dark young men from Pete's past, particularly high school and college, for whom he had yearned romantically at a time when his homosexuality had not yet been acknowledged, even to himself. In this way, the consistent return of these dark young men, literally by the dozens, gave back to Pete what had at the time remained unconscious and unredeemed—his sexual and romantic feelings for the boys and young men he had grown up around but for whom he could not articulate his passion. Thus, the Dark Young Men in Pete's dreams often possessed a certain kind of irresistible or accentuated masculinity: sports heroes in high school, like Pete's first love, Tony, or big muscular bodies, or a kind of commanding presence in which Pete is ordered to serve the man sexually or in other ways. Such dreams as the following illustrate how Pete's homosexuality and his partners' masculinity are two sides of the same coin.

> I'm in a bar and spot a mixed group of guys and girls. The men are all Dark Young Men and one of the more handsome ones, a sharp looking Mexican with black hair, picks me up even though his girlfriend is there. He lays down on a bench and takes his shirt off—he is covered with fine black hair everywhere, even on his shoulders, which is very sexy.

> I am talking on the phone to my college friend Larry's brother's lover who is named Rob. As he describes himself to me—six foot one, dark, and big, with a beard, hairy body, wearing flannel shirt and jeans—I become interested in meeting him. He tells me he likes to go hiking, likes to use his body, feel its power and motion. I masturbate as I listen to him and then eat my own semen.

> I am Tom Cruise in this dream, and I have been hired by the captain of the high school football team, Gary, to serve him sexually. He has a big, dark body and a huge penis, and I give him a blow job as women watch. I feel like I am showing them how to do it, how to pleasure a man. At some point, however, he tells me I can leave the room, that I am fired. I'm somewhat upset at being used,

but it was such a turn-on and I know I can get another job. As I get dressed, I look through his underwear drawer, out of sexual fascination with him.

The obverse of this, the way in which the feminine or women seem to have no place in this, has been illustrated above in certain dreams, such as the one in which Pete's mother leaves as he and Tony make love. This theme, the inappropriateness of the feminine in the realm of the Dark Young Men, became repeated at various points in subsequent dreams, for example, "My sister is jealous that I have a boyfriend and she doesn't: a Dark Young Man."

Yet another aspect of the Dark Young Man, consistent throughout many of these dreams, was his Italian ancestry. Many of the boys and men Pete had yearned for and actually been in relationship with were not simply Latin types, but specifically Italian. At first, we wondered together, as above, if this might not simply be compensation for the rather Nordic, Lutheran upbringing at the hands of his parents. The Italians of his dreams were sexy, emotional, flashy, cocky, imbued with music and fire, in control and brash, risk takers. Tony, Frank, and Joseph, the men in his three major relationships, had all been Italian. So also had been many of the guys on whom he had developed crushes in college and continued to dream about: Larry, Rob, and Gary.

However, in time it became apparent that these Dark Young Men were not simply compensatory, but in a certain way they personified a natural part of Pete's psyche that had been given short shrift, a naturally Italian part of himself. We therapists get so involved in our work at times, especially with clients such as Pete for whom the process has begun to unlock something new and wholly different, that we can forget how all of the client's psychological and emotional work does not always occur within the sessions but runs its course in the client's outside life as well. For this reason, I was surprised when nearly two years into our work together and one year after our embarking on the path of the Dark Young Man, Pete came in to session one day and simply announced, "I've finally gotten the letter from the adoption agency I have been waiting for. I am Italian."

"You are Italian?" I wondered what Pete's manner of presenting such important information to me was meant to evoke—wonder, shock, disbelief, anger? I stayed as neutral as I could and asked again. "So, you wrote away for your file at the adoption agency?"

"I didn't say anything in here. I don't know why. Maybe I just felt like I needed to do it completely on my own. But anyway, I did it. All these dreams just kept me wondering, what if I really am Italian? What if these dark young men really are a part of me, you know, not just symbolically, but really and truly, a part of my genetic make-up, like my own flesh and blood. And it turns out, in a funny way, they are, at least the Italian ones. My mother was first-generation Italian, born here. My grandfather, her father, interestingly enough was an architect who came over to this country after the depression with my grandmother. The file says that they never really learned much English, but my mother did, got herself pregnant without really knowing who the father was, and at the age of twenty-five—the same age as when I started work here—had me and gave me up for adoption." Pete looked quite calm as he told me the story, calm and collected.

Reflecting this calmness to him, I understood his equally calm response: "I guess I am so calm in a way because somehow deep down I always knew I had some kind of affinity to all the men I loved, that somewhere these Dark Young Men represented who I am on some basic level."

The word that came to my mind was "soul"—that in a basic way, the Italian dark young men reflected to Pete his very nature, his soul. Hence the erotic attraction and the sexual imagery, as he strove for union with his self. Hence the masculinity and homosexuality that was a basic part of Pete's personality. And hence, finally, their function as guide to the unconscious. Like the brilliant tenor of the tunnel, whose voice accompanies Pete and illuminates his way to the open field of freedom, like Tony and his brothers whose masculine brotherhood brought Pete out of isolation into a deeper relationship with the world and with others, many of the Dark Young Men of Pete's dreams took on the role of teacher, guide, and leader.

> My first English teacher in high school appeared, Mr. Felice. In the dream I say to him, "You are my guide and psychopomp."

> I am discussing a friend of mine, Tony (who in the dream is blended
> with another Tony, an Italian also on the soccer team) who is also
> discussing with me a friend of his. We talk of how we have both had
> a tremendous positive influence on our friends. He says to me,
> "When I met him, all he knew how to do was play soccer. He had
> no culture, had read no real books, heard no music. I made him read
> books, took him places, gave him opportunities."
>
> I go to Rob's therapy office for my appointment. Rob has become
> young, has dark hair, is intense-looking, slim with beautiful eyes—a
> Dark Young Man figure. He is talking to another patient, with
> whom I must share my hour. I am not at all happy with this and tell
> him so.

Fascinated with the results of much of our work around dreams
and spurred on by the various inner discoveries he was making,
Pete asked me what I thought of his doing something he had read
about in one of his dreamwork books, an active imagination, a kind
of disciplined form of fantasy, developed by Jung, to further one's
conscious contact with hitherto unconscious contents. I encouraged
him to experiment with this form of inner work and see what came
up. The result was a long active imagination over a number of
months based initially on a dream he had had of a young, dark
Marlon Brando with a companion named Ben picking Pete up on
the road and basically initiating him, through various sexual and
spiritual practices, into a religion, based on Brando's own knowledge of himself as God. Again the theme of the Dark Young Man as
teacher or leader recurs, with Brando and Ben as guides to the
underworld and to that supraordinate totality that Jung called the
Self, the image of God in the human soul.

When a stream of the unconscious is tapped in the course of psychotherapy, the ensuing eruption can be both deeply transformative
and enormously disturbing. With this series of dreams concerning
the Dark Young Man, I found myself engaged in a process with
Pete around an obviously archetypal figure of great power and importance about which I could find little written. In the first place, so
little had been written concerning the individuation of gay men that

was of any use or depth that I was forced pretty much onto my own devices in making sense of this archetypal flood.[1] Thus, in one way, I could do little else but follow Jung's own phenomenological method, gathering up the various pieces and aspects of this figure in Pete's soul until a consistent picture began to form, and, like Jung, I stayed close to Pete's own understandings of who—and what—this figure represented for him, trying as little as possible to impose upon Pete's process with interpretations.

So, who was he, this Dark Young Man? His darkness suggested what Jung called the shadow, and yet, as I noted early on, this figure was not a shadow figure. His presence was neither frightening nor unacceptable, in fact quite the opposite. He was sought after and longed for. His youth suggested yet another archetypal figure, that of the *puer aeternus,* the Eternal Boy, a figure Jung had written a paper on,[2] the symbol of youth, futurity, spontaneity, and freedom in the souls of men. And yet the Dark Young Man was never really all that much younger than Pete. If anything, he seemed a mirror image of Pete's own youthful sexuality and spontaneity, possessed of a kind of postpubescent masculinity that could be decidedly un-puerile, indeed, even at times imposing and powerful. He was defi-nitely not Peter Pan.

Was the emphasis therefore most properly placed on the latter part of what Pete came to title him, on the "Man" of Dark Young Man? Certainly this figure represented many aspects of Pete's mas-culinity and could be thus seen as a figure of Pete's own ego, a self figure, which presented to him some of the most important and highly charged aspects of his manhood: his gayness, his Italian par-entage, his sexuality, and his love for the masculine and for his man's body. But this figure was not strictly speaking a simple nar-cissistic mirror image of Pete and his personality. The Dark Young Man, at least in Pete's dreams and his various active imaginations, was most definitely an Other, someone else, a figure who often acted in ways quite independent of Pete's thoughts and value judg-ments, a figure who challenged Pete, guided him, and drew him into relationship.

Of course, one of the primary ways in which this occurred was through projection. Many, if not most, of the men with whom Pete had become involved (or had fantasized becoming involved) conformed to the figure of the Dark Young Man of his inner life, and Pete found it difficult, especially in the cases of his lovers, to maintain the relationship as this Dark Young Man projection began to fade and the men with whom he had become involved inevitably showed their real selves to him. In the case of Pete's first adult lover, Frank, Pete found him often uninterested in sex, after an initial burst of hypersexuality early on, and his lover's gradual disinterest in sex came to be replaced by nothing, until Pete found himself cheating on him with other dark young men and finally gathered enough courage to end the relationship. A similar pattern occurred with Pete's second lover Joseph—an initial burst of sexual attraction followed by a waning of interest. This time, however, Pete contained his yearning for the dark young men of his fantasy, only to find himself drawn into growing anger and resentment and even occasional violence as the fights with Joseph escalated. They called a halt to the relationship after a little more than a year.

The dynamic here was a familiar one to many psychotherapists, in which an idealized inner figure is looked for in the people around us, projected onto someone who has sufficient attributes to carry it for us, and then is pursued with erotic compulsion and occasionally obtained, only to have the real person beneath our projection slowly—and disturbingly—emerge before our eyes, warts and all, as our idealized projection fades into the background. Jung noted the frequency of such projection and particularly its psychological importance. Rather than dismissing such projection as a defense mechanism or something inherently pathological, Jung noted that such projections often are precisely the means by which we enter initially into relationships with others, meeting through them those parts of ourselves that we need to embrace in order to grow. A mature relationship, however, would be one in which such initial projections could be gradually replaced by a fuller knowledge and greater appreciation for the real person beneath our idealized image.

The Dark Young Man, therefore, in addition to his darkness, his youth, and his manhood, served a function for Pete that went beyond all of these aspects, bringing Pete through an all too frequent erotic projection into relationship with other men and thereby into relationship with all those hidden, unknown, undreamed-of aspects of his own soul. Given all of the above considerations, it became clear to me that the Dark Young Man of Pete's dreams was neither shadow, nor *puer,* nor self, nor the masculine in some absolute, archetypal sense, but rather acted in every respect the way the anima acts in the souls of heterosexual men: a figure of often enormous erotic charge, all too frequently idealized and projected out onto a man's object of love (or lust), an autonomous figure in men's psyches that serves the function of guide both to the unconscious and to relatedness with others. Jung, however, would have us believe that the anima is an archetype of femininity. Could it be that this is only half the story, a story developed and based on heterosexual models of psychological development and maturity? Might it not be true that the Dark Young Man of Pete's soul was in fact his anima, a male anima whose masculinity corresponded to that essential fact of Pete's erotic life, his homosexuality, his love for other men?

In proposing this expansion of Jung's concept of the anima on the basis of repeated analytic and extra-analytic experiences with gay men, I do not speak alone. Thanks to now almost two decades of an active and vocal reevaluation of patriarchal and heterosexual models of development, it is now self-evident that gay men come to psychological wholeness through a process that differs in many important ways from heterosexual men's process of individuation. Many of these differences are, of course, based on the psychosocial context in which gay men are born and reared, a context that teaches gay men to adopt modes of feeling, thinking, behaving, and fantasizing at odds with what has come increasingly to seem an inborn (or at least constitutional) sexual orientation. To be who they are, therefore, gay men pass through several developmental passages that are conspicuously absent from heterosexual men's individuation, such as the "coming-out" process, the establishment of intimacy and relationship in the face of hostility and the absence of any positive models, and a reevaluation of the meaning of masculinity and femininity.[3] For this reason, traditional psychological models often do not help to shed light on the different developmental tasks faced by gay men and thus require a certain amount of expansion, revision, or even thorough-going rejection.

In proposing that the traditional concept of the anima be expanded (a multi-faceted and evocative concept to begin with, as the previous chapter made amply clear), I find myself within a movement of sorts in contemporary psychology in which the new wine of more objective empirical evidence is being poured into the older wineskins of traditional psychological models, resulting in a distinct and perhaps irreversible change in shape and texture. The deletion of homosexuality as a mental disorder from the list of psychiatric diagnoses occurred on the basis of cumulative empirical evidence showing that gay men and lesbians were not necessarily less functional psychologically due to their homosexuality. Likewise, material from the psychotherapy of gay men like Pete, especially such a wealth of dreams centered around a figure possessing such a distinct personality and psychological function, fairly forces one to consider what we considered earlier in a strictly heterosexual context: namely, that the femininity of the anima may not be essential, but simply accidental, and that at times, and perhaps particularly in the case of gay men, the anima may appear as male.

Nor am I alone in the universe of Jung's followers when I consider the possibility that the anima may at times wear a male face. An invaluable, and unfortunately isolated, contribution to this possibility comes from the pen of Mitch Walker, gay psychotherapist and writer, who as far back as 1976 formulated such a concept and named it the "double" in his article in *Spring* entitled "The Double: An Archetypal Configuration." That his contribution to psychological thought has not been followed and amplified subsequently simply demonstrates how difficult it is to muster support and consideration for the developmental process of people who do not fit standard cultural or social categories. And yet, to read Walker's article is to illuminate precisely what kind of figure the Dark Young Man is to

Pete in his journey toward self-discovery and wholeness. Walker's first two paragraphs, quoted here in full, show exactly how prescient and insightful his proposal was at the time.

> Jung never intended that his conceptualizations were final, or that he was always correct. Rather, he hoped that his tentative interpretations would be developed and revised. In this light, I would like to propose an archetypal concept, the "double," to cover a soul figure with all the erotic and spiritual significances attached to the anima/animus, but of the same sex, and yet not a shadow. This figure has mythological examples and is felt in psychological experience. It is lost if named either shadow or anima/us.
>
> The double is that set of characteristics which give rise, ultimately, to our conscious awareness of identified sex role, although the double is much more than our paltry social idea of manness or womanness, and is entirely lacking in sexist connotations (these are added on later). The double and anima/us are equal and complementary, and form a whole, androgynous in nature. For example, the anima contains the archetypal images of mother, daughter, sister and lover. The male double, then contains those of father, son, brother, lover. Just as a woman can serve for projection of the anima, so a man can serve for projection of the male double, and vice versa for women. The double, as well as the anima/us, can be part of a transcendent function.[4]

Walker supports his proposal for this new archetypal configuration with ample evidence from literature and mythology, showing that the double often does perform the function of "soul guide" for men, facilitates what Walker calls "rapport" (but which Jung might call "relationship" or "the Eros principle"), and serves often as the root of a man's ego identity, that is, his basic sense of himself as a man.

Because archetypal configurations wear many faces and are often interrelated in sometimes complex ways, Walker shows how a clear vision of the double archetype can be confounded when certain variations occur symbolically, such as young-old pairings between men (best known in the famous Greek model of homosexuality in which love relationships occurred between older men and younger

men along a kind of initiatory model) or when the darker aspects of
the archetype appear and are mistaken as simply "shadow." On this
point, Walker writes:

> Every archetype has its destructive features. The double, being a
> multi-faceted archetype (or a group of closely interrelated arche-
> types, just as the anima includes the great mother and the feminine
> soul-guide) has several dark aspects. One of these involves the puer
> aeternus, as we have just seen. Another is the shadow. That is, as-
> pects of the double, such as the tendency toward homosexual ex-
> pression, may be rejected by the ego and fall into the shadow
> personality. This is due to the similarity of the double and the
> shadow in relation to the ego; each is a source deeper than the con-
> scious personality. . . . Therefore, it is to be expected that rejected
> aspects of the double will tend to collect in the shadow-unconscious.
> On the practical level, as misogyny often shows a negative-anima
> projection, so homophobia, fear and hatred of "homosexuals," can
> be the projection of negated double-aspects from the shadow.[5]

In the context of men's individuation, therefore, Walker distinguishes between the anima, which appears in feminine form and
serves all her by-now-familiar psychic functions for a man, and the
double, which appears in male form and complements the anima.
The double serves as the basis for a man's relationship to the masculine, in himself and in others, while the anima serves as the basis
for man's relationship to the feminine, in himself and others. Moreover, both function as soul guides for men and lead men into a
deeper level of experience of their selves and of the unconscious,
but each does so from a different gender position, so to speak, in
relationship to a man's masculine self.

Walker's proposal that another archetypal configuration exists,
and one particularly prominent in the internal psychological universe of homoerotically inclined individuals, makes a great deal of
sense and essentially serves to ground my own intuition that the
Dark Young Man of Pete's dream is a figure of archetypal dimen-
sions. Certainly the Dark Young Man's numinosity, persistent significance, psychological import, and capacity for being projected
and sought after is sufficient to put him into a category of transper-

sonal psychic contents. Walker's elegant and mythologically supported delineation of the double practically reads like a theoretical
description of that figure Pete and I met on the road of our dream
work. Moreover, the newness of Walker's conception of the double
certainly does not impugn the archetypal nature of his figure, for
the primacy of heterosexual, patriarchal values has long obscured
significant aspects of archetypal facets of psyche that only now are
coming to light. If Walker's conception seems fresh or radical or re-
visionist, it is perhaps only because the homoerotic aspects of so
many of the myths he examines—Jonathan and David, Gilgamesh
and Enkidu, Achilles and Patroclus—have in the past been distorted, ignored, or even destroyed.[6]

Walker's answer to our earlier question, "Who is this Dark Young
Man?" would thus be simple. He is the double. However, I wonder
if, by arguing for the addition of yet another figure to the pantheon
of the collective unconscious, Walker is not dulling the edge of Oc-
cam's razor and multiplying explanations beyond the necessary.
There can be no argument with the empirical verifiability of such a
male "soul figure," nor with his distinctness from female "soul figures"; Pete had plenty of dreams in which the anima appeared in the
much more familiar female form and followed much of what might
be expected of the anima, first appearing as a series of firm but be-
neficent black women, then becoming personified in women and
girls whom he knew personally, and finally beginning to show herself to him in more goddess-like forms.

That there are two different faces here is not the issue. My more
radical proposal is that the male and female forms of this archetype
should both be considered "anima"; this proposal is derived from
my more critical attitude toward the way in which patriarchal images of femininity are hung upon the anima concept in Jungian psychology. Here again I am not alone. Hillman, with his usual sharp
eye and daring intellect, notes in his own work on the anima how
this figure often is given its shape by men's images of the feminine,
but as a representative of archetypal femininity, it is essentially part
of women's nature, too. Hillman quotes Jung in this context; our

discussion on the appearance of the anima for Nick is echoed in the following passage.

> . . . The muse . . . belongs also authentically to the potential of women's psychology in its own right and is not only in reflection of men. It is not *man's* anima, and so it is not a man's inner life that the nymph, hetaera, or muse [anima figures in mythology] is reflecting, but anima as archetype, which by other names is psyche or soul.
>
> At this level of distinction Jung himself raises a doubt whether we can truly speak of the anima per se as feminine. He suggests that we may have to confine the archetype's femininity to its projected form. Paradoxically, the very archetype of the feminine may not itself be feminine.[7]

Hillman's quote from Jung makes clear what he means. Jung writes: "When projected, the anima always has a feminine form with definite characteristics. This empirical finding does not mean that the archetype is constituted like that *in itself*."[8]

The real paradox here is how an archetypal configuration, which by definition transcends human form in itself, necessarily must be feminine when projected. One could certainly argue that Jung has every right to define his concept as he wishes: if he wants his idea of the anima to be an archetype of femininity, then so it is. The issue here is whether or not his above statements concerning the anima's femininity when projected are true, empirically supportable, or theoretically helpful. I think they are not.

In the first place, it makes no sense to confine an archetype's appearance to human categories of gender. In admitting doubt himself as to the eternal femininity of the anima, as well as in noting the sometimes androgynous character of this archetype along with what Hillman calls the archetype's "contentless" forms (the anima as "life" or as "world view"), Jung's insistence on the anima's femininity seems to come more out of his own heterosexual vision of the psyche than out of theoretical consistency. If the anima can appear in object or animal form at times, then why not in the form of men or male figures? Second, this "paradox" ends up reinforcing images of femininity and of women that are patriarchal in nature, as Hillman points out, endowing women with a femininity filtered through men's experience rather than acknowledging women's separate, independent, and wholly autonomous femininity. Third, material such as Pete's dreams of the Dark Young Man and Walker's mythological support for his concept of the double demonstrate that a male figure does exist in the psyche of men that acts like the anima and serves the functions of the anima. In my view, if it looks, smells, feels, walks, and talks like the anima, then it is the anima.

Of course, I am aware that to admit the androgyny of the anima so forthrightly may be threatening to many. Such an idea certainly threatens the patriarchal structure of sex-role stereotypes and male-female relationships, particularly as they are internalized and codified into psychological theory. Moreover, this view, that the anima may be both male and female, internally or in projected form, asserts as a kind of corollary that gay men's psychological experience might be a source of enlightenment for heterosexual men: to admit that the anima, an archetypal configuration for all men, might wear a male face in essence opens up the possiblity that heterosexual men might have to begin to understand Eros not simply in male-female terms, but in male-male terms as well.[9]

Far from diluting the concept of the anima, the idea of the male anima might serve to begin to widen the all-too-narrow psychological categories of "male" and "female" imposed on individuals in a kind of undifferentiated, collective manner. Such a concept certainly makes sense of what is often left unexplained and what is perhaps ultimately unexplainable in the psychology of homosexuality, in which gay men find their soul, their essential self, and their fulfillment in relationship in a form that is male. Such an understanding also frees women and femininity from the necessity of having to carry the whole burden of men's psychological wholeness. As men and women move in the direction of increasing androgyny, personally and collectively, is it too radical to imagine that such a movement toward androgyny might occur on an archetypal level as well?

Because this book has as its focus the illumination of male psychology and especially the issues faced by contemporary men in a period of transition as reflected by their dreams and psychotherapeutic process, it is important to follow the lead Pete's dreams have given us. While I have argued above for the possibility of conceptualizing the anima as male at times, especially for gay men, yet another Dark Young Man dream of Pete's helps us work on this problem from another direction.

About four years into our work together, after having had a discussion in therapy about the Dark Young Man and his function as soul figure for Pete, Pete reported the following dream.

> I am in a class on alcoholism which a man from Venus [the planet] is attending. We're all college age, and I act as if coming from Venus is a joke, unable to imagine what it must be like to come from another planet. I and my friends laugh about it, and we're also pretty critical toward certain of the conceptions about alcoholism, for example, that AA doesn't want to change people but simply help them be who they "really" are by going straight. I am surprised at the Venusian's intelligence and culture; he seems almost normal. However, I can't get over it, especially my inability to imagine his culture, growing up, I think, in near solitude with scientist parents. (I have an image in the dream of exploring the darkness of the planet and needing to be called back.)

Needless to say, the Venusian fit Pete's Dark Young Man mold, as we discussed the dream. Handsome and dark, he was an object of Pete's ambivalent fascination, and thus appeared the way the anima often appears: the visitor from another, intriguing realm who draws the dreamer into a deeper, fuller sense of self, symbolized in this dream by Pete's struggle to appreciate the culture of Venus, the Dark Young Man's natural habitat.

However, the most perfect part of the dream, and one that shows the exquisite natural intelligence of the unconscious, is the provenance of this male anima figure from the planet Venus. For Pete, whose soul connection to Italy existed on a literal, biological level, that in this dream Venus, the planet named after the Roman and not Greek goddess of love, appears further reinforces the anima quality of this double figure for Pete. This son of Venus, therefore, served to present Pete once again with what, in my opinion, is often one

function of the male anima for a gay man, namely, a symbolic personification of his homosexuality. At least, that is what Pete himself
made of the dream's setting, a class on alcoholism in which he criticizes the concept of making people who they really are by making
them "straight," a double entendre not lost on Pete. The late-
adolescent joking that occurs in the dream and in which Pete participates to some extent seems quite true to life: men, when presented
with the homoerotic manifestations of love, often hide their insecurity through ridicule and criticism—all those potent verbal defensive skills that the patriarchal emphasis on Logos is especially adept
at providing for men's use against Others in whatever form. For a
gay man, who has been told repeatedly, directly or indirectly, that
his homosexuality is an illness or a disease like alcoholism, a similar
insecurity about homosexuality can be camouflaged with equal dex-
terity by such maneuvers. In Pete's own words: "I am caught in the
dream between my fascination with the Venusian and my need to fit
in with my friends. I make fun of him in the dream, ironically, because I feel so much like him: raised on thought, not feeling, isolated, from another planet because I'm gay." The parenthetical coda
of the dream continues the unconscious psychic logic: Pete's fascination with the Venusian draws him into a fantasized identification
with him, exploring the darkness of his homosexuality, the realm of
Venus, while at the same time needing to be called back into a less
collective realm, because individuation requires our *not* falling
wholesale into such identifications or anima fascinations.

Thus, we see in this dream yet another manifestation of what
Walker would call Pete's "double" or what I have gotten into the
habit of calling the "male anima" of a gay man. However, familiarity with mythology gives us a clue, I think, that allows us to go
even further, beyond merely attempting to revise or correct Jung's
view of the anima. This latest of Pete's dreams puts us onto another
track and provides us with perhaps the more archetypal underpinnings of what gay men meet in their soul figures, namely, the male
face of love, Eros, son of Aphrodite.

Having discussed Jung's use of Eros in the previous chapter, we
have seen that the attribution of Eros, the principle of relatedness,
connection, and feeling, to the feminine, as a feminine principle,

rests on peculiarly patriarchal ideas of sex roles. What Pete's dream shows us and what mythology itself unarguably presents is that far from being feminine, Eros is a male god and has always been. Also unarguable are the many transformations that the image of this god has undergone throughout the ages, so that to get a clear idea of who Eros is, and especially what his archetypal masculinity consists of, requires that we embark on a small archeological dig down through the most modern appearances of this god back to his most primordial beginnings. In doing so, I think we will uncover precisely what missing pieces of sexuality and psyche contemporary gay men such as Pete continue to meet in their dreams and carry for our culture at large.

Our contemporary images of Eros, those most distant from the god's primordial beginnings but closest to the modern individual's collective consciousness, are probably what most people see on their Valentine's Day greeting cards: Cupid as a small child in swaddling clothes, dainty, every bit the ungrounded *puer aeternus,* flying about Peter Pan–style with equally fey bow and arrow, taking aim at the unsuspecting (and thoroughly stylized) human heart, whose penetration causes neither pain nor bleeding. Only the bow and arrow allude to the great god of antiquity, and this remains on the level of mere allusion, for this present image of Eros is a Renaissance refiguration of the Roman borrowing, as Cupid or Amor, from the original Greek. Thus, this twice-removed version of Eros, Cupid (not "love," actually, but closer to "desire," as in "cupidity") constitutes a thoroughly degenerate picture of this archetypal dominant, emasculated into a mere child still held under the dominion of Venus (the Roman name for Aphrodite) by the Renaissance tradition of courtly, spiritualized love and by the poets of late Roman times. (Venus, herself a mighty goddess at one time, seems to have fared no better than her son at the hands of the Italian Renaissance; turned into an icon of ethereal beauty by Botticelli and thus trivialized, she was served on the half-shell to the neo-Platonic male fantasies of the time, with all her original ferocity and, after all, her venereal nature thoroughly tamed.)

Behind this harmless, diluted Cupid, however, lies an image of Eros that begins to approximate the god's original essence: the

Amor who appears in Apuleius's version of the Eros-Psyche myth. This myth, dear to Jung's followers, has been much treated in the literature of analytical psychology because of the way in which its protagonists, Eros as love and Psyche as soul, enact on the stage of imagination what Hillman has called "the myth of analysis": love's redemption of the soul, and the soul's enthrallment of love.[10]

In the myth as told by Apuleius in "The Golden Ass," Venus seeks to punish Psyche for her beauty, which has been robbing the goddess of her rightful worship. She therefore sends her son, Amor (the Roman name for Eros), with his poisonous darts of love, to cause Psyche to fall in love with the worst man on earth. However, by accident Amor wounds himself with his own arrows and falls in love with Psyche himself. Forbidding Psyche to look upon him in an attempt to keep this accident a secret, he takes Psyche as his wife, hiding his identity and, at least for the time being, avoiding his mother's wrath. However, the curious Psyche, goaded on by her sisters, one night takes a lamp and goes into her husband's chamber, discovering that it is the god of love himself to whom she is married. To her surprise, she spills hot oil from her lamp on Amor, awakening him. He flies from her immediately, as angry at her disobedience of his commands as he is afraid of what Venus will do when she discovers his disobedience of her commands.

What Venus does, of course, is to carry out her original intent, punishing Psyche by giving her four impossible tasks—sorting an enormous pile of seeds, stealing a bit of the mythical golden fleece, drawing water from the river Styx, and finally, asking for a gift of beauty from Proserpine (the Roman name for Persephone), Queen of the Underworld, on Venus's behalf. Psyche performs these four tasks with help of various kinds, particularly in the fourth case when it is Amor who comes to her rescue. No longer able to resist his passion for Psyche, his wound now healed, Amor pleads with Jove (the Roman name for Zeus) to overrule his mother's fury and permit him to have Psyche for his wife. Jove consents, pressing his young male lover Ganymede into bringing Psyche the cup of immortality, making her a goddess, and the requisite happy ending is accomplished.

With regard to the image of Eros (as Amor) contained in this version of the myth, we discern a more mature god here, an adolescent with real power, whose own arrows do in fact inflict wounds and from whose passionate inspirations he is not entirely immune himself. Far from being a harmless babe, Eros here is the youthful husband of Psyche, still under the sway of Aphrodite his mother at the beginning of the myth and yet liberated from his thralldom at the end through Zeus's intervention and through Psyche's dedication to her own painful path. This Eros is not quite child yet not quite man, and so the myth can be read both as one of feminine development, as Neumann does, seeing Eros as the animus figure Psyche must work to integrate, or as one of masculine development, as Marie-Louise von Franz suggests, in which Psyche represents Eros's anima, motivating him to separate from mother and become a man in his own right.

This adolescent version of the god, however, is also derivative, a late Roman version of the myth ensconced within a larger tale meant as entertainment more than myth. For our purposes, we must dig even further to recover a more faithful and archetypal image of Eros. In this regard, Neumann's interpretation of the tale is perceptive, for he notices that "it is no accident that the homosexual love relation of Zeus and Ganymede should come to the help of Eros and Psyche." He writes:

> To begin with, there is an evident parallel between Ganymede and Psyche. Both are human beings loved by gods, and both are ultimately carried off to Olympus as earthly-heavenly companions of their divine lovers. This is the first intimation of Zeus' sympathy with Psyche, which decides the final outcome of her story. He sides with his son, Eros, partly out of masculine sympathy, for he too knows the meaning of seizure by love, and partly out of protest against the Great Goddess, who as Hera, strives to check her husband's freedom to love, and as Aphrodite tries to restrict her son in the same way.[11]

Neumann's comment unwittingly directs us back to the third layer of Eros development throughout the ages in the way it ties together masculinity, the unboundedness of love, and homosexual-

ity. The image of Eros we see dimly shining, even through Apuleius's retelling, is the Eros of late Greece, the image we find in
Plato: Eros as a demigod, a daemon born of Poverty through her
scheme to have a child of the God of Plenty; Eros as undifferentiated, unbounded libido to be tamed and trained upon the higher
things. Thus, in the *Symposium,* Plato's discourse on love in the form
of multiple speeches, we find the final word being given to Socrates'
anima figure, Diotima of Mantineia, who acknowledges that as a
child of Poverty he tends to be "hard and rough and unshod and
homeless" and yet "from his father again he has designs upon beautiful and good things, being brave and go-ahead and high-strung, a
mighty hunter, always weaving devices, and a successful coveter of
wisdom, a philosopher all his days, a great wizard and sorcerer and
sophist."[12] Despite Plato's characteristic conclusions, in which Eros,
"neither mortal nor immortal" must be subjugated and in a sense
spirtualized in the philosopher's search for the highest value, the
discernment of wisdom in the good, true, and beautiful, the mythological image of Eros we see here is one much closer to the classical
Greek conception. Plato's images of Eros are masculine in a mature
way. His Eros is no child or adolescent, but a hunter, a wizard, a
philosopher—goal-directed, urgent, never resting, ever renewed by
the sap of his father, the God of Plenty. Eros in his masculinity is
thus an altogether fitting subject for the entire *Symposium,* well
known as perhaps one of the best classical examples of the easy
place homosexuality occupied in Greek culture.

Indeed, though Plato formulated his own version of Eros for his
philosophical purposes, purposes Platonic in both the descriptive
and figurative senses, his Eros, masculine and unfettered in its original state, nevertheless does reflect the typical classical personification of Eros as a strong handsome athletic man, in many ways the
Greek ideal of masculinity, and as such the acknowledged protector
of homosexual love. Thus, in classical times, we come upon what
Walker and others have already discerned: the theme of twinship,
which always seems to appear when the true nature of Eros in his
masculinity is acknowledged. At various places in Greece, Eros was
worshipped alongside Anteros, thus constituting a homosexual pair

of seeking love and responding love. The resident aliens in Athens even set up a statue at the Acropolis to Anteros, the protector god of the mythological pair of homosexual lovers Meles and Timagoras.[13] Neumann's intertwining themes of masculinity, unboundedness, and homosexuality are essential to the classical conception of Eros and Anteros, and his Eros's unboundedness is particularly evident in the multiple genealogies he is given throughout classical literature,[14] almost as if classical authors could not pin the origin of love down because of their awareness of its many forms.

These three attributes of this more basic image of Eros—his masculinity, his unboundedness, and his homosexuality—are derived from an even earlier stratum of Greek mythology in which Eros is worshipped as a fertility god, in the form of phallic statues, at such places as Thespiae and Parium. This association of Eros with phallos thus quite interestingly places him, within the context of early Greek mythology, in proximity to that other god of the phallos, Hermes, whose name is lent to the herms, those columnar portraits of Hermes on Greek highways where travelers offered up their bounty in exchange for protection on their journey. We see in this association of Eros with Hermes the same theme that runs throughout even the most derivative and degraded of his images— the theme of Eros, love, as mediator, go-between, uniter of heaven and earth.

Here we at last arrive at perhaps the most fundamental stratum of Eros's mythology, one that goes beyond human personification, elaborated in the myth of creation attributed to Orpheus, wherein the universe is born of a cosmic egg laid by Night and fertilized by Wind, an egg that splits into Earth and Sky and out of which hatches the fundamental force of the universe, Eros or, as he is also called, Phanes (the "revealer," yet another allusion to phallos, which in Greek is connected to the word for "light" or "shining").

Having thus cleared away some of the later accretions and distortions of Eros's archetypal nature, we come to see that many of the themes contained in the earlier views of Eros's divinity—his phallicism, his mediatory and uniting function, his connection with unbounded sexuality, his homosexual association, and his fertility—

are in many ways exactly that which the Dark Young Man embodied for Pete, and which "male anima" or "double" figures in
general, in my experience, embody for gay men. Such repeated experiences of Eros by gay men, especially Eros's most archetypal
masculine form, seem determined by many factors.

Certainly the way homophobia has robbed gay men of a natural,
instinctual relationship to their homosexuality makes it perhaps all
the more important for gay men to be reconnected to Eros inwardly
and outwardly. Indeed, current stereotypes of gay men—lustful,
sensual, phallic, tightly bound into a like-minded community—
reflect the masculine face of Eros that heterosexual men cannot
admit, since they are caught in a peculiar form of self-alienation
through patriarchy. That such male figures should occupy such an
important and enduring place in the analysis of a gay man is thus
entirely appropriate, if not expectable, just as these figures should
continually remind us of that forgotten side of Eros, his primordial,
phallic masculinity. Because outsiders so often carry precisely that
which has been denied and repressed in the dominant culture, the
epiphanies of Eros in the dreams of gay men like Pete should perhaps be attended to with greater respect and openness, and not
forced into inappropriate models based on the experiences of heterosexual patients and the theories of heterosexual analysts.

On a larger, more collective level, however, I wonder if it might
not be that gay men are carrying Eros in all his masculinity for a
patriarchal culture that has misperceived and distorted Eros into a
feminine principle, something that women embody or are expected
to embody for men but that men cannot or do not dare embody for
themselves. If this were the case, then what we might learn from the
inner life of such men as Pete, and from the lives of gay men like
him, is that the anima and a man's relationship to femininity might
actually be a secondary phenomenon, something that occurs only
after a more basic *coniunctio* has occurred, in which a man is united
with his own masculinity.

We have seen in the progressive distortions of Eros's image, as
Western culture moved farther and farther away from an acceptance
of instinctual sexuality in all it myriad forms, that such a male-male

union, a union of like with like, becomes identified with immaturity, with adolescence, with a psychology of *puer*.[15] This suggests that this union is more fundamental for men, occurring at an earlier stage, and also suggests that such a failure to be initiated into one's own masculinity might lead to the kind of determined projection of wholeness outside oneself, onto literal women or figurative forms of femininity such as the anima or mother figures, that seems so typical of patriarchal male heterosexuality. For this reason, and certainly because men have projected Eros onto the feminine and onto women, it seems a particularly threatening task for heterosexual men to acknowledge and even, when appropriate, enact the very unbounded, masculine, and homoerotic side of Eros, even when this would result in a deeper appreciation of their own soul, their essence as men. In this way, the sexism of Jung's anima theory stands in the way of the psychological development of all men, heterosexual and homosexual. For heterosexual men, the identification of Eros with femininity locates a primordial masculinity outside of themselves and robs them of their natural wholeness available to them in their manhood. For homosexual men, it denies them the unique and fundamental connection to their souls that gay men have *through* their masculinity and forces them to carry the shadowy aspects of Eros that patriarchy's insistence on heterosexual behavior, sometimes called "heterosexism," forces upon gay men.

Out of my experience and by way of the consideration presented above, I have come to believe a number of things. First, the suggestions of various Jungians, including Jung, are correct, and the anima's femininity is not intrinsic to its archetypal nature *an sich,* but its mediatory, uniting, and relational functions are. Second, the peculiar position of gay men in a patriarchal society, as well as their homosexuality, forces them into a different kind of relationship with the archetypal feminine than heterosexual men, thereby assuring that their relationship to the anima is different in certain key ways than for heterosexuals. Third, one of the key differences is that the anima appears personified and projected as male for gay men, and that only by acknowledging and working with this masculinity in a gay man, usually in the form of discrete male figures in the inner lives of such men, can we truly aid the individuation of gay men. Fourth, because of their connection to archetypal masculinity, or, to say it another way, because Eros is so often their anima figure, gay men serve the collective psychological development of a patriarchal society by carrying forth what all men have lost through patriarchal one-sidedness—namely, a connection to the fullness of their masculinity and, thus, a connection to their souls. Fifth, when heterosexual men individually and patriarchal society in general finally begin to stop projecting the shadow of patriarchal sexuality onto individual gay men and the gay community, only then will the collective development presaged by the dreams of such gay men like Pete begin to truly transform consciousness, permitting the soul of the world, the *anima mundi,* to live and breathe through the life force of Eros in all his masculinity.

One interesting result of our nearly four years of work on the Dark Young Man for Pete is that, not unlike a real human figure, this inner archetypal figure began to grow and mature. In our next chapter we will examine the ways in which the Dark Young Man began to connect Pete not only to his own soul but to the larger community of men before him, thus framing an issue that appears for men again and again in the course of their psychotherapeutic work. In a word: Father.

5 The Dream of the Italian Father: Fatherhood as Embodiment and Redemption

The dream starts a split second before a film-review program I am watching cuts to a clip of a film it has reviewed. In Italian, I see and hear Al Pacino, who is a boxer named Maccagnorola, denigrating another boxer, who is named (humorously) Grancchè. There is a crowd in a kitchen which leaves, ready to sit down at the table to eat an Italian meal in the dining room. Al Pacino and his wife are getting things ready, bringing plates of food out. I am waiting to hear him begin using words like "barbaric" and "animal" with regard to the other boxer, but he doesn't. Instead he fusses, making sure everyone is seated and all is ready.

Now I am in the movie, sitting on the kitchen counter, as if my eyes are the camera (you can't see me in the film, but I see everything) and I'm a little kid, eight or nine years old. I ask Dad (Al Pacino) for a piece of bread. He comes very close to me, his chest pressed up against the counter between my legs, so I can feel and smell his body very close. He dips a small piece of bread in olive oil with long thin tongs and gives it to me in the mouth. I barely chew this before I ask for another, which he gives to me in the same manner. I keep asking, expecting him to refuse, hurriedly chewing each morsel so he can't—but even with my mouth full, he continues to feed me. He is extraordinarily tender and generous. I feel very loved.

Occasionally a dream occurs for a man in therapy, especially a man like Pete who came in full of so much rational perfectionism, in which it becomes immediately clear to both him and me that something new is occurring psychically, something quite different and deeply affecting. Jung, borrowing from the central African tribes he visited, often referred to such dreams as "big" dreams, as in the following:

> The Elgonyi . . . explained to me that there are two kinds of dreams: the ordinary dream of the little man, and the "big vision" that only the great man has, e.g., the medicine man or chief. Little dreams are of no account, but if a man has a "big dream," he summons the whole tribe in order to tell it to everybody.
>
> How is a man to know whether his dream is a "big" or a "little" one? He knows it by an instinctive feeling of significance. He feels so overwhelmed by the impression it makes that he would never think of keeping the dream to himself. He *has* to tell it. . . . The collective dream has a feeling of importance about it that impels communication.[1]

The affect accompanying Pete's dream was evident on his face as he told it to me, a kind of wonder along with, I could feel, that "instinctive feeling of significance." We had done so much hard work on dredging up and being with the Dark Young Man of his dreams, a figure who lately began to be paired more and more in his dreams with older men and father figures, that I suspected some kind of shift might have been taking place inwardly. But again, restraining my own galloping intuitions and associations, I stayed close to Pete, by now quite an expert dream interpreter in his own right.

"It was a wonderful dream. I woke up incredibly refreshed and alive. It was so vivid and real. I mean I can still feel the closeness, smell the olive oil. The feeling of being loved so completely, you know, just to ask and to be given so freely."

We sat for a few silent moments just to savor the aliveness and sensuality. I wondered how people can dismiss dreams as unreal when they have such profound effects and remain so long in someone's sensory memory.

"And he was so different than what you might expect," Pete added.

I did not catch his meaning so I asked for clarification. "Different? From . . . ?"

"Well, from the way he seemed at the beginning. You know, he's a boxer. And"—Pete smiled impishly—"and he's Al Pacino, after all. Not really known as the tender-heartedest Italian man in the world."

My own years of dream work and discussion in therapy, as well as my years of dream work with clients, have convinced me that if any modern development could be credited for nearly single-handedly carrying forward the archetypal contents of the collective unconscious into modern consciousness, it would be the movies and the movie stars who populate the mythic universe of film. It is not entirely lax speech to refer to the "gods and goddesses of the silver screen," since again and again, they appear and reappear within the psyche as archetypal figures who bring to us pieces of our deepest self, at first (and sometimes all too disturbingly for the real performers) projected out onto the flickering image, the publicist's creation, the "movie idol," his or her public image, only to be later owned and understood as really a piece of our own common human psychological heritage.

"Are you an Al Pacino fan?"

Pete laughed in a way that suggested not wanting to admit to fanhood—enthusiasm, after all, is too strong a feeling for many men to display openly—and yet I felt some kind of connection.

"Not a fan, really. But lots of associations. What was weird in the dream was how tough I thought he would be, and yet how gentle and erotic it was to have him feed me."

I mulled a bit on how to put what was forming in my mind. "What comes to me is the difference between a public and private self—in public he is a boxer, aggressive; in private, at home, with his son, he is gentle, tender."

Pete nodded. "Which maybe makes sense of the dream within a dream stuff."

Again he had lost me. I looked at him quizzically.

"I mean that the dream is actually both a film that is being reviewed, a film clip, and yet I am in the dream, as if my eyes are the actual camera. I am kind of both on the outside and the inside of what is going on."

I think to myself how common this seems to be when something new is coming up from the unconscious, this motif of duplication, this dream within a dream stuff, but I do not bother to say anything: if something new is appearing, Pete will surely know it, whether I announce it or not.

"It's just like Al Pacino in the dream. From the outside, you'd think he was bad news, like De Niro in 'Raging Bull'—now *he's* someone I have had an ongoing crush on—but up close, he's a wonderful father, generous, giving, warm."

I had learned, perhaps from my psychoanalytic training, to not let any association go unnoticed. "What about De Niro and 'Raging Bull'? Why Al Pacino?" I tactfully left out the part about the crush, but by now, three years into our work, Pete felt free enough to follow it up.

"Well, they're both Italian, and so I guess they are kind of like the Dark Young Man in my fantasies. Sensual, warm, touching. Italian men just seem to have this kind of physical closeness with each other. De Niro I like as an actor because of his unavailability, you know, he acts in a very internal way, detached—you never know what's going on. In fact, I think that's what's so erotically attractive to me about him—he's like an engima; I want to find out more. Pacino seems more volatile to me, more 'out there,' more emotional."

Using his own words, I reframed it to lead in a more psychological direction. "More available?"

"I guess you could say that. He was certainly more available in the dream, wasn't he?"

"And that's *less* erotically attractive?"

Pete struggled here a bit. "I don't know how to put it really. It isn't that he is less erotically attractive, even though I am less attracted to him physically. The physical closeness to him in the dream is really kind of the most unbelievable and wonderful part of the dream. But it's more like—," he paused to find the words, "it's like the difference between a lover and a father. I can think of De

Niro as a boyfriend, but Pacino in this dream is this kind of close, wonderful father."

I sometimes play devil's advocate in a way with clients, especially with clients like Pete who work well on their own with their dreams, picking up loose ends and wondering aloud. "So De Niro is more a Dark Young Man type for you than Al Pacino."

Here Pete smiled. "Yes and no. 'Dog Day Afternoon' was the first movie I went to see with Tony in high school, our first date, so to speak. And that movie is the same kind of thing—Pacino is this tough Brooklyn bank robber on the outside, but then you find out that the reason he is robbing the bank is because he is bisexual and is stealing the money to get his male lover a sex-change operation. Tony and I went to see the movie about ten times."

"So it held quite a fascination for you."

"And not just the movie, as you can imagine. Tony was a large part of it. But now I can look back and see why. I mean the whole subtext of the movie is about homosexuality. So Al Pacino is kind of connected to the Dark Young Man, and yet, at least in this dream, he is fatherly. Like the scene in the kitchen isn't sexually arousing in a genital kind of way—it's more like being made safe with his actual body, with being fed by him."

The mood in the room shifted imperceptibly, became more subdued, as if a shadow of some sort had fallen. Two thoughts came to my mind, the first about the absence of Pete's father in his childhood, the second about the even deeper absence of his biological father, about whom he knew nothing.

"Like being held, in a way," I said quietly.

Pete mused a bit, caught firmly by the mood—sadness? nostalgia? regret? After a few moments' pause, he looked up, a wistful smile holding in pain. He was good at putting a good face on his pain. "Not a frequent experience of my childhood," he murmured with a clinical tone, distant from the feeling. We had moved out of the small child with the "I-am-a-camera" eyes into the posture of the movie reviewer.

"Dad wasn't around much," I empathized.

"And when he was, he sure wasn't shielding me with his body, feeding me with silver tongs as much as I wanted. In fact, I don't really ever remember him hugging or kissing me. Even today, we simply shake hands when I go home." He sighed and I let the mood continue to gather beneath the calm talk. "I have a feeling Italian fathers are different. In fact, I know they are. Tony's dad was much more affectionate and free." Then, with a quick drop into the depths so typical of Pete, he looked at me intensely. "Maybe my father would have been if I had known him—either of them. . . ."

With regard to Pete in particular, we see this dream with its emotion and imagery fit fairly neatly into some of the major themes that Pete and I had been uncovering in the course of his individuation. The first and perhaps most striking was the way in which the compensatory appearance of this Italian father was connected to the figure of the Dark Young Man, sharing many of the same attributes, certainly sharing the physical-erotic attraction: it was almost as if our assiduous work on making the Dark Young Man figure a conscious, integrated piece of Pete's self-image had enabled this inner figure (and thus Pete, too, of course) to grow up, to become more mature and fatherly. No longer simply a double or twin figure, no longer a male anima projected out onto real dark young men who then became objects of fantasy and lust, the figure of Al Pacino in this dream—a youthful father both strong and tender, reflecting Pete's Italian origins and providing both physical containment and sensual nourishment—is an exquisitely appropriate example of how consistent attention to an inner figure of a man's psyche within a safe context does in fact permit growth and change.

Further, the dream demonstrates some of the particularities of the gay male developmental process in the way the Dark Young Man, Pete's male anima figure, is related not to Mother, as a female anima figure often is, but rather to Father, or as Jungians might say, to the Father archetype carried by the patient's personal father. If true (and certainly a whole lot more work on the particularities of gay men's individuation process needs to occur before we can confidently say it is true), then this observation, framed in Jungian terms, provides independent support for some of the more recent thinking within psychological circles concerning the way in which a father's relationship to his gay male son may be more determinative of the son's capacity for intimacy with men and success at love relationships than his relationship with his mother. This, of course, makes intuitive sense: probably no one would dispute the obvious connection between a person's relationship to a parent and that person's subsequent relationship to people of the same gender. Indeed, when it comes to heterosexual development, *cherchez la femme* is practically a commonplace, looking at a man's relationship to his mother in order to decipher the roots of his relationship to women in general and to his wife specifically. With homosexually oriented persons, then, we are equally justified in paying close attention—as Pete's dream would certainly force one to do—to the relationship a gay man has with his father in order to discern the roots of his capacity for intimacy with other men as an adult.

Perhaps one of the keenest ironies in looking at the psychological development of contemporary men is the way in which this all-important relationship between father and son in a patriarchal society is often characterized more by absence or distance than by presence or closeness. Because the very term "patriarchy" means specifically "father rule," one might expect the father-son relationship to be the centerpiece of the male psyche. Indeed, in a certain way it is, but, at least in psychotherapy, not often because that relationship was particularly warm or close or satisfying or helpful. Pete's double experience of the absent father, an emotionally distant adoptive father who was at work most of the time and a biological father unknown even to his genetic mother, is certainly an extreme example, but the theme of the absent father for contemporary men fairly dominates the psychological literature.[2] In my experience, therefore, psychotherapy with men thus often consists of a process of "finding our fathers," to use Samuel Osherson's wonderful title,[3] rather than necessarily shaking off the malign or domineering influence of a true patriarch.

The irony in this situation is again one of those internal inconsistencies inherent in Western patriarchy and its peculiar set of sex roles: by splitting the social role of work and achievement in a culture off from the role of child rearing and nurturing and by assigning the first to the exclusive province of men and the second to women, patriarchy, the system of "father rule," manages a consistent emotional alienation of the son from the father within a network of male dominance. Fathers are not the figures from a boy's childhood who feed, clothe, cuddle, and teach about relationship, body, and feeling. Unfortunately, the best of circumstances often is when a boy's real relationship to his father in contemporary society begins comparatively late in development, around adolescence, at the time when puberty begins to make a physical man of the boy and the father then steps in to provide instruction on sex, shaving, and sports, subjects that are considered a father's province of knowledge in modern patriarchal societies. Thus, a relationship to this largely absent father occurs mostly, if at all, on external, social terms, rather than on internal, emotional terms. The psychological term for this situation is "identification": the young man is expected to find a way to take on the social functions of his father without the foundation of any real emotional or psychological relationship to either his own personal father or to fatherhood as an ongoing, psychological reality. He is expected, in a somewhat superficial way, to identify as a man and look grown up, without really ever having had a deep relationship to that prime carrier of masculinity in his life, his own father.

One way around this especially patriarchal psychological dilemma that many men manage is to fashion a relationship to collective masculinity, and therefore toward a figurative father of sorts. We can spot some of this in men's affiliations with groups: adolescent boys with their clubs and sports teams, adult men with their professional societies, businesses, church groups, or fraternal organizations. Because in a patriarchal society such male-dominated groups not only are valued but actually are given a fair bit of cultural power and prestige, the psychological immaturity of such a collective solution to father absence is not often addressed or challenged. Yet when sports events take on a violent or clownish turn, when corporate politics resemble the infantile greed of children in search of toys, when professional societies function like high school cliques split between "insiders" and "outsiders," we tend to hear that preeminent patriarchal cliché, "Boys will be boys," along with the equally telling characterization of patriarchal systems as "old-boy networks." What such behavior and characterizations reveal, of course, is the fundamental psychological immaturity of contemporary men who, having been largely deprived of a true relationship to father and thus not given any real way to be initiated into adult malehood, must either rely on essentially superficial accoutrements, such as money, cars, clothes, jobs, and possessions, to fulfill the role of patriarch, or they must take refuge in some form of collective masculinity, a developmental dead end that consigns them to a kind of eternal adolescence.

If the absence of father in the developmental process of men has such wide-ranging negative ramifications socially and psychologically in general, such negative effects are magnified for men who are homosexually oriented, whose primary erotic interest and attraction is toward men, that is, toward people who are like father. In these cases, the absence of the father's emotional presence, of his male nurturing and even the touch of his physical body, tends to have a devastating and stultifying effect on the psyche of the incipient gay man who often has little or no experience, by the time of adulthood, in relating intimately to that source of his own masculinity, his own father, and yet who finds himself, because of his homosexuality, impelled to create such relationships anyway. Thus, we see how the older crop of stereotypes concerning homosexuality—that gay relationships do not last, that gay men are narcissistically incapable of relating to others and seek themselves in their partners, that gay relationships are characterized by a kind of father-son sadomasochism—may often actually be the case in particular instances, though not necessarily because of something inherent to homosexuality. Patriarchy's systematic alienation of men from their fathers does not often provide gay men with the erotic objects in childhood that might enable them as adult men to negotiate successful and happy relationships with other adult men. A gay man can count himself fortunate if, unlike Pete and many of the other gay men whom I have seen, he has had a close and satisfying relationship to a father who remained undaunted by his son's budding homosexuality, who responded with care and interest to the son's erotic interest, and who remained continuously open and accepting of his son's homosexuality once the son had become conscious and had begun to structure his life around his homosexuality. Such a rosy portrait of the relationship possible between a gay man and his father has, at least in my experience, been an unfortunately all-too-rare exception to what usually occurs: a father's continuous and subtle discomfort with the son's early erotic interest in his father (that is, if the father is even around), his consistent attempts to "make a man" out of a son whose interests often differ from those socially defined as masculine, followed by denigration or outright ridicule of the gay man's nonstereotypical masculinity, and then, distressingly often, all-out rejection and even violent attack on the son's mature declaration of his homosexual orientation.

Thus, we should not be surprised to see within gay culture an equivalent flight into collective masculinity that corresponds in many ways to the dominant culture's heterosexual male flight into professional societies and sports teams. Certainly the bars and the baths of urban gay life provided many gay men with the masculine peer group long withheld from them by the pernicious intersection of patriarchal values and father absence. Besides creating a space for the free, unhampered sexual explorations necessary to the acceptance of homosexuality as a legitimate and intimate part of one's sexual identity, the bars and the baths gave gay men a community with which to identify and from which to begin to fashion for themselves a workable sense of their own masculinity. As a collective phenomenon, much of this activity on the part of gay men could be seen as psychologically immature, certainly every bit as immature and adolescent as the shenanigans of sports teams, the mindless rapacity of corporate executives, and the cliquishness and foolery of fraternal organizations. Anyone who goes to the bars and those bathhouses that continue to operate today in the age of AIDS cannot help but be struck by the adolescent nature of the social games that still go on—the superficiality of the cruising, the "insider-outsider" dynamic, the sometimes frantic search for pleasure and identity.

Rather than see such collective phenomena as evidence of homosexuality's psychological immaturity, I think it is important to note that on this point both gay men and straight men, in general, suffer from the absence of the father's physical and emotional presence within a patriarchal system, and so are only able to fashion collective solutions to such a deficit, solutions that remain half-way measures to psychological wholeness. That the heterosexual male's collective solutions are valued in our society, while the homosexual male's collective solutions are condemned, seems more a function of social values than a question of psychological maturity. I think it actually serves to obscure the *heterosexual* male's need to find a unique, individual initiation into manhood, since gay men usually already know, because of many experiences that they have had, that something is wrong, either with their own relationship to masculinity or with the dominant culture's ideas of masculinity as applied to their own experience.

Typically, the issue of fatherhood arises at two different points in the developmental process of men. For gay men, like Pete, it arises when issues of true intimacy with another man eventually come to the fore. This powerful dream of sharing the father's body and being generously loved and fed by a father who reflects his own maleness, occurs at a point when the Dark Young Man of his youth has been known and given a chance to be integrated into his conscious sense of self. Rather than continuously seeking this ideal Italian lover outside himself, through our therapy work with this male anima figure Pete realized—as had Nick in the previous chapter—that he was himself the Dark Young Man, that this figure was a part of him. Such a realization paves the way for a true relationship to other men, rather than one based primarily on projection, and at this point one's relationship to one's own masculine source, the Father, enters the picture.

For heterosexual men, on the other hand, my experience has been that the issue of fatherhood appears on the psychological stage not when issues of intimacy with other men grow hot, since all too often male intimacy is subordinated to intimacy with women for the patriarchally trained heterosexual male, but rather when the heterosexual male is faced with the fact of his own fatherhood, when he is given the task of having a baby and literally becoming a father himself. As we will see in the next chapter, when we follow Nick's process forward, dreams of similar power and imagery appear for the heterosexual man, though the issue is framed differently.

Certainly these distinctions remain academic in a world in which real people do not always fit psychological paradigms or expected models of development. As we all know, there are many heterosexual men, especially nowadays, whose life path does not include children, either by choice or by circumstance, just as there are great numbers of self-identified gay men who are indeed fathers, again either through choice, availing themselves of surrogate parenthood or adoption, or through circumstance, such as those gay men who were married and had children before coming out as gay. For these men, obviously, our neat theoretical distinctions blur, and the figure of Father, personally and archetypally, may be dealt with on both fronts. For Pete, however, these two separate issues around fatherhood, having a father versus being a father, remained separate, and in this way, his process allows us to see how a patriarchally imposed father absence, so typical and so harmful to the psychological lives of contemporary men, can be dealt with in psychotherapy.

On the personal level, with Pete, the striking quality of the dream rested on its compensatory function: its vivid sensuality and its father eroticism underlined precisely what was missing from his experience of his father as a child, just as his youthful attempts to retrieve some of these qualities through his relationship to Tony and Tony's family resulted in a kind of "Italian father fantasy" projected out onto such powerful movie idols as De Niro or Pacino, who are seen as possessing and (in the dream) lavishing upon him precisely the feelingful, physical attention his own father did not show him. The dream serves a progressive function, that is, it pushes the dreamer forward psychologically, by making quite a point of demonstrating that macho father masculinity is but the surface of a deeper, more engrossing form of fathering. Not only does the dream-within-a-dream structure make the point that "all is not what it seems," but the details of the dream and Pete's associations reinforce this point as well. As a boxer, the father in the dream at least outwardly fulfills the stereotypical patriarchal male role; he is a public figure whose life and livelihood is built on his attributes of strength, cunning, and ability to dominate other men, physically or through verbal denigration. Yet at home the father has another face entirely, caring for and nurturing not only his guests at the table but his own son in particular.

Pete's associations to the names of the boxers further underlines the duality and complexity of this father figure. "Maccagnorola," the name of Al Pacino, his father, in the dream, had two kinds of associations for Pete. The first was to food, like macaroons and macaroni, an association that we will be examining in great detail when we look at the centrality of food symbolism here. The second and more immediately relevant was to the Italian exclamation "Macchè!", roughly equivalent to the English "No way!", as if the very name of his father in a way refuted, refused, and pushed away the external image he was being presented with. Likewise, "Grancchè," the other boxer, whose name is an Italian expression that means something akin to "big shot" when used to describe a person, is being denigrated in the dream, implying a similar duality between outward appearance and inward importance: Mr. Big Shot in the dream is considered "barbaric," an animal.

The dream thus enabled us to glimpse and experience the emotional underside of Pete's abandonment feelings, made doubly painful by his dual abandonment, first being given up for adoption, second experiencing his adoptive father's physical and emotional absence. If we take the boxing imagery seriously, then certainly what we are seeing is a kind of savage, violent, animal rage inherent in such patriarchal masculinity and its concomitant abandonment of the son. Such rage, at the unknown biological father as well as at the intermittently present adoptive father (Pete tended to say, his "real" father), would expectably lead to what we initially saw in Pete and for most men when they enter therapy, an impossibly tight rein on feelings with a compensatory overemphasis on rationality and perfection for fear that such deep rage at abandonment and absence might erupt in violent, annihilatory form. Whatever one's feelings about boxing in general, inescapable is its primitve quality, with its man-to-man body combat using minimal equipment and structure; it is a sport with masculine struggle and emotional rage as practically its sole content. As a symbol for Pete's feeling level around his personal fathers, it is a powerful image of what father absence bequeathes to men: struggle and rage as the primal context of a man's development in a patriarchal society.

Notable therefore is the dream's distance from Pete's personal issues and feelings, especially the rage and abandonment. His real father is not portrayed. Pete is at first less a participant and more a distant camera-recorder. The dream is not his dream but a film. I picked up on this distance, a patriarchal bequest of the absent father, when I noticed the silences, the wistfulness, and the level of sadness, regret, and anger that remained present and unarticulated. Able to notice in his experience his father's absence and the growing feelings of abandonment as the deeper issues around his adoption sank in, Pete was not yet ready to really experience the depth of this abandonment rage, not until he had a somewhat firmer ground to stand upon, an observing ego more mature than the eight- or nine-year-old dream ego that he is in the dream.

In this way, the dream's second and most important episode moves us beyond the pain and rage at the personal fathers' dual abandonment and the compensatory macho Italian father fantasy. In the kitchen, we come to a place beyond the personal father of Pete's experience, into the realm of the archetypal or transpersonal father.

Two elements of the dream's second episode point beyond Pete's personal father. The presence of a "screen idol" as Pete's father, especially Al Pacino, makes clear the dream's intention to draw Pete's psychic attention away from the absent personal fathers of his experience, and to have him reflect on those elements of fatherhood not present in his personal past but perhaps still available to him psychically through a relationship with the kind of fatherhood Al Pacino would represent. In Jungian terms, the dream's use of Al Pacino presents Pete with the other aspects of the father archetype that have been excluded from consciousness, specifically those aspects Pete himself touched upon—tenderness, nurturing, and eroticism, especially homoeroticism—with the intention, one presumes, of making such fatherly qualities available to Pete.

Along with the presence of this "screen idol," we see a rather exquisite ritual being performed here between father and son, replete with elemental food and instruments, a private ritual certainly designed in some way to impart this fatherhood to Pete in a special and effective way. For this reason certainly, the imagery of food and feeding is central to understanding the dream and portrays in concrete images the deeper layer of Pete's process around fatherhood, that is, his incorporation and digestion of those aspects of fatherhood missing from his personal experience.

It is easy to amplify the psychological process going on here by simply taking seriously the dream's physical analogy to eating, a process whereby necessary and nourishing elements of the outer world are incorporated into our bodies through a process of ingestion, followed by a breakdown into constituent elements, and then eventual digestion. By taking place in a kitchen at mealtime, the dream's context suggests that Pete's process around fatherhood is one of vital import to his psychic life and growth, just as eating is vital to life and growth. Moreover, the imagery points out how the psychological process will parallel the physical one: those aspects of fatherhood will need to be introduced to his consciousness from the outside, broken down into their constituent parts, and eventually digested, that is, incorporated, perhaps even physically, into his existence.

However, the presence of a "screen idol" as father as well as the ritual meal being performed here combine to suggest that the striking quality of the dream is due not only to its relevance and its sensory vividness but perhaps also to what Jung would call its "numinosity," that is, the "deeply stirring emotional affect"[4] that occurs when God images appear for people psychically, whether in a dream, a vision, or, more rarely, in everyday life. This numinous quality is, in fact, what makes the so-called "big dream" big, since the awesome feeling of significance that accompanies it is perhaps the surest sign that we are being confronted with a symbol of transpersonal import.

In the case of this dream, it is not to Greek mythology that we must look to find an appropriate symbolic amplification, though certainly Greek mythology due to its distance from our culture and its age may be more comfortable and more entertaining. Rather, there is a kind of ironic aptness in observing that the truly appropriate symbolic parallel to Pete's dream lies in the central ritual of the very patriarchal religion around which Western culture has been built and maintained, namely, the Eucharistic meal of Christianity.

Of course, we are confronted with a particular set of problems when it is Christian ritual that would deepen our understanding of a psychological process occurring for a modern individual. For the believer, it may seem that we are doing a disservice to sacred truths by simply using Christianity's symbolic forms in an individualistic, psychologizing way, while for the nonbeliever, whether benignly agnostic or forthrightly hostile to organized religion, it might seem proselytizing and apologetic to admit that Christianity is every bit as capable of giving symbolic form to archetypal processes as Greek mythology or modern motion pictures. What is inarguable, regardless of one's religious convictions, is that Christianity, with its images, symbols, theology, and rituals, is largely responsible for Western culture, and so tends to play an enormous role in the unconscious of contemporary men, churchgoing or not.

Moreover, the overwhelmingly patriarchal quality of Christianity in an interesting way makes the Eucharist especially suitable to seeing just how the contemporary man might find a more whole and present relationship to fatherhood. In fact, Christianity and its rituals may indeed be much more instructive on this point than polytheistic and multifaceted religions such as those of ancient Greece or Rome, since in Christian tradition a distinctively patriarchal Godhead, consisting of an ostensibly male trinity, Father, Son, and Holy Spirit, is responsible for the creation of the world and for the redemption of humanity from its state of imperfection and mortality. These patriarchal roots go deep in Western culture and in

Christianity, finding their source in the monotheistic father religion of Judaism, a religion that might be seen as the prototype of patriarchal religion, in which a male God presides and in which a male priesthood carries out a distinctly masculine cult of obedience to laws and ritual worship.

Thus, we see the action of the collective unconscious in the rather strikingly Christian imagery of Pete's dream, sharing what externally at least bears a great resemblance to the central mystery of this religion, the Eucharistic meal, a mystery in its very core bound up with the issues around fatherhood that Pete is facing. As celebrated today by the various denominations of Christianity, though with important theological and ritual differences between them, the Eucharist consists of physically sharing bread and wine, a ritual meal. This meal is both a remembrance of the last supper of Jesus shared with his disciples before his crucifixion and a reenactment of the sacrifice Jesus made of his physical existence, symbolized by the bread as his body and the wine as his blood, through which he attained a higher spiritual state, rising from dead and thereby redeeming an imperfect and mortal creation. Christians, therefore, share this meal not only to remember Christ's sacrifice for them but also to partake of Christ's body and blood, his actual physical essence. In the Eucharist, therefore, Christians actually participate in the life, death, and resurrection of Christ through the ritual incorporation of the bread and wine into their own bodies through eating.

The connection of this ritual and its meaning to the theme of Pete's dream and the psychological process of modern men around fatherhood may seem obscure at first, but it rapidly becomes clear once one understands how Christianity conceives of God and therefore how the life, death, and resurrection of Christ is understood as redemptive. For Christians, God consists of three persons of one substance, eternal in existence and coequal in divinity. The first is God the Father, "maker of heaven and earth, and of all things visible and invisible," according to the formula established at Nicea in A.D. 325 and subsequently approved at Chalcedon in 451.[5] The second is the Son of God, Lord Jesus Christ, whom the Nicene formula makes quite clear was "begotten, not made," a point which is repeated in the Nicene Creed again, "the only-begotten Son of God," and yet again, "begotten of the Father before all the ages." This insistence on Christ's generation from the Father, rather than his creation by God, is derived from the importance early Christianity placed on differentiating its conception of God from the Greek and Roman model of creator gods, as well as from the Gnostic conception of gods subordinate to other gods. However, this insistence shows exactly how patriarchal a model Christianity was using, a father-son model of divinity without even a hint of feminine cocreation. The third person of the Christian Trinity, the Holy Spirit, is not begotten of the Father, strictly speaking, but rather "proceedeth from the Father," and is termed in the creed as the "Lord and Giver of Life," worshipped with the Father and the Son as coequal in divinity.

While many think of Jung as just the sort of person who would be particularly entranced with such an abstract and complex intellectual conception of God, for his part Jung writes:

> The Trinity and its inner life process appear as a closed circle, a self-contained divine drama in which man plays, at most, a passive part. It seizes on him and, for a period of several centuries, forced him to occupy his mind passionately with all sorts of queer problems which today seem incredibly abstruse, if not downright absurd. It is, in the first place, difficult to see what the Trinity could possibly mean for us, either practically, morally or symbolically. Even theologians often feel that speculation on this subject is a more or less otiose juggling with ideas. . . .[6]

And yet we notice that this "self-contained divine drama" is one that is organized around fatherhood and sonhood, and in particular around the divinity of these persons and their action to redeem and save mortal humanity. Such redemption is accomplished, according to the Nicene formula, through the person of Jesus Christ who "for us men and for our salvation came down from the heavens and was made flesh by the Holy Spirit and the Virgin Mary, and became man." One step in this redemption of mortal humanity and of the whole imperfect universe, therefore, consists of the physical incarnation of the divine Son of God, his taking upon himself the body and life of an actual human being. The second step consists of sacrifice, in which the God-man Jesus Christ "was crucified for us under Pontius Pilate, and suffered and was buried." Through his voluntary incarnation as a man and his acceptance, as a divine being, of the conditions of this mortal life, suffering, death, and burial, Jesus Christ accomplishes the third step in the process of redemption through his resurrection from the dead: he "rose again on the third day according to the Scriptures, and ascended into the heavens, and sitteth on the right hand of the Father, and cometh again with glory to judge living and dead, of whose kingdom there shall be no end."

What we see therefore in the Eucharistic meal is a ritual recreation of this process of redemption through the use of bread and wine, actual physical substances, which in the course of their consecration actually become the body and blood of Christ, repeating the very incarnation of divinity that is the first step in God's plan for humanity's salvation. Various ritual operations then proceed, which re-enact Christ's sacrifice, the breaking of the bread and pouring of the wine; the bread and wine are then distributed to the congregation who consume and incorporate Christ's body and blood into their own being, accepting in this way Christ's sacrifice of his mortal existence for their own eternal salvation. The third step in this process, Christ's resurrection, presumably results when the incorporation of Christ through the worshipper's participation in the meal gives Christ new life on earth by way of the community of the believers who share this meal together, the Christian church which, following Christ's ascension into heaven, is considered the Body of Christ on earth.

The Christian myth, therefore, in both its Trinitarian conception of divinity and its understanding of Christ's action of world redemption, uses the father-son relationship as the symbolic vehicle for its central concern: the process of obtaining eternal life, immortality, through a perfection of the human state. The father-son relationship is especially apt in this regard, since it is one place where symbolic immortality resides in human experience, through the biological continuation of the species. Christian symbolism, however, illustrates the complexity of this relationship both in its juxtaposition of divinity and humanity (Jesus, as son, is both God and man, fully God and yet fully human) and in the duality of God himself, who is both Father and Son, both God transcendent and God incarnate.

The Eucharistic meal as a ritual recreation of this process of immortalization or redemption, to use the Christian term, further emphasizes the duality of this father-son relationship in its use of both bread and wine. Bread is a product of the earth and thus linked to the mortality of human life, since it is the earth from which life springs and to which all life returns, while wine, a spirit-based product, is connected by its essential volatility to the higher nature, the part of human existence that like Christ or, for believers, through Christ, is capable of ascending and attaining a higher spiritual state.

Moreover, both these substances in themselves reflect the very process of breakdown, fermentation, or digestion, followed by integration or consolidation that is the symbolic ground of both the Eucharist and the Incarnation, and therefore of psychological individuation. Bread is created through the grinding of grain, which is then combined with yeast, a fermenting substance that causes the bread to rise, after which it is exposed to fire, consolidating these once separate grains into a single unified product. Similarly, wine is made through the crushing of the individual grapes, followed by fermentation and aging, once again producing, out of an original collective state, a united substance with an individual character and body. Not by chance, therefore, is it the sacrament of the Eucharist that in Christian theology creates the Church, Christ's body on earth, a collective consolidation of individual believers who, like the grains that make the bread and the grapes that create the wine, sacrifice their individual natures to take on a union with Christ through the Eucharist and thus incarnate God themselves.

Jung explicates these symbols by noting:

> Bread therefore represents the physical means of subsistence, and wine the spiritual. The offering up of bread and wine is the offering of both the physical and the spiritual fruits of civilization. . . . Grain and wine therefore have something in the nature of a soul, a specific life principle which makes them appropriate symbols not only of

man's cultural achievements but also of the seasonally dying and re-
surgent god who is their life spirit.[7]

Of course, the Christian Eucharistic symbolism sits on an even
earlier stratum of Jewish images that were meant to characterize
Yahweh's special relationship to Israel and, through this nation, to
the entire world. Specifically, the Eucharist recalls the Seder, the
Passover meal celebrated by Jews in remembrance of Yahweh's pro-
tective action in their flight from slavery in Egypt, as well as the
miraculous provision of manna, the "bread from heaven" that fed
the Jews during their wanderings in the wilderness following their
escape from the Pharaoh. Both these allusions touch on that quality
of Father that Pete's dream underscores and that is inherent in the
mystery of the Incarnation symbolized by the Eucharist, namely,
God's providence toward creation, and humanity's reception of this
providence through the symbolic incorporation of the Father's
essence.

The perspicacious reader, however, will remember that Pete's
dream does not really present us with a Eucharistic meal properly
speaking, for instead of bread and wine, what Pete is ritually fed by
his dream father is bread dipped in olive oil. Now of course, for Italians, olive oil is perhaps every bit as important culturally and every
bit as rich a symbol as wine, representing like wine a highly refined
product created through the extraction of the individual essences as
well as the lavish providence of the creative earth. In this way, the
dream does not stray all that far from Eucharistic symbolism, though
the absence of wine suggests, at least for Pete, a less spiritual or
volatile union with Father and a more earthbound, bodily integration of fatherly nurturing.

The greater earthiness of the bread and olive oil symbolically
makes sense for a young man who actually never knew his real father physically and whose search for the father, as a gay man, is
carried out on one level in his erotic relationship with other men.
While such an assessment might be used to condemn or dismiss
Pete's homosexuality, my opinion is that the dream is actually attempting to show Pete the sacred nature of his erotic longings, behind which lies a search for contact with both a personal and trans-

personal source of masculine being. As opposed to a view that sees in such a dream an absence of masculinity, I wonder if Pete's search may not have as its purpose a kind of self-confirmation of who he has sensed himself to be on the deepest level of his soul. If this is in fact the case, then gay men may be healing the wound of the absent patriarchal father through their homosexuality in a way that constitutional heterosexuals may not have available to them. Gay men, like Pete in his dream, incorporate the father physically and symbolically in their union with other beloved men and thus, if they are conscious about it, know their own masculine essence in a way that, like the Eucharist, unites both heaven and earth, profane and sacred, body and soul.

However, the olive oil, this surrogate for the Eucharistic wine in Pete's dream, brings to mind another ritual and therefore another related layer of meaning, namely, anointing and all its purposes. With parallels to baptism (which we shall examine in great detail in the next chapter on Nick's fatherhood dreams), anointing, the pouring of oil on the body, has been an important religious ritual throughout the world and throughout the ages. Because of the essential preciousness of oil, derived from the work its extraction entails and from the clarity and purity that constitute its physical properties, anointing is used as a symbol of status elevation, as in the crowning of kings or the ordination of priests, to confer on an individual a higher spiritual condition or more notable temporal position. Thus, like baptism, anointing marks a new, higher stage in the development of an individual, especially a new religious condition. For this reason, anointing is used as consecration (as with animal sacrifices) or as protection (as with soldiers before battle). It makes holy and brings the anointed into the purview of God's care.

Alongside ordination and consecration, we see perhaps the most common purpose of anointing in its use as a ritual of healing. While in non-Christian religious practice the healing purpose of anointing is no doubt linked to special properties that oil may be seen to have medicinally or magically, we see within Roman Catholicism the elevation of this ritual to sacramental status in the rite of extreme unction. In this rite, individuals in danger of death (*in extremis*) who have confessed and repented of their sins are anointed with pure olive oil that has been blessed by a bishop on Maundy Thursday, the church holiday commemorating the Last Supper before Christ's crucifixion. Though some believers may still hold to a magical view of this rite, with anointing seen as a form of healing, what seems clear is that the rite of extreme unction, nowadays simply called "anointing of the sick," is intended to prepare the penitent for a higher spiritual state, the union with God following death, and, given that the oil is blessed on Maundy Thursday, alludes yet again to the incarnation, death, and resurrection of Jesus at the center of Christian mythology.

Of course, the use of olive oil in Pete's dream simply reinforces the same themes we have discerned previously as he comes to grips with fatherhood and sonhood in himself. As a ritual of elevation, the dream father's use of oil points to the way Pete's individuation is intended to move him beyond a state of unconscious relationship to fatherhood and to men, and elevate him to a more conscious participation in the essence of masculinity, a higher spiritual state. Naturally, the aspect of healing inherent in anointing is central, healing the wound left by the absent fathers through incarnation and union with the archetypal elements of fatherhood—providence, source of life, protection, and masculinity.

The aspect of anointing as preparation for death both in its ritual use within Roman Catholicism and other religions, and in its connection with Christ's own incarnation and sacrifice, leads us to perceive that on a deeper level Pete's search for the origins of his life, the archetypal Father, also brings him into more intimate contact with the finality of death and his own mortality. Thus, we see the arrival of this dream at a point when the Dark Young Men, his psychic doubles, have begun to lose their passionate hold on his soul, a time when Pete turns his face away from exclusively youthful concerns and toward more mature issues: Who am I as a *man?* Whose masculinity do I incarnate? What is my life's purpose?

Of course, for gay men throughout the United States, the reality of death and personal mortality looms large these days. With obituary columns often running two and three pages in gay newspapers in the San Francisco Bay Area, with nearly a dozen of his friends and acquaintances either dead or dying of HIV disease during the course of our analysis, and with his own HIV status unknown at the time of this dream, Pete's individuation process involved more than simply a symbolic preparation for death but actually a quite literal confrontation with the reality of his own mortality. It is impossible these days to discern the individuation process of gay men without taking into account the unbelievable psychic toll that the HIV epidemic has had upon the collective soul of the gay community. The sheer numbers of the dead and the infected—121,000 cases nationwide as of January, 1990, nearly half the gay community in San Francisco estimated to be infected, 70 to 100 deaths per month in San Francisco alone—begin to convey how thoroughly the gay community is saturated with an awareness of mortality. One visit to the Names Project quilt when it is displayed around the country is sufficient to demonstrate visually and viscerally what it must be like to live as a gay man in the midst of such suffering. A sea of over ten thousand multicolored panels laid out like gravestones, each containing the name of someone who has died, behind whom exists a community of friends and loved ones bereaved and shaken, this quilt serves as one of the best symbolic expressions of the community's grief around the loss that is at the heart of AIDS.

That Pete's dream of Father directs us to the theme of death, a theme underscored again and again by the Christian rituals amplifying his dream imagery—the Eucharist as commemoration of Christ's death, the Seder as commemoration of the passover of the angel of death, the rite of extreme unction as preparation for death—shows us how the common experience of death among gay men these days actually furthers the individuation process of those men, like Pete, who are forced by the HIV epidemic to become more conscious of the meaning of their lives. For many gay men, the result of this consciousness raising, this encounter with mortality, has been unprecedented political action around research, treatment, and services for the great number of individuals affected by AIDS. On the internal level, however, my experience has been that gay men, all too often alienated from institutional forms of religious expression, must now create for themselves an individual relationship to some sort of higher power or greater meaning in order to cope with the catastrophic loss of so many friends and lovers. Loath to term such a journey "religious," in part because of the institutional associations of this word, gay men find themselves having increasingly to confront what is more comfortably called "spirituality" in themselves and in the gay community.[8]

Pete's dream, and his process around fatherhood, suggests that such a spiritual meaning for men perhaps cannot be fully discerned until we have established our own individual relationship to the origin of our lives, in a word, to Father, personally and archetypally. Native cultures weave together these diverse themes in their masculine initiation rites; young men are taken from their customary social circumstances by the elder males of the tribe, sometimes by surprise and by force, and then put through trials and tests often resembling sacrifice and death. Once ritually "dead," they are conducted as individuals reborn into a higher state, namely, that of the mature adult male in the tribe. In this way, a young man's entry into fatherhood, that is, adult malehood, requires a sacrifice, a confrontation with death, and a spiritual rebirth. For Christians, the life of Christ is the exemplar of such initiation, physically in his literal resurrection from the dead and spiritually in his incarnation of God on earth, and so the Christian is exhorted to become the *imitatio Christi,* the imitation of Christ.

Our rather extensive examination of the religious symbolism to which Pete's dream alludes is meant to draw our attention to the fact that Pete's incorporation of Father is not simply a personal coming to terms with the real father, the establishment of a relationship in an ordinary psychological way of thinking. The Christian symbolism, as well as the initiatory imagery as it spontaneously appears in Pete's psyche, suggests that something wider and deeper is occurring as Pete struggles with finding and incorporating the Father. The Christian myth, with its Jewish parallels, suggests that what is going on is a search for a higher, more perfect way of being, both in the sense of spiritual perfection or wholeness, as well as in the sense of obtaining some sort of spiritual immortality. His father in the dream is a god, or at least the way gods tend to appear to contemporary men nowadays, in the guise of a movie star. He participates in a ritual of incorporation and sustenance, a continuation of life through the relationship with and ingestion of his father's substance. This entails a confrontation with the reality of death both individually and collectively, a process of digestion and consolidation into something new and different, which results in a rebirth of sorts, an ability to go forward from a youthful condition with a new and more mature sense of self. The dream has all the emotional hallmarks of a vision—numinosity, lingering sensation, and a vivid sense of importance—and can be seen as a manifestation of Pete's psychological process and inward spiritual journey.

If we hold to this dual understanding of Pete's dream, seeing men's individuation both personally and transpersonally, a process of both psychological and spiritual development, the patriarchal one-sidedness we have criticized so frequently in these pages becomes yet even more potentially dangerous. If patriarchy's systematic alienation of sons from fathers is effective, the result is not only the kind of personal psychological brokenness that forces men into therapy, seen in the emotional pain so many men carry at the absence of their fathers from their lives as children and as adults, but there is a transpersonal danger lurking about as well. If men are alienated not only from themselves, but from the personal and transpersonal source of their being as men, namely, Father as the source of immortality literally and figuratively, then the result can only be spiritual malaise and despair, a kind of death-in-life in which hope in a higher, better way of being has been taken away and replaced with materialistic or collective substitutes that lead nowhere.

Believer or not, it is incumbent upon all men to come to grips with what the Christian myth has so perfectly captured in its symbols for Western culture, namely, the way in which we participate both in mortality and immortality, death and life. Rather than simply believing in a figure like Christ, men in psychotherapy on its deepest level are attempting through their individuation process to *be* Christ, to straddle the paradoxes of incarnation and divinity, death and life, to be in contact with the source of their existence as men, and to fully know and realize themselves as unique beings in relationship to that source. In this way, the father-son relationship carries much more than an affectional tie for modern men, but actually may be the locus of spiritual and physical redemption.

Of course, such an understanding requires adopting the rather broader view of psychotherapy held by Jung, in which the strict division of psychology from religion, inherited from modern scientific materialism, is loosened to acknowledge the religious roots of psychotherapy (literally "soul healing" after all) and the psychological roots of religious experience. Likewise, this understanding requires a fuller appreciation of the importance of ritual in the lives of modern men, particularly initiation rituals, which might help men begin to repair the hole in the spiritual fabric of their inner lives left by their absent or neglectful personal fathers. As opposed to male rituals in which the intention toward initiation is honored but remains unconscious and largely unarticulated, as in fraternity hazings among college boys or S&M enactments within the gay community, ritual initiation into manhood can only do what Pete's dream intends—create a new man through psychological integration and spiritual anointing—if such initiation is made conscious and appreciated as such. For this reason, psychotherapy, in its attention to consciousness raising, in its ritual context, and in its greater openness to the spiritual reality of men's lives, has become one of the few effective initiations into manhood open to modern men in an age of individualism.

I think we also see from Pete's dreams that spiritual development and psychological individuation do not seem to be necessarily confined to heterosexual men. While of course there will probably always be those voices who beg to differ, Pete's dreams, especially when interpreted on the deeper archetypal level, I believe show that the individuation process of a man proceeds regardless of sexual orientation, and indeed sometimes acquires its unique shape and texture precisely from a man's homosexuality. This suggestion, that gay men indeed do have an individuation process as gay men, without any requisite conversion to heterosexuality beforehand, is in line with current psychological and anthropological thinking concerning homosexuality. By considering homosexuality to be merely one variation on a continuum of sexual expression, this line of thought throws into relief patriarchal biases and projections on homosexuality rather than pathologizing the homosexuality itself; it also relieves gay men of the burden of having their homosexuality become the sole focus of cure within psychotherapeutic treatment. With an attitude of openness toward gay men, and with the conviction that gay men's individuation is not a process of cure from homosexuality but rather a process of self-realization as *gay*, contemporary psychotherapists may come to see the way to honor what gay men have to offer to the psychology and healing of all men caught in patriarchal traps and blind spots.

With regard to Father, we have touched already on how a gay man such as Pete may come to a deeper relationship to this archetypal dominant of human experience through his homosexuality in ways not available to heterosexual men. A gay man's special experience of the masculinity of Eros, for example, or the way Father can be known in a conscious, mutual, and intimate love relationship with another man, would be difficult, if not impossible, experiences for a man to have in a heterosexual relationship with a woman. And yet many might wonder, does not the gay man's unlikelihood of being a father somehow preclude or limit his experience of the archetypal Father? Acknowledging that many gay men are in fact fathers, as noted earlier, either through circumstance or conscious choice, in part answers this question: no, gay men are not necessarily exempted from being fathers.

However, of the gay men, like Pete, whose exclusive homosexuality does in fact entail childlessness as part of his life's path, my work with gay men makes me wonder if perhaps this might not actually be a sort of psychological advantage by forcing the gay man to forge some sort of relationship to fatherhood primarily on an inner level, rather than rest on a simple biological capacity to have children in order to accomplish this kind of psychological connection to archetypal fatherhood for him. In other words, a gay man's childlessness might illuminate the psychological and spiritual facets of fatherhood more brightly for him than for the heterosexual man and make fatherhood a more consciously integrated part of his sense of self, rather than a simple automatic function expected of him socially and culturally.

Because we will be ending Pete's story here, a final dream, I think, ties together many of these various threads we have been discussing and gives vivid image to the goal of psychotherapeutic healing. Brought into psychotherapy by a creative block for which discipline, perfectionism, and self-beratement was ineffective, Pete was forced in many ways to undertake a kind of excavation of his inner life. The initial work, centered around awareness of feelings and an ongoing wrangle with me about the issue of who in our relationship had authority over his inner life, eventually resulted in a kind of conversion experience, in which the reality and aliveness of his soul became apparent and personified.

In our encounter with the Dark Young Man, a multifaceted archetypal figure for all intents and purposes like the anima of a heterosexual man, Pete and I began slowly to bring to awareness hitherto unsuspected pieces of his personality, such as his eroticism and his capacity for relationship, as well as hitherto unsuspected pieces of his personal history, such as his Italian ancestry. Armed thus with greater knowlege of himself and enlarged by the deeper emotional experiences of himself in the course of our work, his perfectionism lessened, he became more self-accepting, and, during our time together, he even undertook a relationship with a man, slightly older than himself, with whom he is still involved.

As the Dark Young Man slowly transmuted into a figure more closely allied with the father in his dream life, Pete and I embarked on the final stage of his analysis centered around the integration and embodiment of his masculine origins into his conscious sense of self. Following the Al Pacino dream, which we discussed over the course of many sessions, returning again and again to the theme of father embodiment and maturity, Pete graduated from school and obtained a job in the field of architecture commensurate with his skills and with sufficient income to support himself comfortably. The old procrastination habits died hard, still troubling him when new demands were placed on him, but for the most part he remained able to carry on with his work with a minimum of trouble. Because of the intensification of and increased satisfaction of relationship to his inner life, however, many of Pete's ups and downs in the worlds of relationships and work often seemed somewhat incidental.

Knowing himself and his origins placed him on a firmer psychic footing, gave him a center around which reality could swirl with minimal disturbance. One concrete example of such firmer footing was the way in which the successive diagnoses of his friends with AIDS were handled in a way that neither capped the normal grieving process nor allowed their illnesses, and in some cases, their deaths to derail his life. In the course of our work, Pete acquired sufficient courage to go with his lover to be tested for HIV, testing negative himself but discovering instead that his new boyfriend was in fact infected with the virus. As we worked with and to some extent through the waves of fear, anxiety, and grief that this information brought up for him, he was manifestly quite a different person from four years previously, able to feel and articulate his feelings, and able to love and accept love from his boyfriend, whose perfections and imperfections could be held in balance and appreciated with a minimum of projection. Our work with Father actually enabled Pete to conceive of being able to perhaps follow through on the caretaking and support that would be required when his lover eventually would become ill with AIDS, showing him that those aspects of archetypal fatherhood that we had discerned in his dream were by no means confined to literal fathering but were ever-present aspects of male experience.

Near the end of our work together, the following dream occurred for Pete:

> I am with my friend Daniel, a Dark Young Man type, but slightly older and bisexual. We are in bed together and have just made love. I hug him from behind as he sits on the edge of his bed, stroking his navel and the muscles of his abdomen in a kind of absent-minded way, trying to excite him so we can make love again. Suddenly, the muscles begin to contract of their own accord, more and more violently, and I realize that in fact Daniel is going to be giving birth soon!

Pete reported this dream with a great deal of excitement and a little bit of uneasiness. The sight of the birth process, the violent contraction of the muscles, and the feeling of responsibility he felt for having induced labor through the stroking of Daniel's navel all brought home to Pete through symbol what he and I had already spoken of in words and what his dreams had been assiduously demonstrating throughout our psychotherapy. In coming to know oneself, a man must return to his origins, the navel of experience, and, as in this final dream, the result is a birth of oneself inwardly. Unconfined by patriarchal categories or expectations, a man's soul, if given sufficient space and attention, shows how false at times such categories and expectations really are. In this gay man's dream, the Dark Young Man, that focus of relationship and the guide to Pete's deeper sense of self, unites in his bisexuality previously incompatible opposites and takes on what we are told in patriarchal societies is the exclusive province of women, the ability to conceive and give birth to new life. In this way, this dream is the logical successor to the Eucharist dream of Al Pacino. In integrating his fatherhood psychologically and spiritually, through digestion and anointing, Pete unites with a more mature soul figure and accomplishes the husbandry of his soul figure's birth, giving birth to himself as a man through men, through the Father, through masculinity.

For these reasons, I suspect gay men are viewed with suspicion and prejudice by patriarchal supporters of the status quo who quite rightly sense that homosexuality threatens the all-too-rigid distinctions between male and female, man and woman, that are the cornerstones of traditional gender and sex-role definitions. Pete's conscious acceptance of himself as gay entails a kind of fluidity that enables him to bring forth unglimpsed and unappreciated portions of the male psyche, portions that reveal patriarchal rigidity for what it is—stifling, unworkable, ridden with contradictions, and false to the real wholeness of both men and women.

However, it is not only gay men who challenge the patriarchal status quo. For the way in which a heterosexual man's experience makes a "re-visioning" of fatherhood necessary and enlivening, we turn now to the final phase of Nick's psychotherapy, in which his literal fatherhood occupied center stage.

6 The Dream of a Daughter's Baptism: Fatherhood as Initiation and Relationship

> I am watching a newsreel on a policeman who shot two blond boys in a bathroom. I am then in the bathroom and am ordered by the policeman to urinate on the two kids, which I do, without feeling, until they then become my daughter. I continue to urinate, telling her to turn her face to avoid my stream of piss, and suddenly there is great sadness and shame within me. I finish and then quickly take her to the bathtub where I begin to wash her, soaking the sponge full of water and squeezing it over her head and letting it run down over her body. She begins to laugh and I see her joy but know I have hurt her, too.

Nick smiled, preparing to answer the unasked question that followed the report of his dreams in our sessions. "Not too hard to figure out where this one came from. We've been having diaper wars at home lately."

"Diaper wars?" I wondered aloud, not really in the dark about what he meant—his daughter was just under a year old at this point—but interested in his particular experience of the baby and of fatherhood.

"I say 'wars' because in a certain sense it feels like opposing wills, like I'm trying to keep her clean and comfortable while she deliberately continues to mess, sometimes right after I put the new diaper on. My fantasy is that she likes being dirty, you know, enjoys the smell and the warmth."

I notice his circumspect descriptions and decide to allow our speech to get a little less tidy as well. "You mean, of her shit and her piss."

A momentary look from him told me that my directness was unexpected but also welcome. "Right, like she actually likes sitting in her shit and doesn't really appreciate my efforts to keep her dry and clean."

"Which makes you feel . . . ?"

"Pretty angry. I don't know how Judy manages so much equanimity with her. I've just been getting so frustrated lately, and it seems pretty clear in the dream, doesn't it? Not that I would actually contemplate shooting her or pissing on her, but I guess part of me is pretty enraged."

"And ashamed about it, too, it seems."

A lull ensued as the more difficult layer of feelings rose to the surface and permeated the atmosphere. "It seems so destructive and so childish to be mad at an eleven-month-old baby because she won't do what I want. I feel so helpless. I guess I am even a little ashamed at having this kind of dream. Pissing on people is something I think of little kids or animals doing, not adult men." First I heard the quaver in the voice and then realized that there were tears rising in Nick's eyes. "And the sight of her in the dream, huddled in the corner of the bathroom as I continue to piss on her is so painful to remember. I feel so guilty."

"Does she seem to mind in the dream?" I wonder, remembering that in real life it seemed to Nick that his daughter did not have the same diffidence toward her bodily functions, seemed more at home in the mess of her eliminations.

"Actually, no. She's so young, it's almost as if she couldn't tell the difference between my piss and the water in the bathtub. I wouldn't say she enjoyed it, though."

"But in the dream it wasn't really harmful. What was disturbing was your sense of your hostile feelings toward her."

"Over which I didn't have control. I'm thinking about being

ordered to piss on her, as if I become the policeman who has shot the two boys. That makes me think of myself, actually."

"The two boys, you mean?"

"Yeah, it feels a little like—how can I say this?" He spent a moment or two thinking, and I could feel him piecing together his own interpretation of the dream, something that after three years of dream work he was more than capable of doing. "It feels as if part of the struggle my kid faces me with is the conflict over being who I am, good and bad, and loving it no matter what. I am more inclined to be angry, reject, shoot myself than love, respect, own my feelings. Like I am caught in this recycling of my father's judgmentalism toward me, so I can't simply let myself have my feelings, my creativity, my interests, my fantasies. I have to look nice, be nice, act nice. Can't have a dirty diaper, can't let my kid have a dirty diaper, can't let her enjoy herself. I kill the child in me and so in some ways act to stifle her childishness, too, expecting her to control her bowels and bladder."

"So do you think it's important in the dream that you aren't the policeman, you don't shoot the kids, but simply piss, become aware of a more natural way to be."

"But I don't like it directed at her."

"Even if it doesn't really hurt her."

"I should protect her from who I am."

"You're that dangerous?"

"It feels like I might be. I can see how child abuse happens. It's so frustrating."

I intervene here, knowing that at this point his rage is probably not a serious outer threat. "It sounds more like you are trying to control yourself through controlling her, and that the attempt at control comes not out of acceptance but out of rejection—you don't like yourself when you are angry so you attempt to control it, which actually in some ways makes it worse."

He got my point and continued on his own. "As opposed to accepting that it is frustrating, that I am going to get angry, and take steps to manage it." He stopped for a bit, thinking. "Maybe that's the way that I am pissing on her in the dream, the way I am like the policeman." Another silence ensued, longer this time, with a more pensive, introverted feeling to it, wandering about a bit in his own world, away from our conversation and its conclusions.

"I guess that's my idea of what a father is, a policeman. That certainly was the way my father was, as you know. But I don't really want to be that way—it feels too bad; I feel too guilty; it doesn't really feel like I recognize my kid for who she is."

I think to myself of an old supervisor who said that the capacity for remorse was the sign of a mature personality. The dream certainly succeeded in bringing to the surface for Nick his remorse over the diaper wars at home, showing him what was actually happening between him and his daughter on an unconscious emotional level. Of course, it is almost a psychological commonplace by now that the experience of parenthood actually returns us to those primitive emotional states we ourselves experienced as children, the helplessness, rage, attempts at control, and fear that Nick had used the dream to ventilate with me. My hope was that my neutrality and matter-of-factness about these primitive emotional states would stabilize his sense of himself as a capable, caring father, lessen a bit of his guilt.

Yet, my experience consistently taught me with dreams that the quick and easy interpretation was usually the one that the client could probably have gotten to without the benefit of the dream really and that so much of the meat of the deeper layers of the dream lay in some of the smaller details. Nick and I had been seeing one another for some time now, so I decided to probe a bit around the edges, so to speak, to see what else could be lifted off. With issues of authority, masculinity, and femininity so prominent in our work, I wondered if he might be able to see the dream less objectively, less as a comment about the real outer situation of fatherhood, and more subjectively, more as a picture of how his recent fatherhood was dovetailing with his inner psychological growth. With this intention in mind, I asked: "Why boys at first and then your daughter? Do you have any thoughts or associations about the two boys?"

There was a long, long silence this time. He stared out the window away from me and as the time wore on, I realized I had hit some kind of knot. From within me, the seeds of a kind of anxious dread sprouted. Having had too many experiences in which my intuition unwittingly laid its finger on something the patient was not yet ready to talk about, I realized that perhaps the dread I was feeling was shared by Nick. But having already asked the question, I felt in a bind: it was too invasive to insist, but too false to move on to something else. Thus, I resigned myself to a process of waiting— so much of therapy is waiting, waiting for the illumination, the insight, the change, the right symbol, the correct moment, the proper feeling. Patience is not simply a virtue in psychotherapy, but often the actual substance of healing. I waited, deciding to let Nick use the session as he felt he needed to. Was I, too, learning how to cede control, tolerate mess?

He shifted in the chair and sighed. More silence followed. I followed his breathing, calm and quiet, and synchronized my own breathing to match his, thinking that perhaps he might sense my attempt to be with him on an unconscious level. The anxious dread felt like drizzle inside, light, insistent, not crippling but uncomfortable. I wondered what association could have come to him. I could hear the cars pass by outside and every once in a while the mourning doves in the eaves above the inner courtyard would coo. I thought of another client for whom this sound brought back memories of her dead grandmother. I thought of my own dead grandmother, her care and concern.

Nick shifted again, his face dark. Clearing his throat, he said, "When you asked that, it suddenly hit me. I hadn't really thought about it in years. I mean even at the time I didn't really think much about it, but suddenly there it was. Way back in high school, when my old girlfriend Mona and I were together, twice she thought she was pregnant. The first time was kind of uncertain. She had missed two periods and then had an exceptionally heavy period the third month. She didn't go to the doctor at the time, so we don't know for certain, but I guess I always felt like she had been pregnant and there had been a miscarriage. The second time was the next summer, just before college and the same thing happened again, missed periods followed by a heavy third, only this time she did go to the doctor, and he confirmed it was in fact a miscarriage." Nick continued to stare out the window.

"You can probably imagine what it was like. I think at the time, like a normal teenager, I just blocked it out and thanked God for my luck. I don't know if we would have gone ahead with an abortion. Probably not. Probably would have gotten married real quick, with God knows what consequences. Lord knows I felt guilty enough to begin with for even having sex. I think at the time I felt like someone knew that we were not ready and so nothing serious happened. But you know, and I guess this is hard to believe, I still feel so responsible, almost fifteen years later. I have always imagined that those two babies would have been boys, and that in some ways my immaturity was responsible for their deaths." He looked straight at me, dry-eyed but grave. "That's what it feels like the two little boys being killed in the dream are about, and like the birth of my daughter is just part of a larger process."

"Because you have actually been a father before."

He smiled weakly, still caught up in memory, responding slowly, as if taken with inner images and old feelings. "I have, haven't I? I really haven't let myself feel what those pregnancies meant. I mean at the time it felt much more like something which was happening to Mona, something I had no control over but which I needed to handle in some indefinable way. You can just imagine what the two months of missed periods were like, sitting around and waiting to see, waiting to see. I had no doubt in my mind that I was positively, absolutely not ready to become a father or get married. I remember just thinking over and over again that I wish it wasn't true, that it couldn't be happening. But it also felt like—," he winced here and looked straight at me with his intense gaze again, "like it was something out of my hands, something I had nothing to do with."

Remembering his wincing, I asked gently, "And the feelings?"

"I guess it really hurts, as if I had been deprived of an experience of fatherhood, even if it was a fatherhood I didn't want and wasn't ready for. I also feel tremendously guilty in that irrational way I suppose people feel—like my wishing it weren't so had killed the babies, like my irresponsibility had caused their deaths."

"Do you think this has something to do with what's going on with your daughter?"

"It certainly makes me feel like I need to be extra perfect. It also tinges my happiness with a whole lot of grief and sadness that I wasn't even aware of until just now. I mean, the two boys in the dream may have been her older brothers. It also reminds me of that feeling of being kind of out of it, like I am some sort of stranger to her, like Judy is the real parent and I am this kind of stand-in. Which would make sense if I hadn't really grieved the deaths of our other babies."

"Make sense . . . ?" I wondered aloud.

He thought for a minute or two. "I guess maybe I am distancing myself not just because I don't know what it actually means to be a father but because it brings up my sadness, too, to be close to my kid without really feeling as if I have a right, like I am the secondary parent." He waggled his head from side to side, arching an eyebrow. "That kind of overstates the case. I am actually quite proud and possessive, but, maybe on a deeper level, I feel kind of inadequate, distant."

I had wondered for many months how and when I would put the question. Now felt as good a time as any. "Actually, you may not be aware of this, but you have never told me the name of your daughter. I kept wondering when it might come up, but so far it hasn't. And it feels a little bit like the distance you are talking about. You always say 'my daughter' or 'my kid' but I haven't ever heard her name."

I had refrained from asking for so long for fear of embarrassing or disconcerting Nick. It seemed so obvious and so charged. However, he smiled in a genuine way, not particularly overwhelmed by my remark. "I suppose it *is* the kind of distance we are discovering here about my being father. I can't really say why I haven't told you—I am not aware of wanting to cut you out. I feel with you like I feel sometimes with my other male friends, you know the guys I used to work with, like my fatherhood is a sort of nonessential part of me, something I haven't quite taken in yet. This dream certainly makes that clear, doesn't it?" Then he stopped and laughed out loud. "But I still haven't told you her name, have I! It's Stevie." He smiled impishly. "I like the ambiguity."

In the last chapter we looked at the effects of father absence on the psyche of a gay man, and we noted how the lack of an ongoing, embodied emotional closeness with father in childhood can leave a homosexually oriented man in many ways seriously adrift, looking for daddies rather than lovers in his partners, substituting sexuality for erotic intimacy, deprived of a deeply rooted relationship to the cycles of life and death. Some theorists would lay these effects at the door of homosexuality itself, calling them the natural consequences of perversion. However, an equally plausible explanation, as we have seen, is that patriarchal sex roles prescribe a singularly unworkable pattern of father-son relationship, a pattern that ensures alienation rather than bonding between father and son, and thus deprives the son of a relationship to the archetypal aspects of fatherhood and of masculinity itself.

If such a pattern is deleterious to gay men, it is every bit as noxious to the individuation process of heterosexual men like Nick, who find themselves in a situation that many gay men do not have to face, that is, literal fatherhood. Here we see how easily the worst aspects of the patriarchal male role become perpetuated for lack of knowing anything better or different. Having had a distant Sky Father concerned with higher things in his ministerial vocation, Nick naturally understood fatherhood as a matter of distance rather than closeness, and so we see in his dream what we saw previously in Pete's, a psychic situation concerning fatherhood that at first appears as impersonal, a newsreel of a murderous policeman shown on television, a conflict first experienced as something "out there." Likewise, Nick's take on the dream was that it was making a comment on an external situation, his relationship with his daughter, rather than seeing it as a symbol of what may have been going on for him inwardly.

This distant experience of fatherhood, symbolized so well by the initial impersonality of the dream, could perhaps have been deduced given Nick's background, and in fact had been a topic of ongoing exploration for us throughout the nine months preceding his daughter's birth. Unplanned though not unwelcome, his wife's pregnancy caught Nick by surprise and, in an ironic way, the news brought to my awareness how studiously the topic of fatherhood had been avoided throughout the first three years of our work together. When Nick announced the news that "we're pregnant," I realized in a flash that I did not have a clue as to how or what Nick might feel about this important new transformation of his life. Was a baby ardently desired or deeply feared? Did he want a boy or a girl? Would he or she be an imposition, or a joy, a natural occurrence, the fulfillment of a dream? Nick showed all the correct emotions for the occasion—elated, excited—and yet the rather complete silence on the topic beforehand, as well as the unexpectedness of his announcement, tipped me off that more was going on. His somewhat trendy use of the first person plural fashionable in Berkeley at the time, "we're pregnant," struck me thus as being out of place, a way to sidestep the more uncomfortable reality of his situation, namely, "I am going to be a father."

In our subsequent explorations, we uncovered considerably less than rosy feelings. The lack of planning around the pregnancy as well as Nick's own unconsciousness around what fatherhood meant to him were, we found, related to emotional distance. His own father's absence was certainly one powerful source for his feeling, stated on a number of occasions, that contraception, pregnancy, and child rearing were of more importance to Judy than to him, that they were her concerns foremost, affecting her body, and were thus issues over which she should have control, and only secondarily of importance to him. As in most patriarchally organized families, in Nick's family birth and child rearing were the province of Mother, not Father, and so he naturally had gotten married and become a father with this set of feelings and attitudes largely undisturbed.

In an interesting way, his wife's feminism served to reinforce Nick's lack of engagement during the pregnancy. As Judy began to own and celebrate a uniquely feminine transformation of her body and use the occasion to bond closely with other women in her professional circle as she planned for motherhood as a working lawyer, Nick's feeling of outsiderhood became more and more entrenched, and he found himself caught in the very role of the distant Sky Father that he had hoped to avoid. Thus, his experience of fatherhood right from the start was not too unlike watching a newsreel in which something important was happening to someone somewhere that in some ill-defined way affected him but only at a distance, only indirectly.

Even nine months of gestation, outwardly and inwardly, did not change this distance a great deal, though, as we continued to work with this insidious recreation of his own experience of absent fatherhood, Nick became more and more insistent that he would be taking a daily part in the life of his baby. Even the first year of child rearing after her birth, a year when, again quite typically, the breast-feeding mother remained the central figure in the baby's life, Nick still often came to sessions feeling left out and neglected.

However, as this dream shows us, it is not just the external circumstances of patriarchal socialization that continues to alienate fathers from their children, but actually the inward psychic attitudes that perpetuate the outsider status of father. The dream's initial impersonality is not just a comment on Nick's outer life situation, for example his difficulties in becoming engaged in raising and caring for his daughter, but rather a symbol of the *inner* lack of engagement that makes it difficult for him to change his outer relationship. The best signal of his continuing psychic distance from fatherhood is the fact that it took me a year to even learn the baby's name, and then only after I asked.

I think perhaps the impoverishment or cold-heartedness of this experience of fatherhood finally brought Nick to an awareness of how much of his adult experience as a man was being given away to his wife and to women in general. Certainly Judy's continuing joy and excitement over motherhood consistently confronted him with a kind of mystery into which he began to want deeper access. However, much of our previous work on his dreams of unfeeling authoritarianism and lack of emotional connection, as discussed in chapters 2 and 3, had prepared Nick to see how his diffidence and distance were covers for another kind of emotional experience.

Beneath the impersonality and lack of involvement, we found a great deal of fear. Not having had much of an emotional experience of Father in his childhood besides that of being provided for and occasionally lectured, his own fatherhood became a situation of responsibility for which he felt himself singularly ill-prepared. His fear shaped itself into a series of nettling questions that became a kind of unconscious running commentary whenever he attempted to develop various aspects of his relationship to his daughter: How am I going to support this new life? What will she require of me? Am I capable of providing it? What does Judy need from me? Do I have it to give?

We thus came to see how Nick's experience of a largely absent father had created an inner situation of radical insecurity in which the ways and means of fatherhood remained vague, unknown, and ungraspable. For this reason, the outer struggle Nick reported over his daughter's diaper habits was in fact but a reflection of how Nick, like many other men I have seen, attempted to manage the feelings of exclusion, noninvolvement, and insecurity he had in his fathering role. It is not by chance that we see the reappearance of the policeman in his dream, for control all too often becomes the cure for the painful distance and insecurity that afflicts so many contemporary fathers. Rationalized as concern for the child's growth, achievement, and success, unabashedly put forth as paternal pride, control over the child's development is often one way fathers like Nick can assert a type of relationship with their children that appears to overcome the distance and estrangement they feel.

Nick and I were lucky, in a sense. Having already broken open Nick's authority issues to disclose the frightened adolescent beneath the swaggering cop, he was quite capable of deciphering the dream for himself on the personal level, and our ongoing work on his general lack of emotional involvement—with me, with Judy, with himself, and with the pregnancy and birth—enabled him to read the dream quite clearly. Frightened and insecure about being a father, without a solid foundation of experience from his own father, Nick caught himself using the only tool he had been given to cope with this insecurity, namely, control, and caught himself wielding this instrument on the defenseless object of his inner conflict, his baby daughter.

In the often ruthless way dreams have of representing our inner reality, the beginning of Nick's dream showed him the kind of emotional violence that was occurring as he struggled with his daughter. Unable to avoid closeness with a baby whose bodily needs required near constant care and attention, unable to establish control over another human being whose spontaneity and formlessness were perhaps among her most precious qualities, Nick came to see on quite a concrete level of experience just how useless and inhuman the patriarchal model of fatherhood can actually be. Thus, quite fittingly, the dream takes place in the bathroom, that place where most childhood struggles around control and independence take place.

Of course, the literal outer situation of the "diaper wars" certainly contributed to the way in which the dream frames these issues, but a subjective interpretation of the dream, one that disclosed to Nick the more fundamental inner psychic situation, was actually the level of understanding that I felt might be able to move Nick past the distance and control characterizing his experience of fatherhood. In asking him to associate to the two boys, my thought had been to see if Nick could see himself in these victims, to see how his distant fatherhood and insistence on control were harming not just his daughter but his own inner boy, the part of him that was still childlike, still searching for another experience of being fathered and loved. As we saw with Pete, to have an insufficient, inadequate, or distant relationship to the father, who is a man's source of his masculine being, usually means having to deal with a part of himself that remains forever immature, the boy who has never been fathered and so has never grown up. Moreover, as we have also seen throughout this book, the solution to such psychic immaturity can often be for men to grasp at the outward trappings of collective masculinity, aptly symbolized in Nick's dream by the rigid, explosive, phallic gun and the violence it inflicts. My request for his association, therefore, was intended to lead him in the direction of seeing how his lack of patience with his daughter could actually have been more a lack of patience with his own helplessness, as if Nick's daughter faced him with the fatherless little boy who still lived inside him and to whom he now had to try to relate without the impersonal distance of the Sky Father or the violent, exterminatory control of the authoritarian cop.

In his association, I discovered in fact what I expected, that the two boys were indeed symbols of this inner child-self, but in the process I came across a secret fantasy even more poignant than the dream itself. In imagining that the two miscarriages were boys and that his immaturity was responsible in some cosmic way for the spontaneous abortion of these unborn children, Nick revealed by way of projection the very psychic situation that he himself had undergone. Emotionally fatherless, he was the two boys in the dream, the male child who remained unborn, dead in the womb, killed by a collective masculine attitude that does not, cannot, appreciate childhood as its own. These ghosts, quite naturally, continued to haunt him, symbols of the violence that was done to him, symbols of the violence he continues to wreak on his own childlike feelings and impulses, symbols of the violence he now had to find a way to prevent from occurring to his daughter.

The bathroom thus acquires a second layer of meaning as we examine the personal level of Nick's father wounds. As the place of elimination, the bathroom is where the rejected, the shameful, and the offensive is secreted and flushed. In a patriarchal system in which parenthood is given over to women, in which fatherhood equals Sky Fatherhood and is a matter of authoritarian control and impersonal distance, and in which the child is not given a place in the world of adult masculinity, then all the most wonderful aspects of children—their playfulness, mess, physicality, spontaneity, and lack of self-consciousness—become for men a shameful, rejected, offensive part of themselves to be hidden or eliminated. The policeman in the dream thus "wastes" the two boys, to use a bit of contemporary slang, killing them certainly, but also throwing away their potentialities, their creativity, their life.

On the personal level, therefore, we see reflected in Nick's dream the complex web of coldness, fear, insecurity, violence, and longing that pervades the inner life of contemporary men who attempt (or, unfortunately, find themselves compelled by circumstance) to father children with only marginally adequate experiences of being fathered themselves emotionally. By examining the dream not simply as a comment on his outer struggles with his daughter but as a reflection of Nick's own individuation process, we come to see that the outer struggle is but the overt manifestation of a relationship he has to his own past, to his own inner child. On this personal level of interpretation, we see demanded of Nick a kind of fatherhood that he himself never really received, an experience of fathering in which patience, attention, earthiness, and closeness must play a significant role and which must be directed, first and foremost, toward himself. Although his literal fatherhood through his relationship to his daughter provides him an opportunity to develop such qualities in the outside world, what is equally clear is that such patience, attention, earthiness, and closeness must be developed with relationship to his own inner child.

In this task, our long, slow psychotherapeutic process, in which assiduous attention to his real self requires just these qualities, can become at least one arena in which the experience of the absent father can be repaired, in a certain sense perhaps even created *ex nihilo,* out of the safety and neutrality with which we examine and explore his true inner self, who he actually is—good or bad, nice or naughty, strong or weak. I think it is tempting to imagine that psychotherapy repairs these wounds around fathering through an experience, in which the analyst supplies the patient with the ideal fathering that the patient never had. Certainly when difficult and painful feelings arise in men, for example the guilt and shame around violence, the intolerance of one's childishness, and the empty alienation of one's emotional life, it is difficult to resist the urge to reassure, to comfort, to cover over the upset with soothing words. Yet my experience has been that a less active stance allows the patient to develop the fatherly qualities he needs and to create for himself, within the experience of my nonjudgmental presence, the understanding and tolerance for who he is that constitute the most needed aspects of the father experience. In this regard, psychotherapy seems at times to resemble alchemy, a process in which a wholly new and very precious substance, like the experience of being fathered with patience, kindness, understanding, and love, comes to be created out of more

humble material, out of the confused mass of our complex, contra-
dictory feelings, out of the dregs of our pain.

   This creation of something from nothing, like gold from lead, is
not strictly speaking all that magical or mystical. Nick's experience
of fatherhood is not limited merely to what he experienced (or failed
to experience) from his own father. If we begin to understand fatherhood less in the literal way that our culture and its cult of the
family would have us see it, as a simple chain of genetic transmis-
sion in which personal qualities are handed down over generations,
but more creatively and metaphorically, as a multifaceted psychic
experience common to all men, we begin to see that the assiduous
attention devoted to unconscious reality in psychotherapy is the
means by which a more transpersonal experience of fatherhood can
be located and developed. Metaphor, in its radical sense of "carrying beyond," is the way past the personal absence and literal lapses
of our fathers. By way of that most metaphorical of all psychotherapeutic enterprises, dream work, men like Nick can begin to
find within themselves those aspects of fatherhood that they indeed
may never have experienced personally but that nevertheless exist
as archetypal aspects of their masculinity.

   The second episode of the dream thus moves Nick's process forward in an especially unlikely way. At first we think that really
nothing different is going on; Nick has merely become the hated
father figure he himself has suffered from, following the cop's orders
in a way perhaps even more horrifying than the impersonal newsreel, since it is his own daughter whom he is to attack. However, the
importance of this subtle shift must not be missed: we have moved
from an impersonal newsreel, something occurring "over there," to
something a great deal more personal, something that really concerns Nick and his own flesh and blood. Granted, at first glance it
seems disgusting, a shameful and contemptible way to behave, and
yet we must not discount what has been achieved: a move away
from the realm of collective masculinity into a more individualized,
personal sense of action and responsibility. Naturally, to become
aware of the character of his relationship to his daughter is painful,
filling him with shame and guilt, but what must not be overlooked is

that the very pain, shame, and guilt at least denotes a real relationship, a father who at last is truly present to his daughter and to himself psychically and emotionally, however painful the insight, however difficult the truth. Had Nick's own father been able to see the
effect of his impersonality and authoritarian attitudes in such a vivid
way and with an equally unflinching, honest inner eye, no doubt his
shame and guilt might have modified his behavior in a way that
would have made him more present and sensitive to Nick's need for
a fuller experience of his father. Here the birth of the Erinyes, the
agents of remorse, from the blood spilled by Kronos's overthrow of
the Sky Father comes to mind—a herald of progressive movement,
the rounding out of human experience.

Moreover, we see that Nick does not actually follow the policeman's orders. Rather than shoot, a less lethal and considerably more
natural process is substituted, one which, though shocking, is nevertheless far from fatal and in some ways may even denote something
a good deal more magical. To be sure, both the symbolism of urination as well as Nick's visceral emotional response to the dream in a
certain way does represent his compliance to the policeman's order.
Just as the shadow side of patriarchal masculinity is unleashed on
the boys in the newsreel, so too does Nick unleash his own waste
on the head of his daughter, a phallic expulsion of all that is un-
wanted and unloved. The extreme contempt of this gesture constitutes the most negative aspect of this symbol and shows how Nick
personally participates in the very hatred of the body and of the
feminine that is the ground of patriarchal Sky Fatherhood. If this
were to happen in real life, it would be perhaps one of the most
despicable examples of child abuse imaginable, and so one cannot
help but notice the violence and abusiveness that lies within this
gesture. Nick certainly did, his eyes filling with tears as he remembered her look, his voice quavering, ashamed even to admit that
such contempt could exist within him.

Nevertheless, to look at a dream merely through the lenses of our
conscious, daytime attitudes is to do the dream an injustice, for the
dream's language is always and ever symbolic. In this context, other
aspects of urination must be considered as well for the whole of the

dream's unconscious meaning to become clear. As we have already noted, Nick chooses to disobey the authoritarian masculinity, involving his daughter instead in a process that is natural, an everyday occurrence, and that also spares her life. Furthermore, given the outer context of the dream and, by his own report, his daughter's natural infantile enjoyment of her bodily functions, it is not at all clear that his daughter would actually experience his urination as the gesture of extreme contempt that our adult consciousness would understand it to be. I am inclined to think she might actually enjoy the experience, not only for the sensual aspect of its warmth and liquidity but also in the way that Nick would be sharing a natural product of his own body and his own father masculinity with her.

Further support for this more positive interpretation comes from the fact that urine has been regarded throughout the ages as a substance with magical properties, not unlike blood or spit, to be used in potions and alchemical operations as an especially powerful agent. Von Franz, in her lectures on alchemy, for instance, explores at great length the uses to which urine, particularly the urine of an uncorrupted boy, was put in ancient magic and medieval alchemy. In part, such belief derives from the innocent childishness of uncontrolled urination and is based on the closeness that children seem to have to the contents of the unconscious. In her explication of an alchemical image taken from the seventeenth century *Codex Latinus,* von Franz writes, "The alchemical image of the 'pissing mannikin' and the use of 'the urine of an uncorrupted boy' as a solvent, relate to the psychological reality that the unconscious is more responsive to the naive and spontaneous attitudes associated with childhood."[1] If we can abandon our rational, adult prejudices for a moment and follow up on this more imaginative view of urine, we see in Nick's urination a movement toward becoming more childlike, abandoning the rigid adult male Sky Father role and attempting to enter into a more naive and spontaneous relationship with his daughter and with his own propensity for receptivity and playfulness.

Urine as a potent magical substance must also be seen, for obvious reasons, in close association with that other magical substance par excellence, semen, male potency itself, the seed and power of life; and so again the dream symbolism returns us to Nick's central concern, the matter of fatherhood. By bathing her in the potent water of his body, Nick shares his manhood with his daughter, not through a distant, destructive phallic gun, but with a more positive intent, as one way to connect to her as a man and as her father. Having in a certain sense created her through his phallic capacities, Nick's attempt to integrate the psychic reality of his fatherhood leads him to share his phallos with his daughter again, only this time with greater consciousness and with a more childlike inner attitude.

The incestuous nature of this urination makes a symbolic attitude toward the dream especially important. While a Freudian might see in this urination a literal, sexual impulse in Nick toward his daughter, a Jungian perspective would perceive in this father-daughter incest the more fundamental impulse that so often undergirds the literal incestuous act and that makes it such a transgression of a child's autonomy, namely the father's impulse toward enjoying an intimate relationship with a part of his self. Thus, the urination represents Nick's attempt to shower his daughter with himself, to share himself with her fully in a way that necessarily includes his worst aspects but that will not necessarily kill her or damage her permanently, in order to feel at one with her and thus with his fatherhood. The dream incest is thus a *symbol* of how Nick is attempting to actually *move away* from a lethal, collective fatherhood into a more personally present, integrated, individual relationship with his daughter and with his own inner child.

One aspect of this process, as we have seen throughout Nick's psychotherapeutic journey, entails bringing the waste products of his emotional life, the despised, rejected, and shameful parts, into a living, working relationship with the rest of his consciousness. The urination, therefore, can be given a double-edged meaning, seen either negatively, as Nick's dumping his emotional garbage on the head of his daughter, or more positively, as his joining in with his daughter's childish, joyful spontaneity concerning her body—a gesture of sharing, rather than a symbol of hostility. More likely, as any parent knows, the experience of fatherhood is actually both at the

same time, since it is impossible really to spare our children from
having to experience at least some of our own unresolved emotional
waste, an experience that need not be permanently damaging to the
child if handled with honesty, consciousness, and lack of aggres-
sion. For Nick, the urination in the dream represents a kind of midway point, a compromise, neither sparing his daughter his less sa-
vory side nor unleashing it upon her with malevolent glee.

Indeed, we see in the dream that the contemptible side of this
act succeeds in evoking from Nick the very remorse that stimulates
his fatherly instincts. The shamefulness of his behavior ironically
shows him the way to actually love and care for his child. The corollary to my supervisor's observation that remorse is the hallmark of
maturity is that guilt is the beginning of responsibility. Nick's urination is followed by a realization of the effect of such a spilling of self,
and leads us into the final symbol of this interesting dream, the
washing in the tub.

In associating urine with other secretions of the body supposedly
endowed with magic power, we must not overlook perhaps the
most basic association, urine's association with water, the foundation of life itself. To follow alchemical symbolism a little further, we
turn again to von Franz, who writes:

> Water, in general, including urine, carries the projection of knowl-
> edge. In medieval Church symbolism they spoke of the *aqua doc-
> trinae,* and in the Swiss dialect if somebody comes out with a lot of
> nonsense, just a lot of words, we say he is urinating. Psychogenic
> kidney troubles very often have to do with people being filled up
> with such bad water, for they have not the right attitude, or the
> right connection with knowledge; they just blather a lot of undi-
> gested knowledge and that is like urinating. So usually it can be said
> that water has to do with knowledge extracted from the unconscious
> which can either be misused or used positively. In alchemy water
> was either the great healing factor, or poisonous and destructive.[2]

In following this train of imagery, the double-edged quality of
Nick's symbolic urination is reinforced. Filled with father knowledge but of the wrong sort, his urination represents the actual psychic situation quite well. He relieves himself of his stored patriar-

chal refuse in a way that his daughter cannot avoid. And yet the symbolic equivalence of urine with water leads us in a more positive direction as well, into the realm of water as the giver and sustainer of life. Nick's urination and the hard-won consciousness it brings leads him to a higher level of relationship with his daughter and with his own fatherhood as well.

Washing Stevie in the tub at first seems so prosaic, so matter-of-fact. If we look at the dream with the rational eye we have been taught to develop in this age of Logos consciousness, seeing the dream as a literal occurrence, then naturally we would expect any ordinary caring father to take steps to clean off his daughter. There is nothing especially astounding or enlightening here—parents do it every day. But again, to understand a dream requires the more imaginative inner eye, the continued awareness that the dream is not literal reality but a tissue made up of symbol connected to symbol connected to symbol.

In moving from urine, the water of Nick's own body, to a tub of clean, fresh water, we sense a step in the direction of another kind of sharing between father and daughter, to relationship less fraught with ambivalence, anger, and contempt. Nick bathes Stevie here, not in the stored up, destructive, corrosive water of his own rejected fatherly self, but in a new container with water drawn from another, less conflicted source than his own personal fatherhood. To use von Franz's amplification, we might say that Nick has located, through his guilt and responsibility, a higher knowledge, a purer water, with which to bathe his daughter. In bringing to awareness the conflictual relationship he has with Stevie and with childhood in general, both through his outer struggles and the symbolic ambivalence summed up so perfectly in the image of urination, Nick has been spurred to enact a less destructive and childish image of father and embody for his daughter a more mature and caring sort of fatherhood.

In taking the sponge and squeezing it over Stevie's head, allowing the water to run down her body and renew her spirit, Nick in his dream enacts a ritual which, alongside the Eucharist, remains at the center of Christian symbolism. Of course, it is interesting to notice how an explication of the archetypal aspects of fatherhood brings us back again to Christianity for symbolic amplification, but in some ways, this return to Christianity makes sense, for few religions have been so single-mindedly patriarchal and so filled with the imagery of father and fatherhood.

Among all the Christian sacraments, baptism retains a central and abiding place, recognized in some form by all Christian denominations, though the means and meaning of the rite may differ from sect to sect. On its most basic level, baptism (from the Greek *baptein*, to dip) is the Christian rite of initiation into community. For this reason the symbolism of death and rebirth is especially prominent, present in nearly all initiation rites throughout the world but especially central to the Christian myth with its dying and rising god. In the early days of the Christian church, this initiatory aspect was marked, since baptism occurred exclusively with adult converts to Christianity in an annual ceremony that took place during an Easter vigil ceremony. After a lengthy period of instruction and teaching, the initiates, called catechumens, were kept secluded until nightfall, dressed in white robes; they were then brought out into the community where, in a ceremony often held by torchlight in the darkness, they were immersed bodily into a font of water and then raised back into life as new members in the Christian community. In this way, the initiates' experience paralleled Christ's own experience of life, death, and rebirth, emerging from the dark womb of the earth to a new life filled with the Holy Spirit of God the Father. As Paul writes in his letter to the Colossians, "You were buried with him in baptism, in which you were also raised with him through faith in the working of God, who raised him from the dead."[3] Thus, the material aspect of the Christian baptismal rite, like so many other *rites de passage,* can be seen as a symbolic rebirth, with the tub and the water representing the womb of a new second birth, the emergence of a new person into a higher spiritual state and into a community of believers who, as we have already seen in our discussion concerning the Eucharist, are considered to be the actual Body of Christ on earth.

Although Paul's later interpretation of the rite as a parallel to

Christ's death and resurrection is largely responsible for this stratum of baptismal symbolism within Christianity, baptism itself did not originate with Christianity; indeed, all four accounts of Jesus' life in the New Testament report Jesus himself being baptized in the Jordan River in a Jewish ritual presided over by John the Baptist. Thus, a more basic layer of baptismal symbolism emerges, one connected to Jewish ritual cleansing and thus to repentance and forgiveness. Indeed, the account of Jesus' life as told by Mark begins with his baptism by John, who is seen here as the classic "wild man," the social outsider bringing wisdom and enlightenment.

> John the baptizer appeared in the wilderness, preaching a baptism of repentance or the forgiveness of sins. And there went out to him all the country of Judea, and all the people of Jerusalem; and they were baptized by him in the river Jordan, confessing their sins. Now John was clothed with camel's hair and had a leather girdle around his waist, and ate locusts and wild honey. And he preached saying, "After me comes he who is mightier than I, the thong of whose sandals I am not worthy to stoop down and untie. I have baptized you with water; but he will baptize you with the Holy Spirit."
>
> In those days Jesus came from Nazareth of Galilee and was baptized by John in the Jordan. And when he came up out of the water, immediately he saw the heavens opened and the Spirit descending upon him like a dove; and a voice came from heaven, "Thou art my beloved Son, with thee I am well pleased."[4]

As one of four differing accounts of Jesus' life all written some years after the events in question, Mark's account should be considered less an example of historical reportage and more as a story that reflects an early Christian understanding of who Jesus was and what his purpose had been. In Mark's story of Jesus' baptism, we see woven together the earlier layer of symbolism, derived from a Jewish understanding of cleanliness, forgiveness, and devotion to God, and the newer Christian understanding of the rite. By contrast, John's considerably more interpretive and mystical account of Christ's life portrays Jesus weaving these two aspects of baptism together himself, combining both initiation and ritual purification, in his conversation with Nicodemus.

Now there was a man of the Pharisees, named Nicodemus, a ruler of the Jews. This man came to Jesus by night and said to him, "Rabbi, we know that you are a teacher come from God; for no one can do these signs that you do, unless God is with him." Jesus answered him, "Truly, truly I say to you, unless one is born anew, he cannot see the kingdom of God." Nicodemus said to him, "How can a man be born when he is old? Can he enter a second time into his mother's womb and be born?" Jesus answered, "Truly, truly, I say to you, unless one is born of water and the Spirit, he cannot enter the kingdom of God. That which is born of the flesh is flesh, and that which is born of the Spirit is spirit."[5]

One can see how this combination of ritual purification from the Jewish tradition and initiatory symbolism from the newer Christian theology would lead to a view of baptism that would accommodate the essentially historical, that is, nontheological development of infant baptism. From its earliest use as a rite of conversion and initiation (echoes of which can be seen in the Jewish conversion ritual, *mikvah,* with its parallel immersion symbolism), baptism soon became less used for adult converts, who were far fewer as Christianity became established and succeeding generations already considered themselves Christian, and turned instead into a ritual used primarily with infants as a sign of their initiation into the Christian community through their parents' religious faith. The purification symbolism of baptism survives in an understanding, prominent in Roman Catholic theology thanks to Augustine, that the sacrament is effective in removing an infant from the state of original sin, that is, the condition of spiritual imperfection into which all humanity is born, and inaugurating the infant's soul instead into a state of grace, that is, into a state of acknowledged relationship to God through membership in the Christian church established by Jesus' death and resurrection.

The subsequent development of infant baptism strays from the historical roots of Christian practice and constitutes an errancy that numerous Protestant denominations have sought to rectify. Nevertheless, from a vantage point outside of doctrinal concerns, we notice that the essential elements of baptism as both purification

and initiation remain even today, with subsequent customs continuing to make the distinction Jesus is reported to have made with
Nicodemus, differentiating between mere biological parenthood and
a more spiritual acknowledgement of our relationship to a higher
reality. For instance, the institution of baptismal sponsors for the
still unconscious infant results in a custom that further reinforces
the initiatory level of baptismal symbolism. To have "godparents"
as a Christian makes clear how baptism is a rite in which literal,
biological parenthood is subordinated, transformed, and brought
into relationship with a higher form of parenthood, in which Christians are seen as children of God the Father through his Son Jesus
Christ. Likewise, the confluence of the baptismal ritual with the for-
mal naming of the child within a community, as in the "christening"
ceremony of English tradition, points to how a Christian's very
existence as an individual, denoted by his or her name, depends not
on biological parentage but rather on initiation into the Christian
church, understood theologically as the living body of Christ on
earth. Baptism in this way moves the individual out of the realm of
the personal and into a higher reality, into an acknowledgement of
his or her relationship to the ultimate origin of existence, a transpersonal source of life.

One does not necessarily need to subscribe to the metaphysical
truth of a Christian understanding of reality in order to appreciate
how this symbolism, and especially the complex web of meaning
surrounding the ritual of baptism, has a particular kind of power
when men like Nick struggle to find a relationship to a fatherhood
they have never known. His baptism of his daughter in the dream,
first out of the waters of his own body and then, quite appropriately,
using an ancient ritual of initiation and purification, points to how in
his psyche there exists the impulse to break the cycle of a literal and
limited experience of fatherhood in order to inaugurate his daughter
and, through her, himself as a father into a wider community of men
based on a higher, more spiritual understanding of what fatherhood
could be. Through his guilt and repentance, Nick comes to recognize his daughter in her own individuality, and so the baptism is the
symbol of a momentous occasion and the seal of this newer under-

standing of fatherhood. It stands in Nick's soul as the beginning of a love for her that goes beyond his own personal fatherhood and is based instead on a relationship to her that acknowledges her divinity as well as his own.

In this baptism, therefore, we see the abusive, fascistic, patriarchal father authority of the first part of the dream initiated into another way of being. In a word, Nick's consciousness leads him to love and to all that love entails—the ability to recognize, value, and care for another person, the capacity to seek another's happiness before one's own, and the continuing awareness that we all exist in relationship to something greater than ourselves that is the source of our being, from which our own parenthood is ultimately derived and to which it will ultimately return.

What is especially powerful in this dream is to see Nick's awareness of his own patriarchal violence and disrespect leading to a repentance that in turn leads him to integrate and enact the very role his father played in his life, that of minister or priest. Father absence in this way is healed by breaking out of a superficial identification with external attributes and by coming to terms with the inward sacredness of a fatherhood beyond mere reproduction. The result of such integration of a higher form of fatherhood is well represented by Stevie's reaction to Nick's baptism in the dream: joy and laughter, a sense of cleanliness, wholeness, completion, and oneness, despite the hurt, unconsciousness, and other limits of her father's human existence.

Nick's dream and his experience of fatherhood returns us, therefore, to the same theme we discerned in Pete's dream and his experience of fatherhood: the distinction between fatherhood as a biological fact and fatherhood as a mode of physical and spiritual immortality. Clearly, as far as the psychological development of contemporary men is concerned, this distinction is of vital importance, for as our patriarchal system of male domination slowly begins to give way to a more balanced relationship between masculinity and femininity, between man and woman, men like Nick and Pete quite accurately sense that mere literal fatherhood is sufficient neither for providing individual men's psychological and spiritual fulfillment, nor for the development of the new conceptions of masculinity, femininity, and family that will be required as we enter a newer age.

In the period following this dream, which became the final phase of my work with Nick, many of the seeds we had planted throughout our relationship gradually came to fruition. In coming to know his inner authoritarianism and in beginning to learn a less controlled, rigid, and performance-oriented way of being, it increasingly became clear to Nick that his work as a tile setter, however financially lucrative, would never really give him the sense of contentment he sought from his work. As Stevie matured and his wife's career in law became more and more secure, Nick used these circumstances to make a radical change, resigning from the contracting firm to pursue a much earlier dream that his parents had long discouraged, a career in industrial design.

Of course, before the switch was actually accomplished, there was considerable waffling and insecurity, in part because it would entail his depending on Judy's income during the years of training, and in part because returning to studenthood would mean becoming the primary parent in the family. Negative parental voices rose within him, discouraging him from seeking something better, introducing doubt as to his competency, belittling him for his abdication of his role as provider and man of the family to become a dependent and a student. In favor of the plan, of course, was his considerable experience in construction work, Judy's own encouragement of his greater participation in parenting, and the growing closeness he began to feel toward his daughter as his insecurities and feelings of distance calmed down with Stevie's ever-increasing responsiveness toward him. Most powerful, however, was the call to a more creative, open-ended, personally fulfilling use of his many talents and interests that a career in design might actually afford him.

Clients may perhaps intuit how rewarding it is for a therapist to be a party to such sweeping changes in people's lives, and in Nick's case the changes he made were especially gratifying to assist. From a fairly depressed, inhibited, and somewhat callow young adult,

Nick slowly became someone with a constant inner sense of self out of which flowed an ability to give and receive in relationship to his wife and his daughter, as well as a talent for creating and implementing industrial designs that not only made functional sense but had an aesthetic value, making them pleasurable and inviting. Though I would never say that our psychotherapy work alone was responsible for such changes, what is certainly true is that our work provided the kind of open space, direction, and focus to Nick's process of individuation that he needed to use his potentialities to their fullest.

Like Pete, Nick's individuation required straying from the path laid out for him by patriarchal sex roles and attitudes and required his living a life that many people would probably term "unconventional"—supported by his wife, primary parent to his daughter, and involved in a career centered on creative and aesthetic concerns, rather than prestige, achievement, or money. For this reason, I wonder if Nick could have tolerated such a transformation of himself without the ongoing support that my nonjudgmental presence and our continued mutual commitment to his growth provided through his psychotherapy. His individuation process certainly required of me everything it required of him—an ability to tolerate disruption and mess, a capacity for reflection and empathy, an ability to hold hope in the face of opposition and negativity, and a dogged commitment to being able to imagine and "re-vision" all the old definitions until we discovered just what kind of path actually fit. And at times, infected myself with hopelessness and fatigue and anger, it was Nick's patience, understanding, tolerance, and imagination with his own inner figures that rekindled in me a belief in the capacity of men to transform their lives.

Because much of our discussion has taken place with attention to the archetypal aspects of men's experience, and thus has waxed at times high-flown and abstract, we must remember that the point of psychotherapy is not simply increased intellectual understanding but, at least in my view, a true change of life. We have noted how such a change of life occurred for Pete in the course of our work, with our inner explorations beginning and supporting a transformation that led him to find a new self and a fuller sense of satisfaction. A similar process eventually occurred for Nick, though the process was slower and more fraught with difficulty.

Just as the psychotherapeutic process is centered on transformation, a change of life, so too have this book and its explorations been centered on the transformation occurring for contemporary men as they deepen their awareness of themselves. We have seen guns and bullets transformed first into phalluses and urine and then into sponge and water, tools of a softer, more natural, more responsive pattern of fatherhood. We have seen boxers who live by the power of their fists come to their sons with a milder but no less transformative force, feeding and anointing their sons as they hold them close to their own maleness, to their own bodies.

We have seen images of union begin to occur for contemporary men. Women have sprung from the shackles of an oppressive set of projections and are freed to enter into intimate relationship with men, who must find their own femininity inside them if they are to be successful at all in sharing the fullness of their lives with the women they love. Men themselves have begun to find a pathway to union with their own masculinity, reclaiming for their maleness an erotic tenderness, a physical interaction, a love for other men that is the source of masculine wholeness.

We have seen images of a social order in need of transformation—brutality exposed as immaturity, and arrogance and one-sidedness opposed through rebellion, courage, and plain-speaking—while images of new life have emerged, small and humble like ants and spiders, from the rubble of centuries-old oppression. At times this new inner life for men seems miraculous, about as miraculous as the repopulation of Oenopia or the return of Persephone, and yet continued attention to the dreams of contemporary men within the context of psychotherapy seems to give us hope. Men need not be the opponents of this shift away from a patriarchal social order, but, as Nick's and Pete's dreams demonstrate, men may in fact be among the primary beneficiaries of the greater psychological and social freedom that comes from a rejection of one-sidedness and a determined search for inner and outer wholeness.

In the course of writing this book, I took a break one day at my kitchen table and, leafing through piles of books distractedly while sipping a cup of coffee, I came across a poem by Jalal-al-Din Rumi, medieval Persian poet and Sufi mystic, which says in thirteen lines what this entire book on men's dreams and men's healing through the psychotherapy relationship has been about. Thus, I leave the last word to a poet whose love for men and spiritual wisdom has enlightened many throughout the Western world. Rumi writes:

> I tried to think of some way
> to let my face become his.
>
> "Could I whisper in your ear
> a dream I've had? You're the only one
> I've told this to."
>
> He tilts his head, laughing,
> as if, "I know the trick you're hatching,
> but go ahead."
>
> I am an image he stitches with gold thread
> on a tapestry, the least figure,
> a playful addition.
>
> But nothing he works on is dull.
> I am part of the beauty.[6]

Notes

In the notes, CW refers to *The Collected Works of C. G. Jung,* 20 vols. (Princeton: Princeton University Press, 1967–1978).

CHAPTER 1. A DREAM OF ANTS AND SPIDERS: MEN AND FEELINGS

1. The academically minded reader may wish to read James Hillman's comprehensive excursus on insects as psychic symbols entitled "Going Bugs" (included in *Spring,* 1988, pp. 40–72) in which Hillman marshalls historical sources to document the pervasive execration of insects through the ages and the psychic effects insects as symbols have on us through our dreams and fantasies.

2. Robert Graves, *The Greek Myths,* vol. 1 (London: Penguin Books, 1955), pp. 212–216; Karl Kerenyi, *The Gods of the Greeks* (1951; reprint, New York: Thames and Hudson, 1979), p. 210.

3. For a detailed, arresting, and politically progressive account of this religious-political conflict in Greek civilization, see Arthur Evans, *The God of Ecstasy: Sex Roles and the Madness of Dionysos* (New York: St. Martin's Press, 1988). From a more traditional and psychological angle, Erich Neumann's magnum opus, *The Origins and History of Consciousness* (Princeton: Princeton University Press, 1954), must also be consulted for the relationship between previous matriarchal religions and the emergence of modern patriarchal modes of thought.

4. Jung, CW 13, p. 41; CW 14, p. 179.

5. Graves, *Greek Myths,* p. 215–216.

6. Graves, *Greek Myths,* p. 213.

7. Erich Neumann, *The Great Mother: An Analysis of the Archetype* (Princeton: Princeton University Press, 1955), especially p. 233.

8. Carol Gilligan, *In a Different Voice* (Cambridge, Mass.: Harvard University Press, 1982), p. 57.

CHAPTER 2. THE DREAM OF THE ADOLESCENT COP: MEN AND AUTHORITY

1. For varying views on the definition and importance of the initial dream, the reader may wish to consult Marie-Louise von Franz's discussion in *On Dreams and Death: A Jungian Interpretation* (Boston: Shambhala, 1987), especially pp. 46–48. Both Mary Ann Mattoon in *Understanding Dreams* (Dallas: Spring Publications, 1984), pp. 153–155, and James Hall in "The Use of Dreams and Dream Interpretation in Analysis," in *Jungian Analysis*, ed. Murray Stein (Boston: Shambhala, 1984), p. 135, devote attention to the initial dream in analysis. Hans Dieckmann, a senior Jungian analyst in Berlin, summarizes his work on the topic for an English-speaking audience in "Some Aspects of the Development of Authority," in *The Father: Contemporary Jungian Perspectives,* ed. Andrew Samuels (New York: New York University Press, 1986), pp. 219–227. This article is especially relevant to the topic we will be examining here, namely, that of authority and its psychological roots for men.

2. My translation.

3. Arnold Van Gennep's classic, *The Rites of Passage* (Chicago: University of Chicago Press, 1960), along with Victor Turner's equally classic *The Ritual Process: Structure and Anti-Structure* (Chicago: Aldine, 1969), should both be consulted as sources on initiation. For Jung on the subject, see CW 7. *Betwixt and Between: Patterns of Masculine and Feminine Initiation,* ed. Louise Carus Mahdi, Steven Foster, and Meredith Little (La Salle, Ill.: Open Court, 1987) provides a substantial look at current Jungian thought on the topic, as does Italian analyst Luigi Zoja's interpretation of one social phenomenon, drug addiction, from this position on initiation, in *Drugs, Addiction and Initiation: The Modern Search for Ritual* (Boston: Sigo Press, 1989).

4. CW 7, p. 112.

5. Arthur and Libby Colman, *The Father: Mythology and Changing Roles* (Chicago: Chiron Publications, 1988).

6. See Robert H. Hopcke, *Jung, Jungians, and Homosexuality* (Boston: Shambhala, 1989), especially pp. 156–172.

7. For Jung's own definitions and discussion of the persona, see CW 6, pp. 463–470, and CW 7, pp. 123–241 and pp. 269–304.

8. This version of the myth is based on Kerenyi's retelling (Kerenyi, *Gods of the Greeks,* pp. 20–25).

9. Graves, *Greek Myths,* p. 39.

10. A classic paper on this topic by British analyst John Layard, "Homoeroticism in Primitive Societies as a Function of the Self," *Journal of Analytical Psychology,* July 1959, is interesting in many ways but also flawed and biased. My discussion and critique of Layard's contribution is in Hopcke, *Jung, Jungians, and Homosexuality,* pp. 85–95.

11. James Hillman, "Senex and Puer," in *Puer Papers* (Dallas: Spring Publications, 1979).

12. Mario Jacoby, lecture entitled "Authority and Revolt," given at the Notre Dame Conference, April 1974. Transcribed from audio recording.

CHAPTER 3. FROM IRON LUNG TO *MÉNAGE À TROIS:* HETEROSEXUAL MEN, FEMININITY, AND THE ANIMA

1. CW 6, p. 470.

2. CW 6, p. 463.

3. James Hillman again is one writer who has spent a great part of his career struggling with—and elucidating—the connections among "psyche," "soul," and "anima." His own complex excursion into this thicket of Jungian thought around the anima, entitled *Anima: An Anatomy of a Personified Notion* (Dallas: Spring Publications, 1985), has a section especially devoted to the connections among "psyche," "soul," and "anima" in Jung's thought and the difficulties in translating Jung's meaning from German into English.

4. CW 6, pp. 470–471.

5. CW 7, pp. 188–190.

6. At times attributed by Jung to biology: "The smaller number of feminine genes seems to form a feminine character, which usually remains unconscious because of its subordinate position" (CW 9, Part I, p. 28).

7. CW 9, Part II, pp. 13–14.

8. CW 9, Part I, p. 70.

9. CW 9, Part II, p. 14.

10. CW 9, Part II, p. 13.

11. This problem is endemic to the phenomenological approach used by Jung and Jungians in discerning the character of archetypal reality: if an archetype is given form through the sum total of cultural images of a particular dominant of psychic life, then all the biases, blindspots, stereotypes, and prejudices of the various cultures surveyed inhere in the archetypal image as well. For this reason, a phenomenological approach needs to be supplemented by a sophisticated sociopolitical analysis of those very subjective biases and stereotypes within a culture that can lead to such falsification and distortion. This problem is especially acute when the archetypal reality under examination is something as controverted and uncertain as the nature of masculinity or femininity. Happily, a number of contemporary writers, mostly women, have put their hand to the task of providing insight concerning sexism within Jungian psychology; among them are Demaris Wehr, Estella Lauter, and Christine Downing, to name just a few.

12. Graves, *Greek Myths*, p. 93.

13. Jung, CW 6, p. 467.

14. Again, James Hillman's treatment of this mediatory aspect of the anima is probably the most evocative and useful currently in print (*Anima*, pp. 128–145).

15. Jung, *Memories, Dreams, Reflections* (New York: Vintage Books, 1965), p. 187.

16. Jung, *Memories*, p. 191.

CHAPTER 4. DREAMS OF THE DARK YOUNG MAN:
GAY MEN, MASCULINITY, AND THE MALE ANIMA

1. See Hopcke, *Jung, Jungians, and Homosexuality*.

2. Jung, CW 9, Part I, pp. 151–181.

3. The best recent addition to the literature on this topic is Richard A. Isay, *Being Homosexual: Gay Men and Their Development* (New York: Farrar, Straus, Giroux, 1989), along with the articles contained in John C. Gonsiorek, ed., *A Guide to Psychotherapy with Gay and Lesbian Clients* (New York: Harrington Park Press, 1985). The chapter on gay men and the feminine from my own book, *Jung, Jungians, and Homosexuality*, looks at similar issues by way of *The Wizard of Oz* as a myth of gay male individuation.

4. Mitchell Walker, "The Double: An Archetypal Configuration," *Spring*, 1976, p. 165.

5. Walker, "The Double," p. 173.

6. In *The Myths and Mysteries of Same-Sex Love* (New York: Continuum, 1989), Christine Downing provides an excellent critique of the process by which gay and lesbian imagery is suppressed within psychology and literature and reconstitutes some of the same-sex symbolism from Greek mythology for a fuller view of homosexuality from an archetypal perspective.

7. Hillman, *Anima,* p. 65.

8. cw 9, Part I, pp. 69–70.

9. This latter point is the fundamental critique launched by Eugene Monick in *Phallos: Sacred Image of the Masculine,* in which he argues that the patriarchal consignment of the unconscious, the body, and sexuality (all aspects of the anima, note) to femininity and to women serves to alienate men from the fullness of the masculine, from the multifaceted nature of their own phallos.

10. Four sources from the Jungian literature should make this point clear: Erich Neumann, *Amor and Psyche* (Princeton: Princeton University Press, 1956); James Hillman, *The Myth of Analysis* (San Francisco: Harper & Row, 1983); Robert Johnson, *She: Understanding Feminine Psychology* (San Francisco: Harper & Row, 1986); and finally, Marie-Louise von Franz, *A Psychological Interpretation of the Golden Ass of Apuleius* (New York: Spring Publications, 1970).

11. Neumann, *Amor and Psyche,* p. 104.

12. "*Symposium,*" in *Great Dialogues of Plato,* ed. Eric H. Warmington and Philip G. Rouse, trans. W. H. D. Rouse (New York: The New American Library, 1956), p. 99.

13. Michael Grant and John Hazel, *Gods and Mortals in Classical Mythology* (Springfield, Mass.: G & C Merriam Company, 1973).

14. Pierre Grimal, under "Eros" in *The Dictionary of Classical Mythology* (Oxford: Basil Blackwell Publisher, Ltd., 1986) notes some of these genealogies for Eros: son of Eilithyia or Iris, of Hermes and Artemis, or of Hermes and Aphrodite, with Anteros said to be son of Ares and Aphrodite born of Zeus and Dione.

15. See Hopcke, *Jung, Jungians, and Homosexuality,* pp. 57–58, 97–102.

Chapter 5. The Dream of the Italian Father: Fatherhood as Embodiment and Redemption

1. cw 7, p. 178.

2. In the Jungian literature, two recent books that explore fatherhood, including the psychological effect of the absent father, are *The Father:*

Mythology and Changing Roles by Arthur and Libby Colman and *The Father: Contemporary Jungian Perspectives,* edited by Andrew Samuels (both mentioned above). An excellent bibliography of the contemporary literature on fatherhood from diverse theoretical perspectives can be found in Michael E. Lamb, ed., *The Role of the Father in Child Development,* 2nd ed. (New York: John Wiley & Sons, 1981), pp. 1–70.

3. Samuel Osherson, *Finding Our Fathers: The Unfinished Business of Manhood* (New York: Free Press, 1986).

4. CW 11, p. 303.

5. Bettenson, Henry, ed., *Documents of the Christian Church* (London: Oxford University Press, 1963), p. 26. All quotations from the Nicene Creed are taken from Bettenson's translation.

6. CW 11, p. 152.

7. CW 11, pp. 253–254.

8. This interesting and completely arbitrary distinction between "religion" and "spirituality" seems especially prominent in the gay community, with its understandably difficult relationship to the institutional Christian church's tradition of homophobia. As part of the research team for a study run by Paul Schwartz of the Graduate Theological Union in Berkeley that interviewed gay men with AIDS on religious or spiritual transformation subsequent to their diagnosis, and in my own study of gay male religious experience for my master's degree, I repeatedly found gay men phobic around the word "religion," and yet completely at ease in discussing their inner experiences of the divine as long as these were described as "spiritual." Given the semantic equivalence of these terms, this distinction seems less founded in what these terms have actually meant historically and theologically and seems more a political statement about one's relationship to the institutional church. To my mind, however, the distinction may tend to reinforce gay men's alienation and lack of community around religious issues, since "spirituality" emphasizes the private experience of the divine, in line with the individualistic trend of Western culture, while "religion" with its etymological origin in the Latin verb "to bind together" emphasizes the common experience of the divine shared by a group of people who thus become one with each other through such experience. I think the political point is better made through specifying one's difficulties with the "institutional church," while retaining the word "religion" as a valid and appropriate designation for experiences of the divine that are most certainly shared by others and that serve to bind gay men together around ultimate concerns.

CHAPTER 6. THE DREAM OF A DAUGHTER'S BAPTISM: FATHERHOOD AS INITIATION AND RELATIONSHIP

1. Marie-Louise von Franz, *Alchemy: An Introduction to the Symbolism and the Psychology* (Toronto: Inner City Books, 1980), p. 49.
2. Von Franz, *Alchemy*, pp. 100–101.
3. Colossians 3:12. (All Biblical quotations are from *The New Oxford Annotated Bible: Revised Standard Version* [New York: Oxford University Press, 1973]).
4. Mark 1:4–11.
5. John 3:1–6.
6. Rumi, *These Branching Moments: Forty Odes by Rumi*. Trans. John Moyne and Coleman Barks (Providence, R.I.: Copper Beech Press, 1988), p. 40.

Bibliography

Boswell, John. *Christianity, Social Tolerance and Homosexuality: Gay People in Western Europe from the Beginning of the Christian Era to the Fourteenth Century.* Chicago: University of Chicago Press, 1980.

Centola, Steven R. "Individuation in E. M. Forster's *Maurice.*" *Journal of Analytical Psychology,* vol. 26, 1981, pp. 49–63.

Colman, Arthur, and Libby Colman. *The Father: Mythology and Changing Roles.* Chicago: Chiron Publications, 1988.

Dieckmann, Hans. "Some aspects of the development of authority." In *The Father: Contemporary Jungian Perspectives,* edited by Andrew Samuels. New York: New York University Press, 1986.

Downing, Christine. *The Myths and Mysteries of Same-Sex Love.* New York: Continuum, 1989.

Edinger, Edward F. *Ego and Archetype: Individuation and the Religious Function of the Psyche.* Baltimore: Penguin Books, 1973.

———. *The Bible and the Psyche: Individuation in the Old Testament.* Toronto: Inner City Books, 1986.

Eliade, Mircea. *Myths, Dreams and Mysteries: The Encounter Between Contemporary Faiths and Archaic Realities.* Translated by Philip Mairet. New York: Harper & Row, 1960.

———. *Shamanism.* Princeton: Princeton University Press, 1964.

Evans, Arthur. *The God of Ecstasy: Sex Roles and the Madness of Dionysos.* New York: St. Martin's Press, 1988.

Franz, Marie-Louise von. *A Psychological Interpretation of the Golden Ass of Apuleius.* New York: Spring Publications, 1970.

———. *Alchemy: An Introduction to the Symbolism and the Psychology.* Toronto: Inner City Books, 1980.

———. *On Dreams and Death: A Jungian Interpretation.* Boston: Shambhala Publications, 1987.

Gilligan, Carol. *In a Different Voice: Psychological Theory and Women's Development.* Cambridge: Harvard University Press, 1982.

Gonsiorek, John C., ed. *A Guide to Psychotherapy with Gay and Lesbian Clients.* New York: Harrington Park Press, 1985.

Grant, Michael and John Hazel, *Gods and Mortals in Classical Mythology.* Springfield, Mass.: G & C Merriam, 1973.

Graves, Robert. *The Greek Myths,* vols. 1 and 2. London: Penguin Books, 1955.

Grimal, Pierre. *The Dictionary of Classical Mythology.* Oxford: Basil Blackwell, 1986.

Hall, James. "The Use of Dreams and Dream Interpretation in Analysis." In *Jungian Analysis,* edited by Murray Stein. Boston: Shambhala Publications, 1984.

———. *Jungian Dream Interpretation: A Handbook of Theory and Practice.* Toronto: Inner City Books, 1983.

Harding, M. Esther. *The Parental Image: Its Injury and Reconstruction.* New York: G. P. Putnam's Sons, 1965.

Hillman, James. "An Essay on Pan." In *Pan and the Nightmare,* edited by James Hillman. Dallas: Spring Publications, 1972.

———. *The Dream and the Underworld.* San Francisco: Harper & Row, 1979.

———. "Senex and Puer." In *Puer Papers,* edited by James Hillman. Dallas: Spring Publications, 1979.

———. *The Myth of Analysis.* San Francisco: Harper & Row, 1983.

———. *Anima: An Anatomy of a Personified Notion.* Dallas: Spring Publications, 1985.

———. "Going Bugs," *Spring,* 1988, pp. 40–72.

Hopcke, Robert H. "Eros in all his masculinity: men as lovers, men as friends." *The Jung Institute Library Journal,* vol. 7, no. 4, 1987, pp. 27–41.

———. "Out of patriarchy, toward a masculine ground of being." *The Jung Institute Library Journal,* vol. 8, no. 3, 1989, pp. 53–66.

———. *A Guided Tour of the* Collected Works *of C. G. Jung.* Boston: Shambhala Publications, 1989.

———. *Jung, Jungians, and Homosexuality.* Boston: Shambhala Publications, 1989.

———. "Counseling Across Sexual Orientation: A Gay Male Therapist Reflects on His Work with Heterosexual Clients." *Journal of Mental Health Counseling* (in press).

———. "Pater Noster." *The San Francisco Jung Institute Library Journal* (in press).

———. "Midway in Life's Journey: The Mid-Life Dreams and Inner Healing of Gay Religious." *The CMI Journal* (in press).

Isay, Richard A. *Being Homosexual: Gay Men and Their Development.* New York: Farrar, Straus, Giroux, 1989.

Jacoby, Mario. "Authority and Revolt." Lecture given at the Notre Dame Conference, April 1974.

Johnson, Robert A., *She: Understanding Feminine Psychology.* San Francisco: Harper & Row, 1986.

Jung, C. G. *Collected Works.* Princeton: Princeton University Press. Translated by R. F. C. Hull. Vol. 6, *Psychological Types,* 1971; vol. 7, *Two Essays on Analytical Psychology,* 1953; vol. 9, Part I, *The Archetypes and the Collective Unconscious,* 1959, 1969; vol. 9, Part II, *Aion: Researches into the Phenomenology of the Self,* 1959; vol. 11, *Psychology and Religion,* 1958; vol. 12, *Psychology and Alchemy,* 2nd ed., 1953; vol. 13, *Alchemical Studies,* 1967.

———. *Dream Analysis: Notes of the Seminar Given in 1928–1930.* Edited by William McGuire. Princeton: Princeton University Press, 1984.

———. *Memories, Dreams, Reflections.* New York: Vintage Books, 1965.

Jung, Emma. *Animus and Anima.* New York: Spring Publications, 1957.

Kerenyi, Karl. *The Gods of the Greeks.* New York: Thames and Hudson, 1979.

Klein, Edward, and Don Erickson, eds. *About Men: Reflections on the Male Experience.* New York: Poseidon Press, 1987.

Lauter, Estella, and Carol Schreier Rupprecht. *Feminist Archetypal Theory: Interdisciplinary Re-Visions of Jungian Thought.* Knoxville: University of Tennessee Press, 1985.

Layard, John. "Homoeroticism in Primitive Societies as a Function of the Self." *Journal of Analytical Psychology,* July 1959.

Lewes, Kenneth. *The Psychoanalytic Theory of Male Homosexuality.* New York: Simon and Schuster, 1988.

López-Pedraza, Rafael. *Hermes and His Children.* Dallas: Spring Publications, 1977.

Mahdi, Louise Carus, Steven Foster, and Meredith Little, eds. *Betwixt and Between: Patterns of Masculine and Feminine Initiation.* La Salle, Ill.: Open Court, 1987.

Mattoon, Mary Ann. *Understanding Dreams.* Dallas: Spring Publications, 1984.

McWhirter, David P., and Andrew M. Mattison. *The Male Couple: How Relationships Develop.* Englewood Cliffs, N.J.: Prentice Hall, 1984.

Michaelis, David. *The Best of Friends: Profiles of Men and Friendship.* New York: William Morrow, 1983.

Miller, Stuart. *Men and Friendship.* San Leandro, Cal.: Gateway Books, 1983.

Monick, Eugene. *Phallos: Sacred Image of the Masculine.* Toronto: Inner City Books, 1987.

Neumann, Erich. *The Origins and History of Consciousness*. Princeton: Princeton University Press, 1954.

———. *The Great Mother: An Analysis of the Archetype*. Princeton: Princeton University Press, 1955.

———. *Amor and Psyche*. Princeton: Princeton University Press, 1956.

New Oxford Annotated Bible, Revised Standard Version. New York: Oxford University Press, 1973.

Osherson, Samuel. *Finding Our Fathers: The Unfinished Business of Manhood*. New York: Free Press, 1986.

Plato, *Great Dialogues of Plato*, edited by Eric H. Warmington and Philip G. Rouse, translated by W. H. D. Rouse. New York: New American Library, 1956.

Rumi. *These Branching Moments: Forty Odes by Rumi*, translated by John Moyne and Coleman Barks. Providence, R.I.: Copper Beech Press, 1988.

Samuels, Andrew, ed. *The Father: Contemporary Jungian Perspectives*. New York: New York University Press, 1985.

Stein, Murray. *In MidLife: A Jungian Perspective*. Dallas: Spring Publications, 1983.

Turner, Victor. *The Ritual Process: Structure and Anti-Structure*. Chicago: Aldine, 1969.

Van Gennep, Arnold. *The Rites of Passage*. Chicago: University of Chicago Press, 1960.

Vries, Ad de. *Dictionary of Symbols and Imagery*. Amsterdam: Elsevier Science Publishers, 1984.

Walker, Mitchell. "The Double: An Archetypal Configuration." *Spring*, 1976.

Wehr, Demaris S. *Jung and Feminism: Liberating Archetypes*. Boston: Beacon Press, 1987.

Wyly, James. *The Phallic Quest: Priapus and Masculine Inflation*. Toronto: Inner City Books, 1989.

Zoja, Luigi. *Drugs, Addiction and Initiation: The Modern Search for Ritual*. Boston: Sigo Press, 1989.

Index

Abandonment, 151–152
Achilles, 30, 126
Acropolis, 135
Acting out, 47–48
Active imagination, 119
Adoption, 15, 111, 117–118, 151
Adolescence, 51
Aeacus, 28–31, 33–34, 39, 95
Aegina, 28–30, 33
AIDS (acquired immunodeficiency syndrome), 148, 161–162, 168, 204
Alchemy, 5, 183–184, 186, 188
Allen, Woody, 37
Amor, 131–132
Amplification, 26–27
Androgyne, 90
Androgyny, 91; of anima, 127–128
Anima, 23, 77–79, 80–84, 97–102, 124, 125, 133, 136–137; *anima mundi,* 85, 138; as archetype, 127; as inner feminine, 85–90, 97–102, 122, 126–127, 137; as intermediary, 99–100; as male, 123, 126–130, 136, 144, 149; as soul or psyche, 80–84; critique of concept, 89–90, 127–128, 137; in gay men, 130–138
Animals, 23–26, 28, 38–39, 199
Animus, 57, 100–101, 133

Annie Hall, 37
Anointment, 160–161, 165, 197
Ant, 9, 23, 24–25, 28–30, 34, 38–39, 197; as goddess symbol, 31, 34; in Aeacus myth, 28–30, 34, 38
Anteros, 134–135
Aphrodite, 32, 33, 62, 69, 130. *See also* Venus
Apuleius, 132, 134
Arachne, 35–36, 37–38, 39
Archetype, 27, 65, 90, 98, 202; polar structure of, 65, 90; critique of approach to, 202
Ash tree, 62
Asopus, 28, 31
Athene, 33, 35–36, 37–38
Athens, 36, 135
Augustine, 192
Authority, 57–59, 61, 63–65, 79; and rebellion, 61, 63, 65
Automobile, 50–51, 53

Baptism, 160, 190–194; infant, 192–193
Bathroom, 181, 182
Birth, 168–169, 177–179
Botticelli, Sandro, 131
Boxing, 139, 141, 151–152, 197
Brando, Marlon, 119

Bread, 157–159
Butterfly, 81

Castration, 62, 63, 68, 69
Chalcedon, 155
Child, inner, 181–183, 187
Childlessness, 166–167
Christening, 193
Christianity, 154–164, 189–195; concept of redemption in, 156–157, 161; concept of church in, 157, 158, 190, 193
Church, 157, 158, 190, 193; institutional, 204
Church Fathers, 27
Clement of Alexandria, 35
Colman, Arthur and Libby, 53
Colossians, Paul's letter to the, 190
Compensation, 52–53
Contrasexuality, *see* Anima, Animus
Conversion, 192
Corneau, Guy, 58
Cosmic Egg, 135
Cupid, 131

Daedalus, 37
Dante, 50
Dark Young Man, 106–122, 125, 129–130, 138, 140, 142, 143, 144, 149, 167–169. *See also* Dreams
Daughter, 170–171, 175–176, 181, 184–185, 186–189, 193, 195, 196
David, 126
Death, 157, 160–162
Demeter, 93–95, 96–97, 101
Demophoon, 94, 97
De Niro, Robert, 142–143, 150
Dependence, 43–44, 48, 50, 57–58, 59, 71, 73
Diotima of Mantineia, 134
Divine Comedy, The, 50
Dog Day Afternoon, 143
Double, 123–126, 130, 136, 144

Dreams, 3–5, 18–20, 26–27, 49–50, 52–53, 56, 72–74, 75–77, 79–80, 82, 103–105, 106–120, 139–144, 150–154, 170–176, 185–189; amplification, 26–27; analysis, 3–4; as image of unconscious situation, 19, 82; as symbolic, 19–20, 185, 187, 189; big dreams, 140, 153–154; compensatory function of, 52–53; dreams within dreams, 20, 142, 150; duplication in, 142; Freudian interpretation of, 187; initial, 49–50; interpretation, 3–5; progressive function of, 150; process of dreamwork in therapy, 3–5, 10, 18–19, 26–27, 41–42, 56, 72–74, 75–77, 79–80, 82, 103–105, 106–120, 140–144, 170–176; symbols of negative feelings, 18–19, 24–25
—Specific dreams cited: Al Pacino as Italian father (Pete), 139–140; ants and spiders (Pete), 9; adolescent cop (Nick), 41; Daniel giving birth (Pete), 168; Dark Young Man (Pete), 106, 109, 110, 112, 113–114, 115, 116, 118–119, 129, 168; escape from reform school (Nick), 74; man and woman making love (Nick), 103; urination on daughter, (Nick), 170; woman in iron lung (Nick), 75; woman on balustrade (Jung), 52
Drug use, 6, 46, 79

Ego, 120, 124, 125. *See also* Self (Ego)
Eleusis, 94
Eleusinian mysteries, 97
Elgonyi, 140
Enkidu, 126
Erinyes, 62, 68–69, 185
Eros (god), 32, 33, 72, 130–138, 166; Eros Phanes, 135

Eros (principle), 3, 32–35, 72, 83, 84, 88–89, 90, 95, 128, 130–131
Eucharist, 154–155, 157–158, 162, 169, 189, 190
Eumenides, 69. *See also* Erinyes
Extraversion, 49, 111

Fairy tales, 22
Family, 53, 178, 195
Fates, 36
Father, 53–54, 58, 59, 64–67, 138, 143–153, 155–169, 177–186; absence of, 58, 145–147, 149–150, 151–152, 177, 181–183; and son, 65–67, 156, 165; archetypal, 152–153, 156, 158, 159, 161, 163, 166, 169, 184; gay fathers, 150, 166; role in patriarchal family, 53–54, 58, 59, 64–66; Sky Father, 53, 64–65, 177, 178, 182, 185, 186
Fatherhood, 150, 166–169, 170–176, 177–189, 193–195, 197
Feeding, *see* Food
Feelings, 9–13, 16–19, 22–23, 25, 41–42, 44, 46–47, 49, 170–173, 175–176, 179, 183–185; men's lack of awareness of, 12–13, 16, 22, 25, 41–42, 44, 49, 179; negative, 9–11, 23, 46–47, 170–173, 175–176, 183–185; unconscious, 16–18
Feminine, archetypal, 31–34, 38–39, 69–70, 86, 89, 91, 92, 98, 127
Femininity, 32–33, 38, 54, 86–90, 95–96, 126–127, 128; anima as image of, 86–88, 126–127; devaluation of, 54, 95–96; idealization of, 54, 95–96; qualities identified with, 38, 54
Feminism, 1, 2, 178–179
Films noirs, 36
Food, 143–144, 151, 153, 197
Fly, The, 25
Freudian dream interpretation, 187

Gaia, 61–64, 68, 70
Ganymede, 132–133
Gay culture, 148
Gay men, 15, 56, 107–113, 115–117, 119–120, 129–130, 136–138, 144–145, 147–149, 159–163, 165–167, 177; and feelings, 15; and fathers, 147–149, 159–160, 166–167, 177; and policemen as symbol, 56; and religion/spirituality, 162–163, 204; stereotypes of, 136, 147. *See also* Homosexuality
Gay relationships, 64, 107–109, 111–112, 113, 115–117, 167
Gilgamesh, 126
Gilligan, Carol, 37
God, 119, 153–159, 190–193; images of, 153; the Father, 155, 158, 190, 193
Godparents, 193
Golden Ass, The, 132–133
Graves, Robert, 30, 31, 35, 63, 95
Greece, ancient, 28, 30, 31–32, 33, 36, 39, 95, 134–135, 156; conflict between patriarchy and matriarchy in, 31–32, 33, 39, 95
Guns, 60, 187, 197

Hades, 93–97
Heart, 21
Hera, 29–30, 31–33, 133; as Mother Goddess, 31, 133
Hermes, 94, 100, 135
Heterosexism, 137, 138
Heterosexual men, 100–102, 137, 149–150, 165–167, 177, 195–196
Hillman, James, 66–67, 126–128
HIV (human immunodeficiency virus), *see* AIDS
Holy Spirit, 154, 156, 190, 191, 192
Homophobia, 101, 125, 136
Homosexuality, 15, 63–64, 102–103, 107–113, 115–117, 119–125,

Homosexuality (*continued*)
    129–130, 133–138, 143–149,
    165–166, 177; and Eros, 134–
    137, and individuation, 119–120,
    122–123, 129–130, 137–138,
    144–145, 147–149, 159, 160, 161,
    165–167, 177; and masculinity,
    116–118; as normal variation,
    166; in ancient Greece, 124–125,
    134–135; in initiation rites, 63–
    64; fear of, 101, 104–105, 130,
    169 (*see also* Homophobia); "la-
    tent," 102; sexuality/eroticism in,
    107–109, 110, 112–113, 115–117,
    121. *See also* Gay culture, Gay
    men, Gay relationships
House, as symbol, 20–21
Hubris, 37–39

Identification, 146
Incarnation, in Christian theology,
    156–158, 159, 161, 163
Incest, 187
Individuation, 39–40, 54, 69, 79–80,
    92, 119–120, 122–123, 129–130,
    136–138, 144–145, 147–150,
    159–161, 165–167, 177, 183,
    195–196; of gay men, 119–120,
    122–123, 129–130, 136–138,
    144–145, 147–149, 159–160,
    161, 165–167; of heterosexual
    men, 137, 149–150, 165–167,
    177, 183, 195–196; as spiritual
    process, 163–165
Initiation, 51–52, 63–64, 119, 137, 163,
    165, 190–193; into masculinity,
    137, 163; modern men's lack of,
    52–52; rituals, 63–64, 165, 190–
    193
Insects, 25, 199. *See also* Ant, Spider
Instinct, 24, 25, 51–52; alienation
    from, 51–52
Introversion, 49
Iron lung, 75, 77

Italians, 117–119, 129, 139–142, 144,
    149, 150, 151, 159, 167

Jacoby, Mario, 69
Jerusalem, 191
Jesus Christ, 155–158, 161, 163, 164,
    190–193
John, Gospel of, 191–192
John the Baptist, 191
Jonathan, 126
Jordan River, 191
Jove, 132
Judaism, 155, 159, 191–193
Judea, 191
Jung, C. G., 3, 4, 5, 19–20, 22, 24, 26–
    27, 32–33, 39–40, 52–53, 59–61,
    64–65, 78, 81, 85–90, 101, 122,
    124, 126–127, 130, 137, 156, 165;
    and alchemy, 5; and dreams, 3–4,
    19–20, 22, 52; feminist critiques
    of, 3; on anima, 78, 81, 85–90,
    101, 122, 126–127, 137, 201; on
    archetype, 26–27, 64–65; on
    compensation, 52–53; on Eros, 3,
    32–33, 124, 130; on individua-
    tion, 39–40; on instinctual self,
    24; on Logos, 3, 32–33, 124, 130;
    on persona, 59–60; on projection,
    60, 121; on psyche, 60, 81; on
    psychotherapy and religion, 165;
    on soul, 81; on shadow, 60; on
    the Trinity, 156

Keleos, 94
Kerényi, Karl, 30, 62
Kore, *see* Persephone
Kronos, 62–65, 67, 68, 185

Logos, 3, 32–35, 83, 88, 130, 189
Lydia, trade rivalry with Athens, 36

Mark, Gospel of, 191
Masculine, archetypal, 31–34, 38–39,
    61, 64, 65–70, 71–72, 90, 184;

conflict with archetypal Feminine, 69–70, 71–72, 90; polarities of, 65–67, 70, 71

Masculinity, 2, 12, 16, 32–33, 51–52, 54–55, 57–58, 71, 101, 109–110, 116–117, 128, 146–148, 181–182, 184, 197; as definition of "health," 54–55; collective, 2, 32–33, 51–52, 109–110, 116–117, 146–148, 181–181, 184; mature vs. immature, 54–55, 57–58, 71; socialization, 12, 16, 101; qualities identified with, 2, 54

Matriarchy, conflict with patriarchy, 31–33, 39, 199

Men, 2, 6, 12, 16–17, 51–52, 54–55, 63–64, 100–101, 146–147; attitudes toward psychotherapy, 12, 16–17; authority conflicts, 63–64; groups of, 146–147; presenting problems in psychotherapy, 2, 6; psychological adolescence of, 51–52, 54–55, 147

Metaneira, 94

Midlife, 50

Mikvah, 192

Miscarriage, 174–175, 182

Misogyny, 125

Mother, 36, 45, 58, 64, 72, 86, 96; Earth Mother, 64; Great Mother, 36

Motherhood, 178, 179

Movies, 25, 36, 37, 141, 142, 143; as carriers of archetypal images, 141, 152–153; *films noirs,* 36

Myrmex, 35, 37–38, 39

Myrmidons, 30, 33, 35

Mytheme, 35

Myths, 28–32, 35–36, 61–65, 71, 93–97, 100–101, 132–135; historical context of, 30–31, 36; of Aeacus, 28–32, of Arachne, 35–36; of Eros, 132–135; of Hades and Persephone, 93–97, 100–101; of Myrmex, 35; of Ouranos and Kronos, 61–65, 71

Nature, alienation from, 24, 25

Neumann, Erich, 36, 133, 135

Nicea, 155

Nicene Creed, 155–157

Nicodemus, 191–192, 193

Numinosity, 153–154

Nymphs, 62

Oak tree, 29

Oedipus, 37

Oenone/Oenopia, 28, 197

Olive oil, 139, 140, 159–161

Orpheus, 135

Osherson, Samuel, 145

Ouranos, 61–65, 68, 73

Ovid, 35

Pacino, Al, 139, 141–143, 144, 150, 151, 152, 167, 169

Parium, 135

Patriarchy, 31–34, 38–40, 52, 53–54, 57–59, 68, 71–72, 81, 87–91, 96–98, 100–101, 127–128, 138, 145–149, 151, 154–155, 164, 169, 177, 178, 181–182, 193–195, 197–198, 199; as oppressive to men, 52, 54, 57–58, 72, 96, 100–101, 138, 147–149; as oppressive to women, 53–54, 89–91, 96–98; attitudes toward men and women, 33, 34, 38–40; concept of authority in, 57–59; conflict with matriarchy, 31–32, 33, 39, 199; family structure in, 53, 178, 181, 182, 193–195; one-sidedness of, 68, 71, 92, 138, 164, 169, 198; religion, 81, 154–155; sex roles and stereotypes in, 87–91, 96, 100–101, 127–128, 145–146, 151, 177; social order in, 197

Patroclus, 126

Paul, Letter to the Colossians, 190

Persephone, 93–95, 96, 97, 100, 101, 197

Persona, 59–60, 78, 99
Phaeton, 37
Phallos, 135, 186–187, 203
Pharmacist, 75, 79
Plato, 27, 134
Police, policemen, 41, 56–57, 59–60, 68, 73, 80, 170, 172, 180, 185; as dream symbols, 56–57, 59–60, 80, 170, 180, 185
Polis, 57
Pregnancy, 174–175, 177–180
Projection, 60, 87, 120–122; anima-projection, 87
Proserpine, 132
Protestantism, 192
Psyche (goddess), 132–133
Psyche (concept), 81–83
Psychotherapy, 2–3, 6–7, 12–16, 19–20, 22, 25, 26, 38–40, 41–49, 52, 72–77, 82–84, 102–105, 106–109, 119, 151, 165, 167–169, 173–174, 183–184, 187, 196–197; acting out in, 47–48; and religion, 165; as confession, 46–47; as initiation, 52, 165; as soul-healing, 82–83, 102; erotic transference in, 108; goal of, 26, 39–40, 102, 167, 196–197; issues for men in, 2–3, 6–7; process for men in, 13–16, 19, 20, 22, 25, 38–39, 41–44, 47–49, 72–74, 75–77, 103–105, 106–109, 119, 151, 167–169, 173–176, 177–180, 183, 187, 195–196; resistance in, 47–48; role of therapist in, 103, 108; structure of, 48; termination of, 167–169
Puer aeternus, 67, 70, 120, 125, 137
Purification, 191–193

Quilt, Names Project, 162

Raging Bull, 142
Rape, 93–94, 95–96, 101

Rebellion, 46–49, 63–65, 68, 69, 79
Rebirth, 163, 190
Religion, 45–46, 80–81, 163, 204
Resistance, 47–48
Resurrection, 157, 159, 161, 163, 190
Revolt, *see* Rebellion
Rhea, 62–64, 70
Roman Catholicism, 160–161, 192
Rome, ancient, 129–131, 132–133, 154, 156
Rumi, Jalal-al-Din, 198

San Francisco, 162
Saturn, 66
Seder, 159, 162
Self (archetype), 69, 90, 101, 119
Self (ego), 122
Semen, 186
Senex, 66–67, 70
Sex roles, 1–2, 54–55, 87–89, 100–101
Sexism, 89, 92
Shadow, 60, 107, 120, 122, 124, 125, 185
Sin, Original, 192
Sister, 41, 45, 53, 64, 72, 96
Sleep, 21–22, 26
Son, 66–67, 197. *See also* Father
Soul, 78–79, 80–82, 99, 102, 118
Soul-figure, 100, 126
Soul-image, 78, 81. *See also* Soul, Soul-figure
Spider, 9, 23–25, 35–40, 197; as feminine symbol, 36–37
Spirituality, 163, 204. *See also* Religion
Styx, 132
Symposium, 134

Technology, modern effects of, 24, 25–26, 51–52, 84–85
Telamon, 29
Thespiae, 135
Tickling, 21
Trinity, 154–157

Transference, 108
Twins, 107, 134–135, 144

Unconscious, personal, 56, 58–59, 61
Unconscious, collective, 56, 65, 92
Union of opposites, 92
Urination, urine, 170–172, 185–189, 197

van Gennep, Arnold, 52
von Franz, Marie-Louise, 133, 186, 188, 189
Venus, 129–133

Walker, Mitch, 123–126, 128, 130

Washing, 170, 188–189
Water, 188–189, 190
Window, 21
Wine, 157–158
Women, 2, 56–57, 86, 88, 96, 100, 197; as carriers of anima, 86, 88, 96, 100; freedom of, 197; policemen in dreams of, 56–57; sex roles of, 2; stereotypes of, 89

Yahweh, 159

Zeus, 28–30, 31, 33, 62–64, 67, 68, 93–94, 132–133; as symbol of patriarchy, 31

Credits